DREAM JOB

Jill &
with love,
JuliAnne

mascotbooks.com

Dream Job

This book is a memoir and a work of creative nonfiction. It reflects the author's present recollections of experiences and events over a period of time, some of which have been consolidated for brevity's sake. Names, places, characteristics, and details have been changed at the author's discretion.

www.JuliAnneMurphy.com

For more information, please contact:
Mascot Books
620 Herndon Parkway #320
Herndon, VA 20170
info@mascotbooks.com

Library of Congress Control Number: 2018903130
CPSIA Code: PBANG0518A
ISBN-13: 978-1-68401-874-1

Printed in the United States of America

DREAM JOB

Shattering the glass ceiling comes at a price.

JULIANNE MURPHY

ACKNOWLEDGMENTS

Words can never express how grateful I am for the experiences that led to the writing of this book.

Special thanks to "Yo" for believing in me and supporting my writing, come hell or high water. (And, both did.)

An endearing shout-out to Jan Williams, from whom I leased a tiny apartment for my writing studio in Veracruz, Panama, for an entire year. More than half of *Dream Job* was composed in Panama, from under a mango tree.

I'm forever grateful to my writing consultant and dearest friend Maya Christobel, for her part in making this book the best it could possibly be over a three-year period. Wow.

Thank you to my husband Yor for being my sounding board and listening over and over and over again as I read the manuscript aloud and then made further edits. His patience with me continues to be unending. Thank you.

And, finally, thank you to the very special man who served as my driver during my time in Panama for five years; he came into my life as if I had called him in. He showed up, day after day after day, during a time period when I was hardly at my best. *Muchas gracias por todo, Señor.*

CONTENTS

PART ONE: *The Adventure Begins*

PART TWO: *All That Glitters*

PART THREE: *Freedom*

PART ONE

CHAPTER 1:
The Realization

The room began to whirl as the shapes around me in the dim light began to fade. Stars appeared before my eyes.

What the fuck?

I inhaled, sucking stale air from the large events hall into my lungs, forcing it down my throat. The sound of my breath roared like a jet engine in my eardrums.

Breathe, JuliAnne, breathe.

Sweat beaded on the back of my neck, as I cast my eyes to either side. Other members of Panama's business elite squeezed in around me, packed in like canned sardines. *I can barely move.*

My throat began to constrict, tension pulling at my chest. I tried to loosen a collar that didn't exist.

I can't breathe.

My vision seemed to freeze, the world around me moving in slow motion. The man's voice started to echo, sounding as if it were a million miles away. I blinked. Once. Twice. A third time.

I can't do this here. Not now.

The people around me turned cartoonish, their bodies bending and swimming before my eyes.

No, I cried. *Not here, please.*

Suddenly, the plane lurched. I was ripped out of my dream and the memory that was still following me in my sleep. I came into consciousness not recognizing my surroundings at first, but then the voice of the stewardess came over the intercom.

"Damas y Caballeros, la puerta en la cabina principal ya esta cerrada. Por favor apaguen sus aparatos eletronicos en este momento."

The announcement crackled from the overhead speakers behind my head and jolted me back to reality from where I sat scrunched in my seat, staring at the small screen in my hand. My heart was pounding as I read the same text, over and over. Hardly anything made sense. My hands were clammy and I suddenly felt faint.

"Flight attendants, please prepare the cabin for take-off." I had heard those words a hundred times, but every word pierced my splitting head.

My fingers released the wadded Kleenex from my hand to free my thumb so it could switch my phone into airplane mode. "Cut off, cut off." The words rang too true. I was about to cut myself off from everyone in Panama, from Joe, from my entire life of the past eight years, and I was terrified.

The voices started again. *Did I do the right thing? Holy Shit! What if I'm making a mistake?*

As I swiped, a quiet voice whispered in my left ear: "Señora?"

"Señora" had become a greeting that I had become so familiar with: so respectful, so right. I felt like I was coming back to earth for a moment. My tear-stained cheeks met the eyes of the young steward in a crisp blue and red uniform. I was suddenly self-conscious that my mascara might be running.

"*Su asiento, por favor,*" he said, jutting his chin toward the slight incline of my posture. "Please bring your seat up." I stared at him as the words began to compute in my brain.

"Ah, sí, sí, sí." My hand shot out for the button. In my haste, my phone fell to the floor at his feet. "*Disculpe.*" I scrambled toward it, but a hand the color of butterscotch caught the escapee and returned it to me. As he flashed his eyes toward mine, the look in them told me that I must look like the wreckage I was leaving behind.

"*Gracias,*" I stammered, my face already flushed from the recent bout of tears that had started days before.

He scanned my face, taking in my puffy eyes, giving me a perfunctory nod before he moved off down the aisle. "*Claro.*"

He has no idea what this flight means for me, I thought. *But then, how could he? I'm like an escaped convict on the run. Did he see in my eyes this incredible guilt I feel for choosing my life over everyone else's? For finally letting my marriage die? Does he know that before boarding this plane I burned my life to the ground?*

I returned to my iPhone screen which now showed a photo of a sleek black Doberman running, ears pressed to either side of her slim face, the ocean splashing beneath her feet. My eyes filled up again, and I shook my head to fend off the rising pain. So many endings. Too many deaths.

Ding. A new text arrived.

I did a quick scan of the cabin to see where the steward stood before I snuck my thumb for the swipe.

It's him, replying to my earlier goodbye. An unfamiliar warmth rose in my chest as I read.

"You are very special to me."

A second ding brought up another line. "Whatever you need. I am here."

My heart swelled as I tapped the phone into airplane mode. But the instant before I could cut everything off again, a third text slipped through. I scanned it before my eyes were drawn to the window as, in the distance, past the tarmac, the shape of the city flashed by.

So, this is it. A sigh rose in my chest. *It was never what I wanted.*

The shadow of the plane rose above the blue cranes in Balboa Port, crossing the muddy waters of the Canal, then the steel expanse of the Bridge of the Americas. Sunlight highlighted the carpeted green of Panorama, my old neighborhood, the gym, and then our expensive condominium building.

My heart expanded with a pang as I reflected on all that this small country had given to me and on all that it had cost me, as well.

The warmth of gratitude spread across my chest as I whispered to myself. "Thank you for all those teachers who were brought into my life, in this chapter. The lessons were so different from what I thought they'd be, including the people who came and went." My soon-to-be ex-husband's face rose in my mind's eye; the dark curl at the nape of his neck. I swallowed hard.

"Including Joe." I returned to my breathing in an attempt to linger with the positives. But beneath the moment lay an ocean of feeling that would take me months to sort out.

And, now I am leaving. Alone. I closed my eyes as loneliness swept over me.

I am here. The soft baritone of another familiar voice sounded in my ears. *You were never alone.*

My eyes blinked open as the vision of him rose, and the images began to cascade. *Well, that's true, but…* And then I saw it for the very first time.

Holy shit! My pupils widened as the realizations broke over me, one after another, like a tsunami. *For all those years…* I clamped my sweaty palms around the armrests as it all became clear: the moments, the conversations, his presence. I shook my head in disbelief. *I never saw it. No matter how hard it was, how complicated it all became, how unforgiving everything seemed…he was always there.*

Oh, my God.

My hand shook as I scrambled for my phone, swiping to bring up the last text.

Stand by me!

Steady and true. Simple. Always there. *Just like he had always been. The unexpected, quiet presence.*

I bowed my head toward the coastline below, which appeared endless to the horizon, as my hands came to my temples. *My God, I never saw it before. How could I not have seen the blessing he was? He was such a big part of my life. Holy shit.* My heart alighted for a moment before a smile broke through my tears.

I could see his face: always smiling. Those transparent eyes had seemed to look right through me all these years.

He had been there all along. My breath caught in my throat, as a half-sob escaped. *The whole time I thought I was so alone.*

I watched the sun spread across the horizon through the small square pane of my window. "Thank you," I said aloud, nodding at the memories coming fast and hard. My hands came up to cover my face, as I continued to nod. "Thank you. Thank you. Thank you."

I wanted nothing more than to sleep, but a flood of what was, what had been my life stood front and center in my mind, and I was dragged back into that first moment I saw Panama, that fateful flight that brought me into a life I could never have expected. I remembered the joy of that moment when Joe and I were full of anticipation of what lay ahead for us.

CHAPTER 2:
The Leap

Eight Years Earlier...

Ding.

My eyes popped open and did a quick scan. *Where am I?*

A sandpaper palm brushed my cheek. "Hey, sleepyhead."

I turned my head to the left, squinting to bring him into view.

"Are we there yet?" A huge yawn interrupted my question. My left hand came up to cover the cavern of my open mouth. "Aye, pardon me."

My husband, who stood six feet four inches, was squeezed like a sardine into the seat next to me. He motioned to the flight map on the monitor on the seat-back in front of him.

"Not yet, Murph, but we're close." He smiled with excitement.

The subdued voice of the female flight attendant oozed over the loudspeaker: "Ladies and gentlemen, we are beginning our final descent into the city of Panama. In preparation for landing, we ask that you bring your trays up to the stowed and locked position and your seat backs to the upright position, as well."

Joe tapped my hand, motioning toward the window beside him. "Check it out." He pointed a long finger at the expanse below. "Look how many freighters are lined up. They must be waiting to go through the Canal."

I shook my head, attempting to shake off my fatigue before I unbuckled my seat belt to lean across him. His lips skimmed my cheek as I crossed over him.

"Holy shit," I quietly said. The tiny ships, dotted along the swath of the Pacific Ocean below us, looked more fake than real, like a game of Battleship.

My eyes scanned a statuesque silver structure bridging a narrow chasm, which appeared like a slit on the horizon. "So, that must be the Canal then?"

"Must be," Joe replied, his cheekbone bouncing against mine as we shared the tiny square of glass. His hand went up to steady me as the plane lurched, grasping the curve of my ass.

"Stop it." My hand swatted his as a slew of tall buildings along the coastline pierced the skyline.

"What?" His voice teased. "Can't I welcome my wife to the tropics in style?"

I smiled before swatting him again. "This city looks way more metropolitan than the pictures I saw online."

The overhead speakers crackled. "Flight attendants, please take your seats."

"So, what do you think: should I say, 'welcome home' yet?" My husband kissed my ear.

Using Joe's armrest as leverage, I pushed myself back toward my seat. "I don't think so." My eyes cut toward him. "This is only an *interview*, remember?"

"Yeah, *right*." I heard the smirk without even seeing his face. "And if you hadn't *really* impressed the owners in your interview last week, we wouldn't be spending our *Thanksgiving* crossing the continent, now would we?" His dark head shook in my periphery. "I know my wife. You accepted this job before you boarded the plane from Miami back to Denver."

Ducking my chin to hide a smile, I slid the metal clasp of my seat belt into the buckle across my lap. He was right, but I wouldn't admit it. "Well then, we'll see, won't we?" I retorted.

An hour and a half later, Joe leaned into a heavy glass door marked *Salida*. As I rolled past him, a wave of humidity hit me like a ton of bricks. I stood, blinking in the partial sunlight as Joe struggled through the narrow exit behind me. On cue, a sea of white shirts and tan pants sprung to life. Dark hands waved placards of all sizes and shapes toward us among the cries of "Taxi, taxi!" and "Señores!"

My eyes scanned the signs as I moved down the line toward the exit. Some were printed, but most were handwritten. The variety of penmanship and font caused my feet to slow as I attempted to make out a few of the signs closest to me. A cluster of bored faces standing at the end of the line did not disperse when we reached it. They just stood there, blinking.

All right then, I set my jaw while using my roller bag as a weapon to part the seas before us and, one by one, they moved.

"What did they say the guy's name was?" I turned my head sideways to catch Joe's shout amidst the din of the *taxistas*.

"They didn't give me a name. They just said it would be someone from the hotel," I shouted back as I continued the slow march forward.

"Jesus," Joe grumbled, as we burst through the end of the crowd into an empty expanse of floor tile that looked like it hadn't been cleaned in a week. He reached up to wipe the sweat from his forehead. "What the heck was that?" he asked, referring to the chaos we had just overcome.

"No kidding," I replied. "There's a bunch more signs I couldn't get to. Let me see if I can go find our guy." As I returned bagless toward the wriggling morass of humanity, I chanted, "Murphy, Murphy, Murphy."

Signs were thrust within inches of my nose as I darted in and out of the cluster of mashed bodies, pushing forward toward each new person that exited Customs. Some came so close I had to step back to read them, causing me to collide with other sweaty, damp heads behind me.

Seven minutes later, I reemerged, shaking my head, bangs now wilted across my forehead.

"Well, do you have a phone number? Anything?" Joe's voice had begun to rise with his body temperature.

"What good will that do since our phones don't work, Joe?" I snapped. "That said, let me see if I can find it, so we can look for a payphone."

"Mr. O'Mealey?" a phantom voice rang out.

We looked up to find a large black man approaching us from across the expanse of tile, wiping his face with a washcloth. The man lumbering toward us resembled a tank with his broad shoulders and his square head.

"Pardon?" I asked, eyes straining toward the placard in his hand, which unlike most of the others was printed.

"Mr. Joseph O'Mealey?" The man's wide smile suddenly felt like a life preserver in the sea of blank faces. "For the Hotel Bristol, yes?" He came toward me in a cloud of cologne so strong it took my breath away. I stepped back as he stepped forward, and released my bag to his grip, without a word. Sensing my discomfort, Joe took a step forward to stand next to him, though his stature seemed dwarfed next to the man's hulking form.

"I'm Joe O'Malley," said my husband, as he enunciated his last name. "It's O'M-all-ey."

"Yes, yes, yes," said the man, his skin wet with sweat. He dragged the washcloth from his shirt pocket and wiped his face again. "My name is Tomas. I am from Hotel Bristol. I am your driver, sir." When he delivered the "sir," he smiled at me. Standing five feet four inches in my bare feet, he towered over me like a sequoia.

"Hi, Tomas, I'm Joe," Joe said as they shook hands before Tomas took the handle of Joe's roller bag.

"Nice to meet you!" His green eyes beamed. "Now, come here." He waved his hand toward us to follow, as he headed for another set of glass doors leading to the airport exit.

We followed, eager to get to any form of air conditioning.

But, then, "Wait." Tomas left us with our bags on the curb. "Five minutes."

"Whew," I panted toward Tomas' clipped head from the backseat of a white SUV when we pulled away 25 minutes later. "That took a lot longer than you thought, I guess."

Tomas pretended not to hear me. "You like air condition, sir?" he said instead.

"Oh, my God, yes! Please!" we exhaled in unison.

"And water?" Tomas asked, handing first one bottle and then a second over his shoulder. Joe snapped the seal on one and handed it to me before wiping another stream of sweat from his face. Then, he cracked the second one, and raised it toward mine in a mock toast.

"Well, we made it!" Joe smiled. "Finally, on Panama ground." He leaned over and gave me a hearty kiss as Tomas' eyes widened in the rearview mirror.

"Okay!" he said as the tires screeched away from the curb. "Welcome to Panama, sirs!"

The three of us burst into laughter.

And thus, the adventure had begun.

CHAPTER 3:
Me

I sat in my office sipping a Starbucks, trying to wake up as the face of the calendar stared back at me: August 20, 2007. I shook my head to clear the early morning cobwebs and pushed the button on my laptop to fire it up. *August. Where is the time going?*

Wow! It's early, and I'm already really tired. Keeping up with the rat race was catching up to me. I worked 10 to 12-hour days between the demands of my corporate job, two volunteer positions on community boards of directors, and the daily grind of managing a two-professional household.

I watched from the corner of my eye as the number on my inbox scrolled skyward. *Ugh. This is where all the time goes.* One hundred and fifty emails! I flipped my appointment book open that was my rudder for the day.

Only three meetings today? Really? I crossed my fingers, hope rising like a balloon. Unscheduled hours meant the piles on my desk and in my drawers might get diminished, and I might get caught up!

The carved name plate sitting atop the round table opposite me caught my attention. JuliAnne Murphy, Vice President of Marketing.

Score! My latest promotion from marketing director had come only six months prior, at the largest redevelopment of a former airport in the United States. It had come as no surprise. "I plan to make vice president within two years," I'd told my boss in our first interview. I took pride in the fact that the achievement had come four months ahead of that timeline. In that moment, there was no glass ceiling for me.

A few months later, however, another surprise announcement had followed.

My boss had shown up one afternoon, coffee in hand, peering over his reading glasses. "Got a minute, JuliAnne?"

I warmed at the sound of Hank Baker's voice.

"Come on in!" I replied. I looked up from proofing the latest version of a magazine in progress, and smiled at the short, grizzled figure in my door. With unruly salt and pepper hair and a penchant for sleeveless Polartec vests, Hank looked more like an aging college professor than he did the executive vice president of the most prominent development project in the U.S. "I was looking for you earlier."

"Oh, yeah?" Hank chuckled as he ambled in and shut the door behind him as I cleared some desk space to make room for his ever-present coffee cup.

"Spit it out then," he said as he pulled the chair close enough to the desk so he could put his feet up. "What's up in that brain of yours today?"

The crease in my eyes deepened as I whipped down my list. While others in the office didn't appreciate Hank's sniper-like, direct approach, I adored it. The man had never failed to encourage me in the short span of our two years together, and it was because of him that numerous doors had opened wide for me within the community, providing this fledgling falcon the opportunity to really fly. This was, by far, the best experience I'd had with a boss in my 15 year career, and though I hadn't voiced it, it was one I deeply cherished.

"So," he said, when I came to the end of my list. I waited, expectant.

Then, Hank dropped a bomb. "I'm leaving," he said in a voice that depicted clear skies and smooth sailing, assuming we'd been talking about the weather. "Getting out of this place. It's about time."

My face fell, along with the Starbucks cup in my hand. Chai tea seeped all over the carpet. "Leaving?" I threw a few tissues toward the floor to clean up the mess, tapping a high-heeled toe atop them, my eyes never leaving his face. "What the hell is that supposed to mean?"

Hank's smile was calm. His shoulders shrugged. "Well, you knew the time would come eventually."

"But, I never expected it to come so fast," I stammered, the weight of his words beginning to sink like a stone in my stomach. "When?"

"A few months, still." Hank's eyes twinkled. "And there's a good chance Clarence won't replace me."

"And?" My voice trilled upwards, following my anxiety.

"And?" His fingers hammered out a drum roll on my desktop. "And…"

He stretched his mouth wide, drawing out the syllables. "That could mean more opportunity for y-o-u."

My eyes narrowed. "Would that opportunity come with more money?" I'd been around the block enough to know that the word "opportunity" didn't always pay off.

"I guess we'll have to see how good your negotiating skills are," Hank said with a wink.

Another ding in my inbox brought me back to the present from that past memory.

"*Senior* vice president," I said the words aloud, tasting the way they rolled off my tongue in the quiet of the office. "Senior, senior, senior." My stomach twisted for a moment at the thought of having to start over with someone new.

But, there's a lot to celebrate, JuliAnne. I reminded myself. *Go back to what you can be thankful for.* It was an age-old habit I'd formed some years prior, something I did when anxiety started to encroach.

My mind began to scan the proverbial checklist, going to the top of the column at the far left corner of the page.

Personal life, I paused. *Overall, going pretty well.*

Salary. Last year, I had finally reached six figures with my bonus. *Financial stability, check.*

Fun Mini Cooper in the driveway, check.

Nice house, check.

Moving here had been my idea, and the proximity was worth it, though I hadn't loved the house as much as I'd hoped I would. *Spilled milk,* I mused, pushing the thought away.

Good friends, check. The women's group I'd started three years earlier was beginning to flourish.

Handsome husband, check, check, check, I thought. A mere eight days earlier, I had finally tied the knot with my long-term boyfriend. Joe O'Malley and I had worked together for two years and lived together for six years, and had been engaged for almost two before we'd finally taken the plunge.

Yes, it was complicated, but he was the tall, handsome prince with a bad boy attitude that had captured my heart years earlier when we'd first met on another construction project, the building of the Denver Broncos Stadium.

You'll be together for the rest of your life. I smiled remembering our first beginnings.

Two and a half years prior, I'd called Joe from my grandmother's funeral. "I know we always said we didn't need a piece of paper," I told him as I stood in the rain outside the church. "But, I changed my mind. I'm ready."

"Really?" The surprise in Joe's voice crackled across the line. "I mean, of course, you know I will, but I'm curious. Can you tell me what changed?"

I paused. "Well, I just want to grow old with you and be that married couple I saw at the funeral today. It's that simple, Joe. I want to call you my husband." I could feel his smile match mine.

With that, I clamped my internal notebook shut.

See? I trilled to myself. *No wonder I'm so tired. I'm only 37 and I have achieved almost the entire American Dream: the husband, the money, the friendships, the house, and absolute flexibility since I don't have children. Except for my fur baby, Lily, of course.*

The sleek black Doberman was anything but furry, but she was very much my baby.

The buzz of the black phone on my desk yanked me back to the present.

I squinted toward the screen to see if the flashing digits were familiar. They weren't.

On any other day, when I didn't recognize the number, I'd let my assistant pick up the call. But it was early, and he had yet to arrive.

"All right, all right." My hand went for the receiver as if some magnetic pull was summoning me forward, toward a new destiny.

CHAPTER 4:
Beware What You Wish For

The photo of our trip to Mexico beckoned me to sink into the warm waters of Puerto Vallarta, forcing me to leave a pile of paperwork behind from where I sat staring at my computer on my desk on a cold January afternoon. I allowed myself the momentary escape, feeling myself slip back to a few weeks earlier when Joe and I had been bouncing through the passing Mexican countryside.

The frenzy of my hair blurred my vision as our taxi bumped down the gravel road. This week had been hard fought for both of us, with work schedules that seemed to block out all suggestions of leisure and fun.

I attempted to harness the snarl of hair around my head to no avail. The ribbon I had tied around my locks when we departed had flashed out the window a moment before and disappeared into the clouds of dust billowing behind us.

You can never really take your vacation experience home with you, the thought bubble hung for a moment in the air beside me before being sucked behind us into the snapshots of the past eight days.

My daydream lurched back to the present when a steamy palm pressed itself to my inner thigh.

Oh.

"Earth to JuliAnne." The butterscotch eyes of my long-time boyfriend and soon-to-be-husband were cloaked in dark sunglasses, a relaxed grin framing his face. His hand reached for mine. "Watcha doin' back there?"

A smile crisscrossed my face. "Taking in every last moment before we return to reality." My voice rose to a shout, struggling to be heard above the din of Mexican mariachis screeching from the radio. My fingers squeezed his.

In the miles we'd covered since leaving the humble *panga* at the boat dock, the view from the backseat through a frame once occupied by glass had morphed from tranquil lanes lined with towering palms to parched hills of ranch land dotted with crops. Tall grass resembling super-sized grains of wheat cropped up from time to time along the highway with fronds rippling in the tailwind as our taxi screamed past a sign that read, "*Aeropuerto Internacional—Puerta Vallarta.*"

Tropical flora and fauna had always intrigued me, and I'd had more than my fill on this most recent adventure to a remote Mexican pueblo for Christmas, but these statuesque wonders had never appeared in any of the travel books I'd studied before our trip. Green stalks climbed toward what branched into golden feathers above.

They kind of remind me of Africa. A vision of my chubby six-year-old face crowded into my reverie, standing with my seven other classmates for the first grade graduation picture against the backdrop of an international one-room schoolhouse. *Snap!* The camera shutter popped as a shout rang out, "You're it!" and our tiny cluster erupted into a cloud of white socks and Buster Browns in every which way.

Bobbing in the lapping waves of the Pacific had all but erased the worry lines that had begun to stretch across my forehead, something I was very conscious of at 35.

What would it be like to be this relaxed all the time? My nostrils flared at the memory of the daily anointing to which we'd woken daily: a pungent bouquet of tiny white flowers framing the open-air palapa where we'd slept. *What would it be like to live life like this, in paradise?*

Images flashed across the screen in my mind, the moments we hadn't lugged cell phones clicking backwards before my eyes: Joe's arms spinning around him, a bent straw hat covering his dark locks, his head thrown back toward the sky; our bare feet trailing from the end of a small wood dock into crystal-clear water; my face peeking from behind a dog-eared novel. The clomp-clomp-clomp of hooves ascending a narrow pathway up a jagged hillside as we clung to wooden saddles. Tears rolling down our faces as we guffawed with laughter, heads rolling, arms folded atop a seaside plastic table littered with Corona bottles.

Isn't this the stuff everyone dreams of? The question scrolled across the ticker tape of my consciousness. *But is it really possible to live like this?*

If anyone can figure it out, you can, a voice said, bringing me back to the present moment. The voice on my shoulder was none other than a microscopic version of me, the one who always had all the answers and never took no for an answer. This mouthy broad never had a hair out of place and her modest three-inch pumps shone as if they'd been freshly polished. Her pint size might have resembled that of another famous pest named Jiminy, but the similarities ended there. This gal screamed into my psyche no less than 60 times a day with lipstick and a boob job to match. I had come to call her Snickety, a condensed version of the word "persnickety" which my grandmother had used with my siblings and I growing up. "Don't get persnickety with me!" she'd exclaim before she swatted at our backsides with a kitchen towel when we got irritated and grumpy.

Somewhere in teenagehood, my sister and I shortened the word to "snickety" as a descriptor for our moods, covering everything from irritable to judgmental to bitchy. In our Religious Right family, expletives and descriptors like "bitch" were not an acceptable form of communication and thus, we had to get creative.

When this miniature inner critic was especially harsh to me in response to any specific situation, I addressed her as "Miss Snickety" in rememberance of a less-than-kind Sunday School teacher from my second grade year.

And now, here she was again. *If anyone can figure it out, you can.*

Shut up! I replied. *I've done just fine without you firing your nonsense into my ear for the past five days and I'd like to keep it that way.*

Snickety put a gloved hand up to frame her bobbed hair and pursed her lips. *I'm just sayin,*' she said as she lifted a manicured eyebrow, *what if?*

I snapped my fingers in an effort to erase her, contempt rising in me like a snake.

There you go again, she cooed. *Try and get rid of me, and it only gets worse.*

Aarrgh! I snarled. *You only ever have negative things to say. I'm trying to imagine a better future for Joe and me.*

Well, what you can believe, you can achieve, said Snickety, mimicking a quote I'd heard from sales training in Mary Kay Cosmetics a lifetime ago. *So, I'm not bitching about anything.* She tossed prim locks over her shoulder. *I'm just trying to make a point. You've just finished reading* The Secret, *after all. Why not give it a spin?*

I glanced sideways at the red backpack in the seat beside me, which held the copy of the recent bestseller I'd finished two days prior. The thought rose in my mind, unbidden. *Hmm. She has a point.* I shrugged as my gaze returned to the sway of the mysterious foliage. *All right, why not?*

My mind rewound like a tape to the part where the author described how to ask for what you want. *Let's see…I want…*I started.

It's desire, Snickety clucked her tongue at me in reproach. *Request what you desire. Want denotes that you don't have it or that you are lacking.*

I inhaled, shutting my eyelids as the fresh air expanded into the passageways of my lungs. *I desire to live in the tropics where Joe and I can enjoy the kind of a lifestyle we have had on this vacation and where we can spend more time together and where this beautiful tall grass grows.*

I glanced toward the front seat where Joe and our English-speaking driver sat. *Did they notice?* My gaze searched the sides of their faces for a sign, the breath stuck in my throat. *And if they did, would they think I was crazy?*

Are you finished? Snickety ground her heel into my shoulder. *Is that all you got? Aren't you supposed to give a few more details than that?*

Let's just see how far we get with that, I zinged back. *We're just taking this for a test drive before we get serious.*

Be careful. Snickety raised a tweezed eyebrow. *Remember what the book says.* She wagged a finger at my nose. *Be prepared to receive. The universe will deliver, every time.*

The words rose against the backdrop of the green and brown blur outside the car as my tongue began to chant them like a mantra:

I desire to live in the tropics.

I desire to live in the tropics

I desire to live in the tropics.

The taxi continued its dusty quest as we barreled toward the airport to return to Denver. Whatever else might manifest on the playing field of our future would have to wait as once we hit the tarmac, this blissful hiatus would come to an end and I would be back to the reality of my life as it was now, and back to the work that kept me landlocked.

The phone suddenly rang and my memory of that day in the tropics with Joe faded. I reluctantly picked up the phone without thinking, which was not my usual choice. I wanted to know who was calling first and determine if it was worth my time. But the soft edges of the recollection had dulled my usual sharpness.

"Hello?" A deep male voice reverberated through the line.

"Yes?" My voice reflected the abrupt change of consciousness I felt, like the needle on a turntable screeching to a stop. *Shit, that was probably too abrupt,* I gritted my teeth.

"May I help you?" I asked again, shifting into a polite tone before the caller could say anything.

"I'm calling for JuliAnne Murphy."

I sat up straighter. This caller sounded like he was used to getting his way.

"May I tell her who's calling?" Now my voice was cheery, a little fake, impersonating the company receptionist. It was an old trick my mother had used to deter telemarketers and other callers with whom she didn't wish to speak.

"My name's Clark Guy," the voice said, "with Eckle and Zurquist."

Someone else trying to sell us advertising, no doubt. A glance at my Blackberry confirmed the time: 8:30 a.m. *I guess this one's read the book about calling first thing early in the morning when all the execs are still at their desks.*

"May I tell her the purpose of your call?" I tried again, hoping this was not someone I had met who would figure out it was me.

The man hesitated, before clearing his throat. "It's a personal business matter," he said. "But it's important I speak with her."

"Please hold a moment," I said, and hit the hold button. *This could be interesting. The guy doesn't sound like the usual.* I could sniff out a cold caller like a greyhound. But this one had been neither aggressive nor harried. *Hmm.* I let the call hold for a moment before pushing another button to reactivate the line.

"JuliAnne Murphy," I said with the deep, confident tone of a future senior vice president.

"Thank you for taking my call." The voice's tenor had not changed. "My name is Clark Guy with Eckle and Zurquist."

"How may I help you, Clark?" I came to my feet in front of my phone.

"I'm with an executive search firm," Clark replied. "We've been hired to conduct an international search for a marketing executive position in the Republic of Panama."

"I appreciate your call, Clark," I replied, my voice even, "but, I'm not looking for a job. I'm very happy here in my current position."

"Of course," Clark's voice turned jovial, as if he'd expected that response. "We're aware you're not looking for a job. You've recently been promoted this year, correct? To vice president? That's pretty exciting. Congratulations."

His familiarity caused my heart to skip a beat. *Where does he get his information?*

"Well, yes." I hesitated, in order to regroup. "I was promoted to V.P. this past February. And, yes, it has been very exciting." I peered at the number again on the face of the phone. "So, as you can see, I'm in good shape," I said. "And, I'm very busy, Clark. I appreciate the call, but please take me off your potential candidate list."

Clark's voice remained pleasant, undeterred. "No worries," he said. "Perhaps you could take a look at the job description, and let me know if you think of anyone else you know who might be a good fit?"

I exhaled, rolling my eyes to the ceiling. *Fricking recruiters!* "I'll do my best," I replied. "Just send it to my assistant. But to be clear, it will be at my convenience, and certainly not today."

"At your convenience," Clark said. "I'd appreciate it." I gave him the email address.

A moment later, the call ended, and I sank back into my ergonomic chair. *What was I doing, again?* The Starbucks cup with a lipstick stain on the rim sat silent and empty beside my keyboard. I chunked it into the empty trash below.

My cursor sat blinking above my open browser. My eyes went to the red number on the mail icon at the bottom of the screen. One hundred fifty-six, it read. "I left last night at 6:45, for God's sake," I groaned. And then like a practiced swimmer, I closed my office door, put both phones on "Do Not Disturb" and dove in.

~

Several days later, I discovered a printed copy of the job description the recruiter had sent to my assistant. It was late on the Thursday before the Labor Day holiday. The hubbub of the office had stilled as most of the staff had left for the long weekend.

After the brief conversation I'd had with the recruiter, my assistant had printed the 30-page attachment and placed it in a blue folder marked "Miscellaneous." Generally, most documents landing in the blue Miscellaneous file only warranted my attention on days like today, when not much else was going on.

"Fuck," I sighed, bemoaning the fact that I'd ever agreed to give the man an ounce of my precious time. Clark Guy had called twice since that original conversation.

"I guess today's your lucky day, Mr. Recruiter," I said, flipping the cover page back and taking a seat at my side table. "Though I'll bet I can get through your 30 pages in about 15 minutes." I simply wanted to get it over and done with so that I could make it home for dinner, a bath, a movie, and maybe a revisit to my tropical wish list from our now distant vacation. All of that sounded like the ticket I needed after a long, stressful week.

An hour later, I lifted my eyes from the last page as an old-time movie projector cranked up in my head. Ethereal projections on a blank white wall became clear as the mist of fatigue fell away. *Panama? Do I even know where Panama is, exactly?* I Googled the location and a beach scene right out of Robinson Crusoe appeared. Suddenly, I saw myself standing on a hill in a sunny, tropical place. Palm trees bowed and waved in the breeze, with the crash of ocean waves behind me.

This is Panama?

My imagination took off like a thoroughbred. The new job—the one I'd just been reading about—was now mine for the taking: the head of marketing for the redevelopment of the former U.S. Air Force base alongside the Panama Canal, a project that would become one of the largest of its kind in the world. To my left, an old landing strip stretched into the distance between swaths of thickly jungled hillsides. To my right, the ghosts of multi-storied buildings sat abandoned, rotting in the tropical heat.

Ding.

I was ripped out of my reverie once again when a text from Joe splashed across my phone, asking why I wasn't home yet. When I saw the time, I jumped before I replied that I'd gotten caught up at the office and would be right home. As I scrambled to clear the cobwebs of the daydream, close the Panama beach photo on my computer, and gather my things, Snickety piped up.

Beware what you wish for, my dear. I thought I heard a slight chuckle behind her words, but I was used to her "mark my words, dearie" attitude. All I could really focus on at that moment was one looming thought: *How the hell am I going to tell Joe about all of this?*

CHAPTER 5:
Joseph Patrick O'Malley

Joseph Michael O'Malley was a force to be reckoned with and was the type of guy you never forget. Not because he was attractive (which he was) and not because he was successful (which he was), but more because he had that kick-ass, take-no-prisoners, winner-takes-all confidence that overwhelmed you when you first met him.

A slow "Hello" was what he'd first said to me after a presentation I had made, and after he'd barreled through two other people in order to cross my path. "I'm Joe O'Malley." His big grin and the self-satisfied look on his face seemed to indicate that he thought I already knew who he was. But my face let him know I was drawing a blank.

The force of his personality came at me like a tsunami when I looked up and saw him heading my direction at that first meeting. As the subsequent wave of energy hit me, I felt my throat catch. I felt overwhelmed when I first met him; it was as if a foul ball had come out of left field and hit me in the chest: the impact of it almost physical. I was instantly defensive.

"I'm sorry." My tone was curt. "And you are?"

My nonplussed look caught Joe off guard and he recoiled slightly, as if he'd been slapped. But, the dismay passed quickly because a moment later, he rearranged his surprise into a broad smile. His voice took on a more formal tone.

"My apologies." He bowed forward, this time with a serious attempt at diplomacy. "I'm the new site manager for the project with Corporate Construction. I thought perhaps Gene had told you I would be here today." He'd reeled back the alpha male within him to reveal a softer side.

My knee jerk defenses relaxed when I heard my colleague's name. *Oh,* I thought. *Well, he must be all right if he knows Gene.* I made a conscious effort to relax my shoulders.

"I see," I replied. "But no, Gene didn't mention it." I extended a tentative hand to Joe, while maintaining a neutral expression. "Nice to meet you." The meeting of our hands was perfunctory, professional.

Then, I moved on toward the door.

"Great presentation," Joe shouted after me. "You really had them eating out of your hand!"

I glanced back with a slight smile to find him staring at my retreating form. The look on his face was blatantly sensual, yet appreciative in a sort of pleasant way that made me pause for a split second. The warmth I had let bleed through my defensiveness a moment earlier exploded into a flood of liquid honey streaming down the middle of my stomach toward my legs.

WTF, Jules? Snickety popped up from her review of all the things we still had pending to get accomplished that afternoon. *Keep walking.*

As my head swung back, Joe had raised hooded eyes toward me and my stomach did a little flip-flop.

Oh, shit. Snickety took one look at my face. *You're in trouble.*

I made the fatal error in turning to glance back at him again. Suddenly, my brain captured the fine details of his physique: dark, curly hair peppered with the tiniest bit of gray, a muscular build, eyes the color of caramel. His palm came up to wave in my direction, but it was the electric stare that followed that let me know something incredible was happening.

"How is it that men always look distinguished when they're going gray, but women just look old?" I muttered this nonsensical question to myself as I started my car to leave. But, on the 45-minute drive home, all I could do is reflect on every detail of that first 90-second meeting.

Joe towered over everyone he met with his muscular shoulders thrown back and a long stride that could be mistaken for arrogance, as if he had the world by the tail. But that little bit of arrogance was like an aphrodisiac. I wanted to know more. And, to be fair, Joe had reason to be confident. At age 50, he was successful by any modern day standard. He'd conquered the world of construction, working his way up from laborer to become project executive of the nation's largest football stadium project in 2001 by age 44. He delighted in sharing colorful stories of how his lack of a college degree hadn't held him back from corporate success. Part of his pedigree revolved around "the way things were done in the field, when

I was coming up."

When I first met Joe, I realized he was the equivalent of the crown prince on the project on which we both worked. With more than 1,400 workers at his beck and call, Joe was the second in charge of the largest construction project in the region, the building of the new Mile High Stadium for our hometown National Football League (NFL) team, the Denver Broncos. In honor of his station (once I had stopped fighting and succumbed to his charms), I teasingly referred to him as "Number Two," a moniker to which he did not take too kindly.

Joe was well known for his handshake of steel and a commanding voice. With confidence that came easy, he never seemed to meet a stranger, whether in the boardroom or at the bar. But an easy-going personality crossed the line to brashness when he'd enjoyed more than a few martinis, often resulting in subsequent vigorous arguments. And as we went headlong into a torrid affair I'd only previously read about in novels, this part of him was a turn-on that I loved.

This hulk of a man was a man used to getting his way, whether through sheer force of will or experience learned by hard knocks. If one of those methods didn't work, he had the uncanny knack of being able to charm the pants off anyone who crossed his path with his Chicago-born wit and an irresistible grin. These were the survival mechanisms he'd learned as a scrappy kid, competing for his parents' attention among older and larger brothers and sisters.

Once his larger-than-life personality had been turned on me, I was toast to his wit and his charm. My usual defenses toward attractive men of his type had been quite literally dismantled within minutes of our second meeting.

Joe's razor-sharp humor disarmed me completely, causing me to burst into laughter at his edgy jokes that were completely inappropriate for the workplace. But, for me, the sexual play lit a fire between us that would not go out. His tone would vary from light to evocative. While schoolboy charm belied the devil in his almond eyes, I felt quite clearly in my body that Joe was no innocent being. The stirring beneath my breast never lied and, by the time our second meeting ended, all I wanted was more.

When business was done and the room was emptying, I noticed out of the corner of my eye that he was walking in my direction instead of toward the exit. I looked up in anticipation, then put my head back down hoping he did not see how eager I was, in case he'd been heading toward someone else. *Could I be wrong? Am I imagining all this chemistry...*

What else could he possibly need to say to you? said Snickety, her arms crossed in front of her chest. *Anything he had to say could have been dealt with in the meeting.*

But my instincts had been correct. After I had gathered my things, I turned to head for the door and ran smack into Joe, not having seen his final approach when my back was turned.

"Hi," he said smoothly, his tone just the slightest bit sensual. I felt my insides melt at the rich chocolate velvet of his voice. And, before a cognitive thought could even form in my brain, I heard my own voice, as if in a dream, agreeing to meet him for lunch. Our eyes locked and all I could wish for in that moment was that lunch would be as soon as possible. Looking back, I realized I had never even had a chance to say no. Nor had I wanted to, to be honest.

We met at the Brown Palace Hotel for lunch, and I made sure I looked better than their five-star desserts. My green silk dress fit me like a glove and my scrappy heels boosted me a few extra inches, but I knew he would still tower over me. Joe led me to a table by the window. His manners surprised me as he pulled out my seat ahead of the waiter before sitting down himself, removing his jacket and giving me a peek of his svelte form.

As we began the dance, talking about the histories and the questions of likes and loves, I learned that he too was a self-described "veteran" of previous marriages with a third one on the way out. I also learned that he was raising five kids in his blended family. While most women would head for the hills when they heard the word "teenager," I ignored the red flags, and instead allowed myself to fall head over heels as he entertained me with tales of the household chaos. I admired the fact that in the midst of everything this engaging man juggled in his life, he still somehow maintained a remarkable level-headedness about him. I was rapidly moving toward total annihilation of the heart, though my brain knew better.

A married man with teenage kids? Snickety scolded. *Are you crazy?*

I too was married, though it was not a happy one.

But, our laughter was arousing, his smile smoldering. Behind the bravado and the charisma, I came to know another side of this elusive man. He became the romantic who brought me gerber daisies every year on the anniversary of the night we had first made love. That night was full of heat and abandon as he engulfed me under his body, bringing me to climax over and over. We couldn't sleep and as the hours unfolded, our sexual exploration peaked after seven hours and we fell asleep in each other's arms. The deal was sealed. I loved this man beyond anything I had ever experienced.

Over the years, Joe became the lover of my dreams. I became sexually alive and he took on a new role as my knight in shining armor.

Steaming chemistry between us swept me away, but it was this tender side of Joe that caused me to step away from my lifelong fear of both men and of failing at marriage, leave behind all the shoulds, the "have-tos," and all the taboos that came with growing up in a hyper-religious family related to getting involved with a man with grown children, and fall head over heels in love with him.

Because both Joe and I were previous offenders in marriage, we took our time in getting to the altar. But seven years to the day after we decided to be together, Joe and I took the plunge: marrying on a weekday afternoon in a private ceremony with our three closest friends. Joe donned his favorite Hawaiian shirt and I wore a favorite sundress, and we came together in a beloved city park, holding hands and reading our handwritten vows to each other in the middle of a flower garden. I knew I had hit gold and this was finally the forever relationship that would see me through the rest of my life.

Now, as I drove home with the image of Panama burned into my mind, I was apprehensive. Joe was my rock, but even in the solidarity of our marriage, I felt a little tentative, bringing up the topic of Panama at all.

Holy shit. Had I gone off the deep end of sanity to think that I might trash a new promotion here in the States and go after this crazy adventure? What if this wasn't Joe's idea of a dream at all?

Joe was mixing himself a drink when I sauntered into the kitchen, tossing my keys on the counter and giving him a big kiss. He turned to me with passion, like it wasn't the thousandth time we had kissed, to hold me close for a few seconds longer than usual. I reached past him and took a sip of his gin and tonic to get the nerve.

"O'Malley," I said, turning to take off my jacket so I could avoid eye contact. It was an affectionate habit of ours to call each other by our last names from the days we'd worked together. "I got a call from a recruiter this week."

"Really?" was his muffled reply as he went back to chopping something on the butcher block. "And?"

"Actually, the guy has been calling me for weeks," I replied.

"Anything interesting?" Joe put down the knife to take a swig.

I paused for a moment, unsure of what to say as I felt a bout of uncharacteristic butterflies fluttering in my stomach, as if I was getting ready to step onto a tightrope.

But why? Snickety frowned at me from her knitting. *You have nothing to hide.*

"It's kind of a crazy thing," I said, as I took a gulp of air to calm my restless stomach. "It's a pretty cool job in… Panama." I paused to gauge his response.

Joe put down his glass to wash his hands. "Panama?" he asked. He lifted a bushy eyebrow at me in query as I pulled myself up straighter and continued.

"I know, right?" I said, as if I was back in sixth grade presenting my first paper in front of the entire class. My fingers started twisting together, evidence of my discomfort, but I quieted them before Joe could notice.

"Well, it's a project similar to what I'm doing now," I said. "But bigger, way bigger and better. Plus, the pay is almost double what I make now." I knew that would get his attention.

Joe shot a broad smile my way and it was full of affection. He always told me he loved the fact that I was as smart as I was beautiful. Then, he went on to tell me that from the beginning of our courtship my brain was my sexiest attribute. That said, he also knew that I was in love with everything exotic which often led me in random directions. His smile put me to rest and I knew the game was on. We were about to seriously entertain a wild hare idea. Together.

He poured another drink and we went out on the front porch to watch the sun set behind the Rockies. "The position is actually very interesting," I said, reaching up to sweep an errant curl from his forehead. "Would you have any problem with me talking to them further?"

"Have they already asked you for an interview?" Joe took his drink in one hand and my arm in the other and led me upstairs to the bedroom.

"So no interview?" he repeated.

"Not yet," I replied, relieved that that was the truth. "But they will call me." I sat on the edge of our bed as Joe leaned in for a kiss.

Joe grinned at my confidence. My sheer force of will to go after what

I wanted was another thing he loved about me.

"Okay," he said. "Talk to them." I leaned toward my husband and pressed my lips to his in a manner that suggested we might simply end the conversation here. I squeezed his hand in silent victory and lingered with his lips a few more seconds. Joe pulled me to my feet, unhooking my bra under my blouse, and squeezing me tight.

"But, we're not moving to Panama," he added.

I grinned. "Right, honey," I replied as I settled back into the wall of pillows on our bed, happy to have received the answer I wanted.

CHAPTER 6:
The Meeting in Miami

After all my fantasies had spun the stuff of dreams, my dreary office suddenly felt like someone had thrown cold water in my face and I was alert in a way I could not remember feeling before. The sound of the ocean evaporated. What really caught me off guard, however, was that I had only read the damn job description to help the recruiter out. I was not prepared to have been drawn in hook, line, and sinker. Now I was in a full-blown obsession. I had never expected that what those pages held would ignite a flame of hope in my belly, but it had. I was now nervous. Very nervous. And, over the years, I had come to know this feeling as a signal that I was about to embark on a new adventure with no clear outcome. Risk loomed large. I tried to tamp down my heart-pounding desires as they pushed through the soil of my heart like a seed seeking the sun.

You have everything you really want, don't you? said the little voice inside my head. *Why make waves?*

But the truth was that there wasn't much in my day-to-day life that excited me anymore. With all I had achieved—the accolades, the responsibility, the big budgets, the climbing salary, the nice bonuses—it really wasn't lighting my fire anymore, even though my internal success-in-life checklist added up to 10. The measurement of inspiration I had once used to determine if I was meeting my goals was rapidly looking more like a five, which had me off-balance. I didn't feel all that revved up about much of anything at the moment. Instead I just felt tired. *Was I ever that excited?* I wondered.

Had I settled for so much less and called it perfection, called it enough, when it was me accepting a diluted life?

And, that's where the surprise came in. The stuff I had read in those

30 pages was in fact *very* interesting. The opportunity I'd seen there—to be at the beginning of a huge development project in the middle of the tropics, in the Republic of Panama, in Latin America—well, it was definitely exotic and I was definitely excited.

But what made it even more intriguing was that this development wasn't just some mega-bridge being built over a river, or a new, flashy resort being plunked down on a remote beach. This project sounded like it was going to have an enormous impact on the entire country. All of a sudden I saw that I could be a change agent on a whole new plane. My heart swelled with pride at what I could accomplish, the role I might play in this very important project. Giving back to the community was something that made me feel good, and it was such a bonus that it came with the money and prestige and the tropical life.

Wow!

The idea of working abroad had always intrigued me. In fact, Joe and I had talked about it for years, but we had always assumed that it would be Joe's job—in large-scale construction—that would take us there. Joe had even been recruited once or twice for some foreign jobs in past years, but we'd decided against them as his two boys were still teenagers, and he wanted to be around until they were grown.

But Panama was different. The enormous plot of land was adjacent to the country's capital city and had been the site of a former military base. Panama had plenty of old military installations according to the brief, which said that until recent years, the U.S. had been occupiers of all the land on either side of the Panama Canal.

I tried to think what I knew about Panama. My recollection didn't bring up much.

I winced as I pulled up a map of Latin America to see where Panama was actually located—was it Central or South America? I hadn't paid much attention to geography in seventh grade.

Two things did surface, however.

First, I had learned about the engineering marvel that many called the "Eighth Wonder of the World," the man-made Panama Canal, that had been dug out almost 100 years prior by the U.S. to connect the Atlantic and Pacific Oceans.

Second, there had been some dictator the U.S. had taken out of power, by force, when I was in college, if I remembered correctly. *Is that guy still in power?* I flipped through the 30 pages to see if his name was anywhere.

I had never heard of the developers who were conducting the job search. I knew most of the ones in the U.S., but these guys were based out of Europe and South America. The plan was to create a new town from scratch on this old, abandoned military site. In fact, these people had already been awarded the contract by the government to do so.

What had impressed me was that these guys—whoever they were— had their shit together. The package Clark had sent me included detailed information on the company, the project, the country, and the position. These investors were serious.

Overall, I thought the entire thing sounded incredibly ambitious, but exciting. This was the beginning of a 25-year project! The chance to be in at the start of something this scale and size was a once-in-a-lifetime opportunity. The cherry on top was that they were seeking someone with my expertise and I, as always, would be the only female executive on the project. Could I do it? Could I measure up? Did they have a hundred other people they were scouting?

Correction, the little voice inside my head retorted. *The recruiter has called three times already. They are looking for* you.

They are looking for me? I smiled and felt a bit indulgent. *Well, of course, they should be! I'm a pretty rare bird.*

And, rare birds come at a very high price! the little voice said.

I flipped back through the position description the recruiter had sent and I almost laughed as I did. It read as if it had been written based on my very own profile.

Real estate sales executive with more than fifteen years of experience working on high-profile development projects. Experience working with master plans and various builders, as well as a track record of successful marketing campaigns to various sectors and industries with high-level communication skills. Spanish language desired but not required.

You really need to relax, the voice inside my head piped up. *You've got everything right here that you need, everything you've worked so hard for. You're already in a perfect position.*

But there was something nagging inside my heart, an itch just out of reach begging to be scratched. It was that part of me that always was on the lookout for something more. That part that dreamed that there could be something more, beyond what I already had.

Well, what if? I wondered. *Could it hurt just to see where this might go?*

~

I pulled on the jacket of my navy blue suit and adjusted the collar of my crisp white cotton shirt underneath the lapel. Particular about first impressions, I wanted to be sure this one was perfect.

I tested my smile in the mirror and carefully applied a conservative shade of plum to my lips. *Not too flashy, not too conservative.*

The search firm had booked me a hotel on the same street as their offices, just three blocks away from where the interview would be held in Miami. I decided to walk.

No matter the outcome, I adored interviewing. To me, interviewing felt very much like a chess match and I was good at the game.

Use your best strategy to outsmart the players, I mused. *But skillfully make them think you're giving them the outcome they're looking for, just before you take their queen,* I smiled.

Ding! rang the elevator bell as the doors opened before me on the 10th floor, facing a set of wide doors leading to a boardroom overlooking a river.

"May I bring you something to drink?" The receptionist interrupted my thoughts.

"Just water, thanks," I replied with a pleasant smile as I scanned the empty room's elegant high-backed chairs to determine which one I preferred.

I knew from years of experience that where you sat in a room set the tone for the entire conversation. Sitting directly across from someone could be construed as combative or competitive, whereas sitting adjacent to someone was friendly or collaborative. I selected a chair facing the door, so that I could stand and greet Ethan and Julio as they entered. I sat at the end of the table on one side, so that one man could sit beside me, and the other just across from me.

I licked my lips in anticipation. But as I did, my tongue discovered something on my upper lip.

Shit! My heart started to race, and I fumbled for the Chanel compact in my handbag. I didn't want to take the chance of smearing my lipstick right before they came in. Nothing like having lipstick on your teeth to ruin a first impression! What if they came in right that moment? Quickly locating the offending hair, I removed it and gave myself one last appraising glance in the tiny mirror. My hand was just dropping the compact back into my bag when the mahogany doors opened. I arranged my face into a pleasant smile, pushed back my chair, and rose to my feet.

Ethan marched across the room toward me with firm, decisive strides. Julio entered quietly and closed the door behind him.

"Good morning," Julio and Ethan said in unison as they approached.

Ethan's clear blue eyes were respectful as they met mine, and a slight smile graced his coffee-colored face.

"JuliAnne Murphy," I said as my hand met his in a firm handshake. "Great to meet you."

"You, as well," Ethan replied in a slight Latin accent, though his English was perfect.

Julio came close behind in a wrinkled, open-collared suit. His posture was bowed, older than his years, and he lumbered at me like a big fuzzy bear. I stifled a grin as he took my hand and placed his other hand atop mine, covering it with his own. He peered at me over the spectacles perched low on his nose.

"Good morning, Ms. Murphy," he said. "Thank you for coming all this way." I heard European roots in his grammar, though it seemed to hide behind Ivy League educated enunciation.

"Make yourself comfortable," Ethan said, as he motioned me to the table, before he settled himself into the chair, at its head, next to me.

"So, you're the girl from Denver," Ethan observed, as his eyes appraised the clean lines of my wool suit from top to bottom.

"Yes, I am," I replied as I returned his sardonic gaze in quiet confidence. If his demeanor toward me was a test, I was going to set him straight right from the start. The even look in my eyes told him right off the bat I would be taking no bullshit and certainly no advances.

His pupils widened as the message registered. A slight smile teased his lips in return.

So, you're the one that charms them, my mind said silently as it scribbled notes furiously into my memory, *and Julio's the anchor. I wonder who closes the deal?*

"Where would you like to start?" I summoned my most professional tone, taking the helm of the meeting as if I were already the pilot of this ship.

And, in the back of my mind, I heard, *Now, let the games begin*.

CHAPTER 7:
A Panama Welcome and Juan Carlos

When the pilot announced our final descent into the city of Panama, Joe grabbed my hand.

"Are you ready?" he asked with a sparkle in his eye. "This is your adventure, after all. I'm just along for the ride."

"I think I am." I gave him a quick peck on the lips.

We turned to the window, eyes wide for that first glimpse of our final destination. Our eyes were met with the outline of what looked like tiny battleships lined up against the dark waters of the Pacific Ocean.

"Look," said Joe, "all those ships are waiting to go through the Panama Canal! They have to be in line, with their fee paid for the passage, at least three days in advance." Joe had been consuming books about Panama's economy since the call had come through from Miami.

The plane banked left to follow the coastline. As it did, Joe pointed toward the arc of a large steel bridge. "And I believe that's the Bridge of the Americas across the Panama Canal."

"That's it?" I whispered. I'd read so much about the Panama Canal in the prior weeks that I'd kind of expected it to appear nostalgic with rays of sun bursting from the clouds behind it. I saw a large boat coming toward us from under the bridge. Spires of blue and green steel rose high in the air, in the distance, behind the bridge.

Joe followed my vision. "Those are cranes for Panama's two Pacific side ports," he said. "They're the most active ports in Latin America." He sounded proud of all his newly acquired knowledge and I appreciated it all since packing to leave had consumed me.

I stopped myself from blurting what I was thinking, *I don't even know what that means, "Pacific side ports."*

As the plane continued its descent, my eyes widened at the number of skyscrapers towering above the city landscape. The variety of colors and sizes and styles of the buildings exploded across the landscape like a sunburst. And, mirroring what I'd seen online, the new towers were dotted with slums. I'd read that Panama was undergoing a massive explosion of foreign investment; this was visual proof.

The landscape changed as the airport came into view. The skyscrapers abruptly disappeared. Tin roofs on metal shacks with laundry strung on wire strips outside belied the abject poverty of the poor neighborhoods next to the airport. The dirt roads between the shacks were overflowing with a dark red mud, sure evidence of Panama's rainy season that I understood was at its height this time of year. The line of tiny structures seemed to go on and on. Palm tree fronds waved in the wind behind them.

Two minutes later, the pilot set the plane down on the tarmac. Applause broke out within the cabin. We looked at each other. *What does that mean?*

Joe began to fight the stream of oncomers from overtaking him while he attempted to retrieve the second bag from the overhead compartment, but passengers seemed to be lit on fire to exit the plane faster than was needed. The flow of bodies was overwhelming. Finally, he fell back down in his seat with disgust.

"First time in Panama?" A passenger posed the question to us as if the answer wasn't already obvious.

"Well, yes, this is our first time," I said.

Her face spread into an amused grin as she held out her hands. "Welcome to Panama!"

Once we were at our accomodations and just five minutes after Joe and I began to unpack, the phone in the hotel room rang.

"Miss JuliAnne?" a woman's voice asked.

"Yes," I replied, the exhaustion causing my voice to tremor as I sat down on the quilted bed.

"My name is Ana. I'm working with Señor Juan Carlos and I'll be taking you around tomorrow to see some houses." I lifted an eyebrow at Joe, who was hanging clothes up in the narrow closet. *Funny,* I thought, *I figured we would do that at some point, but no one had brought it up yet.*

"What time would you like to go?" Ana asked.

"I'm not sure what the plans are," I stumbled, wondering about the protocol of accepting an invitation before it was discussed.

"How about noon, then?" Ana replied. "I know you have a breakfast with Mr. Juan Carlos, so that should give you plenty of time."

I agreed and we hung up. No sooner had I stepped toward the open suitcase lying on the bed when the phone rang again.

"Yes, Ana?" I lifted the receiver back to my ear, expecting she had forgotten something.

"Hello? Hello?" A man's voice blasted through in unaccented English.

"Hello?" I assumed an executive tone when I realized the caller was my new potential boss.

"Juan Carlos?"

"Can you hear me?" Juan Carlos' voice blasted through so loud the line buzzed. In the background, the backup alarm on a delivery truck was accompanied by a cacophony of honking horns.

"How are you?" Juan Carlos asked. "Did you get in all right? Was everything okay with your flight?"

Before I could answer, he continued, "Look, I lined up a relocation gal who is going to call later to set up an appointment for you to go see some apartments tomorrow."

I decided to break in. "Juan Carlos?" There was a long pause. Had the man hung up?

"Oh, yeah, sorry," his voice said, and being a wife, my instinct told me the man's attention had wandered elsewhere.

I waited since he was clearly multitasking which was a pet peeve of mine.

Juan Carlos' voice resurfaced. "Umm, yeah. So, we have dinner tonight at eight, and we'll pick you up at 7:30. Does that work?"

I decided not to bother him with the news that Ana had already called; we could discuss it at dinner. "Okay then, we'll see you at 7:30," I said. "Thank you."

"Wow!" I hung up the phone. "Two calls in 10 minutes. This is not what I expected in Latin America. These guys are on the ball!"

Since the dinner that night was the first time I had ever laid eyes on Juan Carlos, the butterflies in my stomach started their dance an hour prior to our pickup time. I didn't get unnerved easily, but I cut myself some slack reminding myself that I had every right to be nervous in a new country where my entire future hung in the balance. This one interview could mean a new city, new lifestyle, new culture, *and* new job.

I rifled through my closet and picked out a long-sleeve fitted white cotton shirt with navy blue pants for dinner. I didn't love the outfit, but I had packed frugally in order to limit the size of my bag, so options were limited. I would have preferred a dress knowing that the boss' wife would be wearing one, but the few I flipped through in my closet as I'd packed hadn't felt right for the trip.

"You'll be wearing a sports jacket and khakis," I informed Joe.

Joe tossed his eyes skyward. "Anything for you, dear." My husband despised dressing up.

"Who wears this crap when it's this hot?" Joe swore, as we stood perspiring outside at 7:30 p.m. on the sidewalk waiting for Juan Carlos to pick us up. He wiped a bead of sweat off my melting forehead.

I stood, hands on hips, hoping that our hosts would not notice where the sheer places of my shirt were already sticking to my skin.

Moments later, an attractive couple leapt energetically out of a slick SUV with jet black windows and chrome wheels. The descending activity caught us off guard.

"Good evening! Hello!" the two called out as they approached. "How are you? Welcome!" The man who we assumed must be my new boss gave Joe's hand an energetic shake and kissed my left cheek. His wife followed suit with the kiss.

The rush of close physical contact put me on my defense, bringing a frozen smile to my face, as we accepted the warm greetings. *It's like we're long lost family members*, I thought, as I resisted the inclination to step backwards at what felt like an invasion. "Juan Carlos, I assume?" I stammered, since neither of the two had introduced themselves. I tried to make my tone light so I didn't sound rude.

We sailed through the drive to dinner without a hitch. Juan Carlos and Alejandra were talkative, informative, and polite—full of facts about Panama and the history of the real estate project I was interviewing for.

Dinner was an endless flow of tapas in a dimly-lit restaurant in Panama's historic city. Though it was dark when the SUV entered the UNESCO World Heritage site, it was as if history unfurled before us as we looked out at picturesque, tree-lined squares, colonial architecture, and narrow, cobblestoned streets.

This is still an interview, Snickety reminded me. *Don't mess it up by getting too familiar.* I had survived enough company Christmas parties over the years to not mistake merriment for friendship. *Could it be a test?*

Meanwhile, my husband was relaxed and convivial, enjoying himself with the other couple. When the topic of his business in construction management surfaced, Juan Carlos' ears perked up as he called the waiter over and ordered Joe another gin and tonic.

"We'll need someone like you as we go along." My new boss gestured at Joe with his wine glass. "Why don't you send me your resume?"

Joe looked pleased at the request, but I felt a stab of jealousy. *What if they end up wanting him and not me?*

"Great." Joe winked at me across the large table. "If you're lucky enough to get my wife down here, then I'd be happy to talk to you when the time comes." My chest flushed with warmth at his compliment. *He has my back,* I winked back. *I'm lucky to have a husband that gets how the game is played.*

I couldn't wait to get back to the hotel so Joe and I could compare notes.

"What do you think?" The question flew out of my mouth before the lobby doors closed behind us. Joe laughed out loud as we crossed toward the elevator.

"Whoa there, Nelly," he said, patting my backside. "Give me a minute." Onlookers did a double-take as his hand caressed my ass.

Aware that his antics might have offended, Joe turned with a wide grin to an elegant couple behind us. "Buenas noches," they said in unison with a nod. The man smiled; the woman did not.

"Let me get out of these clothes before I pass out. Then, let's go down to the cigar bar downstairs and have a drink." Joe needed to decompress and so did I. The only question my mind was chewing on was, *Will we be coming to Panama?*

~

The following morning, I discovered Juan Carlos in a back booth in the hotel restaurant. His voice reached me first, ricocheting off the empty tables and chairs.

Is it necessary to talk that loud? The volume irritated me until I realized it was him. As I approached, I saw that he was on the phone.

From the looks of him, Juan was upset with the party on the other end. His voice climbed up and down, punctuated with a few, "*De que?*" which were delivered with force. The thick black hair on his head stood at attention, as if they'd been subjected to a windstorm.

Surely he'll get off the phone soon, now that I've arrived, I thought. That would be courteous, at least in my world.

But, every time, I thought the call was winding down due to the return of calmer speech and several "*Sí, sí, sí,*" his animated gestures became minimal, but then the entire roller coaster ride would start all over again. I shot a discrete peek at my watch.

Twenty-five minutes after my arrival, my coffee made its appearance and the waiter invited me to partake in the buffet. Growing irritable at the wait, I got up to take a look.

A whopping 45 minutes after I'd arrived, Juan Carlos blew a loud sigh from his lips as he punched the end button on his phone. His eyes appraised my empty cup and plate. "Sorry 'bout that," he said. "That was one of the government people I've been trying to reach for a week. The funny thing about the government people here is that once you have them on the phone, you'd better talk to them, because you'll have a helluva time catching them again."

"Don't they have cell phones?"

Juan Carlos shot me a quizzical look. "Well, yes. But that doesn't mean they answer them." I nodded and tucked the information away for the future.

Three hours later, we rose from the table and shook hands.

I departed for the short commute to our room upstairs. Once safely inside the elevator, I leaned my head back against the wall. "Whew." The loudness of my sigh surprised me. *Wow, that man put me through the ringer.* I looked at my watch, surprised to see the grilling had only been 180 minutes; it had felt like a million years. *Is this what lab rats feel like, under the microscope?* The entire interview had had the trappings of an interrogation.

I wandered off the elevator feeling the adrenaline begin to subside as I placed the key in the lock of the hotel room. Joe looked up from a magazine as I entered, noting the presence of dark clouds swimming across my features.

"Hey, baby! How'd it go?" His voice was bright.

I was not bright or cheery, just the opposite. "I'm not sure yet." My briefcase dropped to the floor with a thud. "My head is still spinning from all the questions." I paused.

"And, now that I think about it, Juan Carlos ended things so abruptly!" I'd felt like I was on the edge of a precipice when the man had suddenly stopped. Something felt very unfinished in the way we'd concluded.

"All right then," Juan Carlos had said. "We're done here. I'll pick you up in the morning to take you to the project, so you can see it for yourself." He had risen, extended his hand, and given mine a firm shake. All I could say was, "Thank you. Thanks for your time, and for considering me, Juan Carlos. I really appreciate it."

But the ending bewildered me. I reflected to my husband in our hotel room. "I hope it didn't show. But Joe, I mean, while he acted totally unmoved by the meeting, his eyes were wary like a fox. Like he had somehow secured his prey which was…me. Something feels off, but I can't put my finger on it."

CHAPTER 8:
The House Hunt

Joe and I were standing in front of the hotel in the blazing heat. Ana, the relocation agent, had said she would pick us up at noon to go house hunting. In typical North American fashion, there we were—notebooks and camera in hand—when the clock struck noon, but no car in sight.

I hated nothing more than being late. Joe often ribbed me about it. "No one else in the world cares about punctuality like you do," he'd tell me.

"I'm sure we agreed on noon," I said, the effects of not yet having had lunch started to impact my mood.

"Relax," said Joe. "Do we need to get you something to eat?" Part of my husband's job in our relationship was to make sure I got fed at semi-regular hours when we were together. As such, he always made sure to have an eye out for places that could provide sustenance. It was a habit of mine to forego food when I was stressed, which often made my company less than enjoyable.

"I'm fine," I snapped, a telltale sign I had no idea I was slipping into a mood, but not wanting to change plans. My stomach began to growl. "Let's just see a couple of properties, and then we'll get something to eat."

At 25 minutes past the hour, the temporary cell phone I was carrying rang.

"I'll be there in a just a minute." The phone clicked off. It was already 12:30 and my dress dripped with perspiration. After what felt like an interminable amount of time, a small SUV screeched to a stop in front of the hotel. A petite, dark-haired woman waved at the valet, rolling down her window to speak to him. The valet motioned to us to come outside.

Ana motioned for us to enter on the passenger side in front and back. "*Sí, sí, sí.*" Ana was waving her right arm in front of her, talking in an exorbitant volume into an oversized flip phone at her ear, as we entered. "*Sí, señor. No hay problema. Estoy ocupada con clientes ahora y no puedo hablarle en este momento.*"

The second we were inside the car and the doors were latched, Ana squealed into the street, one hand on the wheel and the other on her phone. She still had yet to speak to us as her phone was still glued to her ear. "*Sí, yo se. Yo se! No le puedo responder en este momento. Pero, lo haré. Lo haré, no se preocupa!*" The woman gestured wildly as she drove. My anxiety mounted as I realized her driving resembled that of someone who was under the influence.

Joe turned around and said in a hushed tone, "Hold on, baby! Like I said, we are having an adventure!"

I rolled my eyes as I fumbled for the seat belt strap behind my shoulder, but quickly discovered the lack of a bottom buckle to secure my lap into the seat. *Great,* I thought. *Not only is this woman late, but now she's going to kill us.*

Ana's cell phone sailed from her hand into a large brightly-colored purse at Joe's feet, indicating the call had ended as she peeled through a red light.

"*Aye, disculpe!*" she said, extending a hand to Joe. "How do you do? It's so nice to meet you!" She turned around to extend the same hand at me, missing a head-on collision by an inch before she turned back. "How has your trip been so far?"

I was sure at that very moment my grinding teeth were audible to the entire car. "Uh! Okay! No need to turn around! It's nice to meet you too." Ana whipped back around and slammed on the brakes, causing the three of us to lurch forward toward the windshield. Fortunately, my hands were already braced on the back of Joe's seat.

"So, do you know what are you looking for?" The cheer in the woman's demeanor indicated she was oblivious to the ill will her lateness had caused, or to the wild ride she was giving us through the streets of Panama. Joe began to tick down the list of specifics he and I had discussed, hoping to distract me from my growing anxiety.

"Mmhmm," Ana replied, as she pulled up behind a truck so close that I was sure we were going to scratch its bumper. In a flash, another car screeched so close to my door that I jumped to the other side of the backseat. I looked up, expecting to see concern on Ana's face, but she didn't seem to notice.

"Well, I set up some appointments today so you can get a feel of so[me] apartments and houses that are currently available," Ana mused. "But [it's] important to note that there's a housing shortage in Panama, so if you see something you like, then we may want to put a deposit down on it right away."

"That would be hard to do," I began, but my voice was lost in a cacophony of loud honks. Ana hit the gas pedal and sped up, pulling into a morass of cars blocking the intersection. The stoplight right above our car turned red and once again, we jolted to a sudden stop.

"What I meant to say was," I started again, but again my words were lost as a multitude of cars began to protest the blockade we had caused. A number of them charged forward toward the SUV and were now within inches of us on one side. I shrank into my seat as I saw them approach, raising my arms around my head, and squeezing my eyes shut in anticipation of impact. I clenched my jaw.

But, the impact never came. Instead, a moment later, I felt Joe's hand on my leg. "Everything okay, honey?" He gave me a pat.

"Did they hit us?" I asked, though Ana was now pulling the car forward into an endless stream of vehicles. My eyes darted to the left and the right.

"Everything's fine, babe."

Relief flooded me and my muscles began to relax when I saw his reassuring smile. Tears sprung up behind my eyes. *Was I so unaware of the impact our four-day travel to this country to interview for a potential new job and a new life amidst the chaos of a new culture would have on me? I need to get a grip!* At that moment, Joe became my rock. I inhaled, forcing myself to recall a mantra of relaxation to just be in the moment.

Meanwhile, Ana dodged and darted, injecting the SUV in and out, up and down, among, behind, and between the sea of chaos around us. I tried to surrender to the experience, the way you just let go as a roller coaster plummets over the crest of the ride and sends you screaming to the bottom.

"Ana," I stammered. "Is this traffic normal?"

"Ah, the *tranque*," Ana sighed, noting my look of terror in the rearview mirror. "Yes, this is normal. But, don't worry. If you come here, you'll probably get a driver. That's what most of the *extranjeros* do."

Joe and I nodded as the cars outside lunged closer and closer to us, like sharks going after bait, their bumpers like teeth gnashing just inches away.

I had always dreamed of getting a driver. But, the scenario I'd had in mind had been a decision based on *luxury*, not the only way in which to *survive*.

~

Once the disappointment was over, having seen apartments that I would not wish on my worst enemy, we headed for the hotel bar to decompress. The places we had seen were so substandard, so '80s and so disappointing, full of mold and critters I couldn't even recognize. Suddenly, I missed our fabulous Denver home and wondered if relocating to Panama would even work for us.

"What did you think of our real estate endeavors?" I asked Joe. My limbs hung heavy. This was the moment when we would unload our true feelings about the four homes we'd viewed with Ana.

"I hope we'll see something else we like tomorrow," Joe replied. "It's a mixed bag, isn't it?"

I nodded, downing my cocktail in one fell swoop. I waved my finger at the white-uniformed bartender to bring me a second.

Joe took a look around to see who else was in the bar before he laughed out loud and put a palm to his forehead. "Actually, those two apartments were fine. I was actually thinking about putting a deposit on the third one. You know, the one with the beveled windows and the 1980s décor? I thought the carved lion faucets in gold were kind of appealing."

My guffaw came out as an unladylike snort. "Though the view on that place was quite lovely, don't you think, darling?" It had faced the Pacific Ocean, which had been the only selling point. "But the last place was what caught my fancy!" My eyes began to stream. "The house that had such low ceilings, you could barely see across the room even when the windows were open? Plus, that bathroom tile in pink really brought it up to the top of my list."

The bartender set a new drink in front of me and I downed it in no time. The weight of the day slid off of me like water and suddenly all I could see was the absolute absurdity of everything that had happened since we arrived in Panama. It was nothing like I had expected. What we had seen thus far was so far from my imagined reality that I couldn't even begin to connect my dreams to it.

We were scheduled to meet Juan Carlos the following day at the project site. The former military base had been shuttered by the U.S. government in the late 90s when the 52-mile stretch of land along the entire length of the Canal had been returned to the country of Panama. Everything I had read about the land seemed full of promise: more than 10,000 abandoned structures sat empty surrounding a now-quiet airport. The company I was interviewing with had won the international bid from the government to redevelop the massive project into a new city.

If I were hired, I would be the sole woman on the five-person executive team to kick off the redevelopment. Shivers ran up and down my spine as I pondered this: the chance to redevelop something from the very beginning, an incredible opportunity! I reflected back on the briefing materials the recruiter had sent me. They had included a European newspaper article printed earlier in the summer, detailing that this particular project, Panorama, had been the largest swath of land in the *world* to be awarded to a single real estate developer to date.

My chest swelled with pride. *And they chose me to come interview for a prominent position on the launch team! Holy shit.*

As if he could read my mind, Joe leaned over and brought his face in front of mine. "I am so proud of you," he said, our eyelashes touching. "No matter if we decide to take this job or not, you are a rock star! They'd be damn lucky to have you." I gazed into his ever-present butterscotch eyes and knew that he meant every word. I was lucky he was here with me.

"Thank you," I said, returning his gaze before I kissed him full on the mouth. Joe lingered with my lips while reaching for his drink on the bar. I slipped my hand over the edge of the glass hoping he would abandon his third drink of the night and focus on me seducing him.

He left the glass full and took his hand down to the small of my back where it rested, waiting for my invitation. My eyes narrowed. "I think there's some other real estate I'd like you to take a look at…upstairs." I hopped off my barstool and tugged at his hand, leaning in for a wet kiss. My tongue searched for his as I slid my fingers down his thigh reaching the hardening that was well under way. The bartender was looking the other way as we laughed and began to pick up our things.

Joe's pupils widened as his eyes trailed down my lithe frame. "I'm pretty tired this afternoon, señorita. Are you sure this piece of real estate will interest me?"

"I'm pretty sure it will." I brushed a finger across his mouth, lingering just for a moment on the space between his lips.

Right on cue, the bartender lay the check at Joe's knuckles. "Señor?" he said with a raised brow.

"Well." Joe opened the folio, signed, and got up to follow me. "I guess there's no translation needed for *that*." He laughed when the bartender winked.

We headed up to our hotel room. We were two ships in a new port, but we could always land on safe ground in bed, in each other's arms, and forget all the rest.

CHAPTER 9:
The Fun Begins

My flowery signature graced the line of my offer letter by mid-December after Joe and I had hammered out my counter-offer specifics, all of which my new company had accepted. Sweat gathered on my brow when my pen poised above the dotted line of the contract, and I thought, again, *Am I really going to do this?*

"Eyes wide open," I said aloud, swallowing my fear as I scrawled my name in cursive. And with that, it was done. I would start work in Panama on March 1 of the new year.

The morning after the FedEx with my acceptance had been sent, Joe was examining a calendar when I entered the kitchen with my head wrapped in a turban from my long customary shower.

I crossed over to where he was sitting on a barstool to plant a kiss on his grizzled cheek.

Tapping the calendar on the wall beside him, he glanced over at me above the rim of his reading glasses. "You do realize, don't you, that we have less than nine weeks to go before we move?"

I could feel the anxiety begin to tighten in my stomach. I grimaced as I reached up for my favorite Wonder Woman mug, filling it with water and adding a tea bag. "Can't we just enjoy this for a few days? You know—the awe, the wonder, the excitement? I mean, we're moving to the tropics!"

Joe's right eyebrow lifted at me. "I don't know…*can* we?" His voice increased in volume to be heard over the drone of the microwave. "Can *you*?"

"Mmmm…" I said, turning my head over my shoulder to look back at him. "Maybe…baby." My eyes smiled back at him.

"You know, Joe, just thinking about the weather down there, I get so very *hot*." I turned toward him, leaving my mug on the counter and untied the velvet belt of my robe as I shimmied toward him. "I mean, there won't be much need for comfy things like *this*." The burgundy robe slipped off my shoulders and fell halfway down my body before I caught it at my hips, revealing the luminescent skin of my naked torso.

I could see the jackhammer of lust begin to pulse in Joe's groin, as his eyes took in my playful moves. His fingers dropped the pen he'd been holding before he shoved the barstool back.

"You're so right, my love." His voice dripping honey as his muscular form approached me slowly. "There won't be any need for clothes like that."

My hands released their hold and the velvet robe piled luxuriously around my feet. "With less clothes, we'll be a lot more naked, I think." My open palm traveled to cover my naked pubic mound, and the other hand settled in front of my pursed lips, now forming a suggestive Betty Boop "O."

"I certainly hope so." Joe panted as his eyes traveled up and down my petite curves. His strong hands reached out to encircle my nakedness, one grasping at my voluptuous ass, bringing my body to his; the other palming my right breast, his fingers circling my nipple. His mouth captured mine voraciously. I returned his devouring kiss, my tongue intertwining with his in a game.

"Let's not forget about these flannel pants." I whispered into Joe's ear, as my fingers searched for the tie to loosen them. Lowering his pants, his hard-on popped free from the material, finding its way into the softness of my palm.

"Mmm hmm…," Joe moaned as I began to stroke his hardness lengthwise, up and down.

"Yes, baby," my silky voice replied. "I want you." I lowered to my knees, pushing him back against the kitchen cabinets and spreading his legs apart. Finding his balls with my right hand, I took the length of his cock in my mouth, sucking slightly. Joe's muscles stiffened as his head threw back in pleasure.

"You've always been so good at that," he moaned as his hand dug into my hair, guiding the sumptuous entry and exit into my open mouth. "Mmm," I returned, fiery eyes gazing up as I took him.

Suddenly, Joe withdrew, reaching down below my arms to lift me into the air. "My turn!" he announced, as he tantalized my lips with his own mouth again, kissing me so hard it took my breath away. My bare ass found the cold stone of the countertops as Joe pushed my body back to lean on the bar. His hands kneaded my inner thighs as he lowered his mouth to my pussy. His tongue flickered out gently to lick the wetness of my engorged lips.

"Mmmmm, my little Georgia peach." His voice was muffled as his tongue began to lather me with sweet attention. Sounds of ecstasy escaped my throat, and my pulse began to pound as my lady parts began to throb. "Oohhh, baby, oooh, baby, ooooh."

"Just think of how good this is going to feel in the sand, on the open beach." Joe lifted his head to give a devilish wink.

"Don't stop, don't stop." I pulled his head back, where his mouth took me yet again. His hands continued stroking my thighs and my outer lips as his tongue found that sacred spot. A moment later, I exploded into delicious blankness as I climaxed. "Yes! Yes! Yes! Oh God! Oh God, baby!" I screamed.

Joe's tongue continued its gentle lapping, as the waves of pleasure subsided.

"Oh, thank you, baby. Thank you, thank you, thank you." My voice soothed though my eyes remained closed.

"Oh, we're not done yet," he said, as his hands gripped my hips and slid me toward the edge of their perch. He took the edge of his cock and circled the inside of me. "Oh yes," I said. "Oh yes, I want you in me." I pulled my body upwards to meet his, my tongue searching for his.

In a split second, he entered me, my wet folds taking him in. His breath caught in his throat as he traveled my length, every cell of his body feeling my sensuousness to his hilt.

I began to ride him, one hand behind me on the counter, the other holding on to his muscular back. His hips thrust into me, and withdrew, then thrust again, and again, and again. Joe's face contorted as his pleasure mounted. Guttural sounds escaped his lips, as I tugged and sucked at them.

"I can't wait to conquer new territories with you," I whispered.

Joe's pupils widened as he gazed into mine, nodding, as he came close to the brink, riding me like only a well-practiced stallion could. "Oh, yeah, baby, yeah, yeah, yeah!"

Our lips met again, as his eyes closed this time and he exploded into me.

~

The days ahead stretched before us as we began the arduous task of preparing to move. While the new company would provide support, the logistics and the organization fell on our shoulders.

My spiral notebook began to fill with list upon list in preparation. One task would be checked off, and another three would take its place. My normal cheery demeanor was soon giving way to a perpetual state of anxiety. There were jobs to resign from, relocation quotes to request, decisions to be made about the house—would we keep it, sell it, rent it, what? I began a close study of Panama's weather, eyeing my wardrobe with mounting suspicion. Would any of the clothing I already had work down there?

Every evening, we fell into bed exhausted after reviewing the day's progress, amidst a growing number of boxes and forms on the kitchen table related to the move. It seemed the more we did, the more there was to do.

One night, we realized we had seen nothing from the relocation agent in Panama. Our move was only six weeks out and we still had nowhere to live! I picked up the phone and called Juan Carlos.

"Do you really think it's necessary for you to come back to Panama to find a house?" he asked. Irritation rose in me like a cobra. *Is he serious?*

"Juan Carlos, I'm moving my family to another country in order to come to work for you. It's absolutely necessary we have a place to live before we move; we're bringing our pets with us."

This last piece of information wasn't really necessary, but sometimes I added details, just to drive the nail into the coffin.

"Hmm," Juan Carlos' voice implied doubt.

I let the silence hang like a cinder between us. In a leadership class I'd taken the year before, I'd learned that the person who speaks first often loses the negotiation.

"Well, if you need to come, then it'd be best if you came for the board meeting we already have planned in late January. Ethan and Julio will be here, and you can attend at least part of it, if you're coming all this way."

"Great, Juan Carlos." I injected a dose of fake cheer into my reply. "Just send me the dates and I'll be glad to sit in on the meetings a day or two during the trip."

Careful! Snickety warned. *Don't let them take advantage of you before you start getting paid.*

Three weeks later, the same smiling driver was waiting for Joe and me as we emerged, sweating, out of Customs. "Hello Mistah Joe and Mizz JuliAnne." The large man with skin the color of ebony waved his handwritten sign as we approached.

"Hello, Tomas." Joe strode forward with a smile to shake the sweaty hand.

"*Hola, Tomas, como esta usted?*" I stepped forward in light-colored linen as Tomas collected our bags and led us toward the exit.

"*Muy bien, muy bien, gracias a Dios,*" Tomas returned, green eyes sparkling. "So, you come to live in Panama?" He beamed a smile in our direction.

"Sí, señor. We are coming to live in Panama next month." Joe winked, as he offered a hand to help me ascend into the SUV waiting at the curb.

"Very good," said Tomas in stilted English as he took the wheel and began the journey toward downtown, speeding into the night. "And, me thinks you need a driver when you come." Tomas flashed a glance in the rearview mirror to see my reaction to his quick application for a good job.

"We probably will," Joe arched an eyebrow at me over his shoulder as Tomas made a left-hand turn to merge onto the four-lane highway. It was close to 11 p.m., but the traffic was still out in full force.

"I like to come work for you," Tomas said, "and, you can pay me 650 dollars a month."

But Joe played along. "I see, Tomas. That's a very kind offer. Thank you. Tell me, what kind of responsibilities does a driver usually have in Panama that you feel you could offer us for so much American money?"

"Well, I dunno," Tomas said. "Most of the time, you give me a schedule and I do drive you or Mizz JuliAnne wherever you need to go…" The Panamanian's voice trailed off.

"I see." Joe's eyes crinkled in amusement at the mock negotiation. But Tomas broke the tension.

"*Sí, sí, sí*, let me think, let me think," nodded the driver, wiping the sweat from his brow with a white embroidered handkerchief and placing it in the breast pocket of his traditional guayabera shirt. "*A la orden.* I am with you all week. At your service, at your service."

~

The following afternoon, I arrived in the banking district. Tomas pulled up in front of a six-story glass and cement building. A crowd of people were waiting at the door, including two armed security guards wearing thick bulletproof vests and black pistols on their belts.

Droplets of sweat ran down my inner thighs as the humidity enveloped me like a glove. Tomas followed my glance down the long line of people sweltering in the morning sun, and noticed that I was on edge. He nodded his head in my direction with a reassuring smile which did, in fact, help calm me.

For him, this situation must be a regular occurrence in Panama, I thought. So I took his cue and stood a little straighter.

"Oh, no, no, no. Don't worry," he said, pointing. "You go here."

My wide eyes followed his gesture toward the main door, where two security guards stood, eyeing us with suspicion. "Where?" I asked. "Past the line?"

He nodded as I reached toward the glass double doors.

"*Permiso!*" a hostile voice rang out. I turned to find one of the guards waving a finger in my direction. He pointed at my handbag, and then indicated a square wand the other guard was holding.

"Oh," I said, as I turned. "Sorry." The guard motioned for me to open the zipper on my handbag, which I did, assuming he would take a look. Instead, the man stuck a sweaty hand inside and moved my things from one side to the other.

The other guard waved his wand up and down my body. Satisfied that I didn't appear to be a terrorist, the first guard then waved me through. Once inside, I took a deep breath and shot a thankful look back in Tomas' direction, who still stood by the idling car. He gave a thumbs up.

A moment later, Joe arrived, tumbling out from one of the local taxis after spending the entire morning in search of new furniture, and rushed to the doors only to be greeted by the same version of a military coup. As he burst through the doors, sweat dripped from his eyebrows and his back was wet with perspiration. I wrinkled my forehead as we came face to face and he shot me a "WTF is going on in this country" look. We both stifled a laugh.

Finding the second set of glass doors and entering the offices marked "Premiere." I looked around, half expecting to find a receptionist just inside. But there was none.

"Tomas said to go up." Joe pushed past me. "What are you waiting for?" He sounded on edge, for which I didn't blame him; this second encounter with Panama had been challenging and we hadn't yet been there a day! I brushed off the uneasiness I felt when I smelled alcohol on Joe's breath. *Was that from last night or has he been drinking this morning?*

At the top of the stairs a wood podium stood empty. Just past it were two leather couches facing one another and a small coffee table that offered an array of glossy magazines. Joe and I glanced around, only to find not a single person in sight.

"Well, someone needs to know we are here, don't you think?" The irritation of not being able to read or speak the local language was beginning to fray on Joe's nerves. This is when my rusty Spanish put him to ease, just a little.

"*Buenas tardes!*" I called out in a bright voice, as I walked down the hallway a few steps and discovered a woman sitting at her desk, head down. I rapped my knuckles on her door three times.

The woman looked up from applying a coat of mascara to her long lashes. "*Sí?*" A slight look of annoyance crossed her face.

"I have an appointment with this person," I said as I held out the business card. "Juanita Diaz."

"*No hablo ingles.*" She pointed her mascara tube toward the next office. I fought to keep annoyance from registering on my face at her dismissal.

I backed out. "Okay, gracias." The woman resumed her singular attention to her makeup application.

"Can you help me please?" I said, boldly entering the second small office and standing alongside the desk. "We have an appointment with Juanita Diaz, and I don't know where to find her." I stood there for a moment before the man reached out a hand—without making eye contact—and took the damp business card from me.

"Please wait," he said in a heavy accent, and motioned back toward the waiting room where Joe had settled.

Twenty minutes passed. The man walked by but hadn't returned. The waiting room was stuffy, with neither a drinking fountain nor a vending machine in sight. "Go talk to that other woman and see what is going on."

Joe's bark was uncustomary, though clearly the rude treatment was taking its toll.

I walked back to the first office and poked my head inside.

"*Perdoname.*" I struggled with the unfamiliar words. "*Pero el Señor aqui,*" I pointed at the other office, "*left y no se nada.*" I moved my fingers back and forth in a verbal translation for walking, so the woman would understand.

The amply endowed woman nodded. She picked up her phone and dialed. After conversing rapidly in Spanish with the person on the other end, her round face returned.

"He come now." My eyes narrowed at the English words.

Another 30 minutes ticked by before the elevator bell rang again. Joe and I looked up as a tall woman in a dark suit emerged and approached. *This person looks promising,* I thought.

"Miss Murphy?" the pleasant voice said. "Mr. Joe? I'm Juanita Diaz."

That's it? I thought, annoyed as I stood. *It's been almost an hour since our appointment and she doesn't even apologize?* "Yes, that's us." My tone had an edge to it.

"You know, there must have been a mistake. Juan Carlos told us you would be meeting us at one o'clock." I flipped my gaze to my watch. "We've been waiting almost an hour." Joe's head was bobbing alongside mine.

"I'm so sorry." Juanita's expression looked sincere. "I just came back from my lunch break. Please," she said, motioning us toward her empty office further down the hall.

"Now," she purred after the two of us were stuffed into two tiny plastic chairs facing the wooden desk. "How can I help you?"

Our mouths dropped open, my voice rising in surprise. "I'm sorry. I thought Juan Carlos had explained who we were, and what we needed?" Joe let out an audible sigh of frustration.

"One moment." Juanita picked up the handset of a small black phone and dialed three digits. Joe shot an annoyed look at me as her phone conversation stretched on for five minutes.

"Okay," Juanita said after she hung up the phone. "So you want to open a checking account, and you have a check from Señor Juan Carlos. May I see the check please?"

I retrieved the handwritten check from my wallet.

Juanita reviewed it. "Okay. This should be no problem." She rose to leave. "I'll need to gather some forms for you to fill out." Joe's knees knocked against the desktop as she shuffled behind his chair to get out the door.

"Ma'am, is there any way we can speed this up?" Joe's eyes were like daggers pointed at Juanita as she returned.

"Yes, of course," Juanita said, seemingly unruffled by Joe's displeasure. "Let me just ask you a few questions, so we can get these forms filled out." She requested our passports, which we produced, and then a home address, phone, and the usual statistics needed for opening a new account.

"Personal references?" I asked in amazement when Juanita explained we'd need two for our account application. Joe and I stared at one another. "For what? We don't know anyone here yet, other than my new boss."

Juanita wrote down Juan Carlos' name on the line. "Don't worry, I have his phone number. But we can't open the account without a second contact." It was at this moment it seemed to both Joe and me that Ms. Diaz was some sort of expert torturer taking great pleasure in stringing along the outsiders.

Steam began to pour out of my husband's ears. He'd been doing his best this long to stay silent and not simply run the woman down. Here, he took a breath to gather a fraction of composure. "Let me just put down our attorney in Chicago," he said in a calm voice.

"Oh no, that won't work." Juanita wagged her index finger back and forth. "The personal reference has to come from someone in Panama." She smiled in triumph.

"How the hell is that possible, if we are new here and don't know anybody?" Joe's voice rose to a shout. I grabbed his arm to try and calm him down, but it was too late. He had lost his cool in the sizzling heat of this office.

"Isn't there anyone else you know?" Juanita asked. "It's a *requisito* by the bank. Unfortunately, I can't change the rules, Señor Joe."

Joe's face suddenly lit up. He stood up, knocking his knees again, to reach for a slip of paper in his pocket. Taking the pen from her hand, he wrote in the name and telephone number himself. The strain on my face lifted into amusement when I saw what he'd written. It was the name of our driver, Tomas.

As Joe pushed the application form back across to Juanita, with his own triumphant grin, the phone on the desk rang. Juanita answered it and my face fell as I listened to the voice on the other end of the line. As she replaced the receiver, she informed us, "I'm very sorry, but I've been called into a meeting with my boss. You'll have to finish up your papers with Mr. Juan." Without a hello or goodbye, Ms. Diaz disappeared out the door.

"But, wait! We had an appointment with you! We need to complete this process in order to secure a lease on an apartment!" I cried as the woman pushed around Joe a final time. "You were an hour late, which is why we aren't finished yet!" Juanita shrugged her shoulders and went to the office next door to inform the insolent young man with whom I had spoken earlier.

"Please," the young man mumbled, appearing behind us a moment later as Juanita disappeared down the hall. "Please. Come. *Aqui*." He motioned to his office as any hopes we'd had of getting the new account that day vanished into thin air.

CHAPTER 10:
Curt

My new dream job had instigated a niggling flaw lingering in the back of my mind. The man who would become my counterpart on the development side of the project was not a likeable man, yet with all the pluses of the job I was hoping my first impressions about him were off. But I would find that, in fact, my first intuition would become more validated as my time in Panama unfolded. Everyone has their own personal nemesis and as time went on, this man became mine.

His name was Curt and he was a peculiar man. He came from Asian stock with a sharp nose and an angular face. He had a habit of squinting his beady, narrowly-set eyes, as if he couldn't quite see you clearly. I surmised he'd probably worn glasses as a kid.

Though Curt would not be described as handsome, he didn't fall into the unattractive category either. His jet black hair, which fell in waves and stopped short just below his ears, had been dyed a kind of auburn color. On most days in the office, Curt kept this unruly bob of sorts tucked behind his ears, which resembled the look of an aging surfer.

The oldest son of a wealthy family, Curt had grown up in a pampered home in Massachusetts, near Boston. The child had wanted for nothing. A doting mother had spoiled him, which had contributed to the development of his annoying habit of making requests in a whining, whimpering sort of way.

When his parents divorced while he was still in primary school, the broken-hearted child had learned to manipulate them to get whatever he wanted with smiles and tears and whining. If that didn't work, the boy's tactics would turn to screaming, yelling bursts of anger and rage, which were more often than not successful. Unfortunately, Curt had not left those unattractive tendencies in his childhood but had, in fact, incorporated them into his daily business.

Having admired his father who had successfully managed big investment business deals like a shark over the years (alternatively maneuvering in and out of them with aggression and stealth), he leveraged his parent's wealthy connections into a well sought-after first job with a major technology company.

Once in the door, he'd ascended the dog-eat-dog corporate food chain by mastering the art of sales negotiations and quick decision making. At age 40, he'd achieved the illustrious title of chief information officer with a new division his company was launching in the faraway country of Japan.

The lifestyle afforded to Curt as a high-ranking foreign executive—with maids and drivers and employees who did what you told them without asking why—had accelerated his penchant for ordering people around at whim, and expecting them to wait on him hand and foot.

Curt's physical presence gave away his mood on any given day. While his athletic body was lithe and fit from obvious time at the gym, his stride was long and purposeful on the days he felt confident, and his gaze direct. But then there were the dark days, when he seemed to avoid human contact altogether, slinking in and out of rooms like a snake trying to escape notice.

One didn't need to work with Curt long to be able to identify those darker days. When his mood was sullen, he rarely looked you straight in the eye when he was speaking. Instead, his focus would be on a notebook, a pen, the wall, or most often, his computer.

It took six months before I learned that this type of behavior was one of the primary symptoms of bipolar disorder, and although I had no idea whether this diagnosis might indeed be the reason for his behavior, my experiences with him on a day-to-day basis were nothing short of harrowing.

Curt wore his angst and his upset on his sleeve for all to see. One moment, his voice was pleasant and soothing; the next, he was screaming and yelling. Curt seemed to operate at the office as if he were on a roller coaster, dissolving in five seconds flat from a happy-go-lucky pleasant executive into a snarling, sniveling mess of a man that would attack anyone and everyone with personal insults and expletives bouncing off the walls.

As if Moses were parting the Red Sea, bodies in the office hallways would scatter like mice when Curt's angry voice indicated he was approaching from a certain direction.

At our first introduction, which in my case was on the phone when I was finalizing my employment contract, Curt came across as extremely self-assured when his friendly voice boomed at me over the line from thousands of miles away.

My uncertainty had been quickly replaced with a red flag when I'd observed this abrupt switch from nice to nasty in Curt's voice. I just figured that I would learn to surf his moods and stay out of harm's way but, all in all, the man was just simply not a likeable guy.

What a jerk, had been my initial thought. However, I liked to give people the benefit of the doubt. *Perhaps he's just having a bad day*, I had speculated after the first three interruptions during that first phone call with him during my hiring process. He, of course, acted as if nothing had happened. But at the fourth interruption, Curt had suddenly exclaimed, "Yep, I've got to go. A call I've been waiting on just came through. I'll get back to you." And, the line went dead before I'd even had the chance to reply.

Surprise turned to shock as if a door had been slammed in my face. But, I pushed down the ugly insult. I came to learn that this would certainly not be the last time I felt this way.

Who the hell is this guy? I thought angrily. *It's a complete pain in the ass that he's been introduced into the picture this late in the ballgame. This is my hiring process...my ballgame! Who the hell does he think he is, hanging up on me like that?* But I swallowed my pride and let it pass.

As eager as I was to be able to report to the top guy in Panama, I didn't feel I could do that with a clear conscience until Curt and I had at least had a complete conversation with niceties at the end and all of that.

In a follow up email, Curt had replied that he couldn't fit me in again until four days later. *Are you kidding?* My face registered dismay as I read it. *Four days!? I can tell this conversation ranks right up there as unimportant in the new guy's estimation.*

But what really pissed me off was that this call was holding up my job offer. And in my life, I didn't like anything to derail my schedules or plans. At the moment, whether he meant to or not, Curt was doing both.

My new job—the marketing director position for which I'd spent almost four months interviewing—had been presented as answering to Juan Carlos, after all. And, since I'd already had four great interviews, I felt in my gut like I had this job in the bag. I was wrong.

The top guy in Panama, Juan Carlos, sent an email saying that Curt had been hired as the new number two guy, and of course, the ownership wanted to be sure that he and I got along before they finalized my offer, as we would be working very closely together…blah blah blah. I recall now that "closely together" jumped out of that email; I resisted a gut feeling in that instant that I was facing a job-long challenge.

My blood had risen to boiling when I had received that email. I hated the politics of corporate life with a vengeance. I hated that I had to kiss ass and take names in order to get things moving.

It took three more phone calls for Curt and me to complete our conversation. By the end he was, apparently, having one of his good days, which made things appear a little more promising.

"I do apologize for how abrupt I must have seemed in ending our last call," he started. "I hope you can forgive me. There's a lot going on here right now, with me attempting to get my family moved to Panama in the coming month."

I allowed silence to hang in the air. *Humph,* Snickety turned up her nose in indignance.

Well, at least he's trying, I thought. I relaxed a bit. Then I heard myself say, "Don't worry about it, I completely understand." I cringed as the sentence escaped my lips. *How do I sound so measured and controlled when what I really want to do is hit him?* "I imagine this is a pretty stressful time for all of you."

"It is," Curt admitted, "but let's get down to business."

Finally! I thought.

"Great," I said and turned to open my notebook to resume with the questions I'd written down. "All right, we left off…"

But Curt interrupted with the force of a tsunami: "I'd like to know why you feel you're the right person for the marketing job."

My heart jumped. *What? Since when had this turned into an interview? This was supposed to be a get-to-know-you friendly discussion, right?*

My inner businesswoman came to the rescue.

"I'm sorry, Curt," I said. "I thought we'd start where we left off earlier this week. It sounds like you have something else in mind?"

"I do," Curt replied in an even voice. "Since I didn't have the benefit of sitting in on your interviews with Juan Carlos and the others, I'd like to understand what it is that they feel qualifies you for the job. I have ideas of my own about how real estate products should be marketed, and to be frank, I don't know that your background is one that I would choose for this position."

The gauntlet had been thrown down.

My heart landed like a thud in my stomach. *Fuck.* I drew in a deep, quiet breath, calculating my response. "I see."

Snickety was waving her fist from my shoulder. *We'll take that as a challenge, you asshole!*

I narrowed my eyes. *Not only will I win you over, but you're going to be my biggest fucking fan by the time all this is said and done.*

Snickety nodded vehemently. *Once she puts her mind to something, it becomes our sole focus!*

I pulled out all the stops. I answered all his questions. I was charming. I got excited, but not too excited. I was passionate when I needed to be, and let the silence hang between sentences when I needed to make a point. But overall, I was an astute professional.

A get-to-know-you call, my ass! I mumbled, when I pushed the end button on my cell.

"Holy moly," Joe said from the couch where he'd been eavesdropping from the adjoining room with a beer and the newspaper.

"He doesn't sound like someone I'd want to work with, just from overhearing your end of the conversation," he said. "Sounds like he's a bit overbearing."

"Controlling is the word," I groaned. "But, unfortunately, I don't have a choice. He's already signed his deal and he starts on January 15."

"Bummer," said Joe.

"The good news is that we only have to work together," I replied. "I mean, at least I don't have to answer to this guy."

CHAPTER 11:
The Quandary

The following week, my hand shook as my finger punched the recruiter's cell number. My breath came in short, shallow rasps.

The line rang. Once. Twice. Three times. I inhaled, expecting voicemail, when a man's voice came on.

"Yeah, yeah, yeah, we'll see." Clark laughed as he answered, cupping the phone to his mouth. "Hello? This is Clark."

Relief burst in my chest when I heard his voice. A childish shred of hope emerged from my psyche: *Maybe he can fix it!* "Clark, it's me!" My voice was shrill, uneven.

"JuliAnne! How are you?" On the other end, Clark's voice quickened with familiarity. "Did you see their offer? I have to tell you I think it's pretty good."

I struggled to keep the emotion out of my voice. "I saw it, Clark. That's why I'm calling. I have to tell you, I'm not happy. All the agreements we made verbally seem to constantly be in flux and change."

"What?" Clark's perpetual cheerfulness evaporated. "Did I miss something? It looked like they gave you everything you asked for."

"Well, yes and no." My tone was grim. "It looks as if they've changed a pretty big piece of it. Specifically, the piece about the position answering to Curt Sampson. Everything the company sent me prior and everything we've discussed up 'til now was that I'd be reporting directly to Juan Carlos."

There was a long pause. *Busted!* shrieked Snickety.

Clark cleared his throat. "Well," he stammered. "You are correct. That is a significant change."

So, you did see it, the lines at my temples tightened. *Why wouldn't you call me first to give me a heads up?* "What the hell happened, Clark?"

"I'm not quite sure, to be honest. I…," his voice trailed off. "This was a change Juan Carlos himself requested yesterday."

"So, they expect me to accept a job working for a guy I've never even met?" The muscles around my breastbone began to screw closed as my volume climbed.

"JuliAnne, listen, I can tell you're upset," Clark replied. "But didn't you tell me that you and Curt got along fine on the phone?"

"Getting along with someone on the phone and reporting directly to them without ever having laid eyes on them are two completely different things, Clark!" I spat, as regret washed over me.

Clark's silence on the other end of the line told me everything I needed to know. *This man holds no power; he's just the messenger.*

Come on, JuliAnne, do you really need to rock the boat right off the bat? It was the side of me that hated conflict, the side that wanted smooth sailing and hoped for the best, even when it was unreasonable. *Can't you just take the job—your job, the one you fought for, the one you called into your life straight off your vision board—and see how it goes? I mean, you've dealt with assholes before. Maybe the man was just having a bad few days when you guys talked.*

Are you kidding me? Every ounce of my sense of propriety screamed back, *You'd be a fucking idiot to take a job without even meeting this guy. If he's that bad on the telephone, imagine what he'll be like in person. The man is a frickin' nightmare! Don't do it. You're setting yourself up to be fucked! Fight for yourself. This is your job, but they need to honor what they told you. They can't just change the rules at the last minute and not even fucking mention it! It's not fair!*

But, this is your job. Your dream job, the first voice soothed. *It'll be all right. It'll work out. You just have to trust them.*

Trust, my ass! The second voice seethed, *If you trust anyone but yourself on this, you're going to live to regret it.*

The cloud that had enveloped my brain parted for the first time in days, and in an instant, I felt clear.

"That's it, I'm calling him," my inner warrioress announced aloud.

"Excuse me?" said Clark.

"I need to call you back, Clark," I said, and with that, I ended the call.

~

Juan Carlos' tone did not match the words tumbling through the line. "I'm sorry, JuliAnne," he said. "Perhaps I should have called you. But you convinced me that you and Curt had such good synergy, I didn't think it would be that big a deal."

Something in what Juan Carlos was saying didn't ring true. *Humph,* I pursed my face, digesting the line of bullshit he was serving up. *Is he putting this back on me?*

I dug my heels into the carpet. "Juan Carlos, while it's true that I believe Curt and I can work together as colleagues, answering to him is a significant change to the position. I went through the entire interview process understanding that I would report to you. Something big must have happened to alter that. Do you mind sharing with me what that was?"

Juan Carlos blew a loud sigh into the phone, as if he were surrendering a fight. "The truth is Curt negotiated a larger role in the project than we'd anticipated."

I held my tongue, letting the stillness hang between us.

Juan Carlos said nothing.

Finally, I broke the silence. "All right, Juan Carlos. I'll give it some thought. Thank you for your candor. I'll get back to Clark in short order with my decision."

My gaze went inward. *Well, it's up to me now. What do I want to do?*

And, then the answer came. Bubbling up from the depths of my belly to the warmth of my heart, it continued its ascension into the folds of my brain.

Just like that, I knew. The change didn't matter. Whatever was going to happen didn't matter. What mattered was me, what I wanted. The rest of it could go to hell in a handbag, as my grandmother used to say. I was making this decision, eyes wide open.

This was *my* adventure. And, we *were* going to Panama.

CHAPTER 12:
The Move

"*Whaaat*?" The timbre of my voice caused Joe's head to shoot up from where he sat on the carpet, tape gun in hand.

"But, but…what does that *mean*?" I screeched into the phone tucked under my chin as the beer bottles in my hand clanged and my feet came to an abrupt stop at the top of the carpeted stairs.

Joe wiped a gingham towel to his brow before opening an empty hand in my direction, fingers beckoning toward the beer.

But, my ability to multitask had evaporated with the information coming across the wire. The furrow between my eyes deepened as my ears struggled to make sense of the stilted English coming from the other end of the line.

Joe cast a dirty look in my direction before crossing the room to pry the bottles from my hand. I covered the receiver to whisper, "Our apartment just fell through."

The lit cigar between his lips fell to the floor. "What?!?" he hissed, before dipping down to rescue the carpet from the burning cinder.

My head bobbed as his face reemerged. "Apparently, they found out the guy that leased it to us doesn't really own it." My teeth were now chattering to match the snow on the ground outside.

Joe stuck the cigar butt back in his mouth as his head shook. He motioned toward the phone I held in my hand. "*What the fuck*?!?!"

"Look, Ana, I don't *care* about the money at this point," I interrupted. "What I *do* care about is that we are moving to Panama *tomorrow*. Did you hear me, Ana? *Mañana*!" My eyes searched the empty space of the wall where a clock had once hung before I crossed the kitchen to read the digital numbers on the microwave.

"We leave at 5:30 a.m. in the morning *tomorrow*, Ana! That's less than 12 hours from now. I need you to tell me what our options are for when we get off the plane in Panama tomorrow night with 12 boxes and three pets!" Crimson filled my cheeks as my blood pressure climbed.

"No, no, *no*!" My right hand waved as if the caller was standing in front of me. "Don't tell me not to worry! In fact, at this very moment, I am *very worried*, Ana. And, I am also very *upset*." My mouth enunciated the words, stressing each syllable as if the volume of my voice could somehow aid the translation to our frazzled real estate agent on the other end.

"All right, all right, all right." My voice started its descent back to earth. I nodded. "Okay. Please call me back as *soon* as you have information." I glanced at the silver timepiece on my wrist.

"Yes, we'll be up late, it's fine. I need to hear from you as soon as possible, Ana." My thumb pressed end as my head shook and my chin dropped to my chest. "Holy shit."

"Jesus," said Joe, bringing the beer bottle up to press it against his brow. "And they just found this out *today*? We put the deposit down on that apartment three weeks ago!"

"I don't get it." I shook my head from side to side before I lifted my chin, defiant. "But what does it matter, at this point? What does it matter that we have nowhere to go?" I ventured a small smile.

"Fuck." Joe shook his head, taking a swig of his Corona. "Well," he raised an eyebrow toward me, "you said you wanted an adventure." His lips curled into a wan grin.

My eyelids shot open, ready to shoot 1,000 arrows in his direction for any sign of malice. But there was none. I lowered my body down to the step to sit beside him. A sigh escaped my lips. "Well, yes...but this was *definitely* not what I had in mind."

Joe reached out to pat my thigh. "Come on, Murphy," he said. "Don't let this get you down. This is just a ripple." Another pat. "Someday we'll look back on this and laugh." His eyes crinkled at me, hoping for me to relax a bit.

"You think?" I turned toward him, pupils the size of platters, swallowing the sobs rising in my throat. "Fuck." My head jerked from side to side. "I don't think I can take any more stress right now." My previous effort at humor was dissolving fast, and in its place was a rising panic.

~

In the still of the night, my eyes flew open, searching out of habit for the clock. But there was none. A stream of ambient light from the streetlight illuminated a patch of carpet through a gap in the blinds. My hand shot out for the sixth time, fumbling for the Blackberry on the floor. Clicking the tiny keyboard with my thumb, my pupils struggled to focus on the numbers at the top. 3:58 a.m. *Fuck*, I shook my head to clear the cobwebs, as I disabled the alarm scheduled to sound two minutes later. Stretching an arm behind me to locate my sleeping husband amidst a lone blanket, my fingers grazed two warm, fuzzy bodies.

"Whaaa?" Joe roused as my fingertips found the smooth skin of his backside. He jerked into a sitting position. "Is it time?"

"It's 4 o'clock." I gave him a few pats before forcing my legs from below the quilt into the chilled air. Ana had called back at 11 p.m. to report that she had secured a small apartment which would allow all three of our pets. We'd had a hard time getting our adrenaline to meld into a good night of sleep so soon after her call.

I scanned the empty room, save for a couple of plastic bins. The movers had come the week before to pack up. The usual chaos of sorting and boxing had added more intrigue to the game between two different trucks: the smaller one for the things to be shipped to Panama, and a larger one for storage. Joe had stood, arms hugging his body as snowflakes floated around him, as he watched the workmen struggle up the ramp with the last of the large pieces. "Two years," he said. "I wonder what stories we'll be telling at Christmas 2010."

I headed for the shower to clear my head and breathe.

"I'm leaving the water on for you," my voice rang out as I exited the shower, vapor rising off my skin. "Did you check the forecast yet? Oh, sorry…," my voice trailed off when I saw naked knees protruding from the toilet. "I didn't realize you were in here."

"Not yet," he replied. "It's freezing outside, but no snow I hope."

The familiar clamp of anxiety gripped my stomach as I stepped out and punched the buttons on the side of the TV to get to the Weather Channel. Toweling my short hair as the screen scrolled through various cities' forecasts, my stomach gave a lurch when the screen highlighted Denver. "Six degrees," I read aloud. "Sunrise at 7:15 a.m., 19 degrees by

9 a.m." An exhale left my lips as I lifted eyes to the sky and crossed my fingers. "Oh, please, please, please."

Airline guidelines prohibited the passage of pets in stowage during extreme temperatures, both high and low. The previous three weeks, I had jumped through hoops to find a vet who would vouch that my brood was fit enough to travel beyond the norms. Even so, our all-day itinerary was stretching the limits. I could only hope that Customs in each location would be lenient. On any day in February in Denver, the mercury would be lucky to reach freezing at 32 degrees Fahrenheit. The opposite was true in Panama, as it was, of course, summer.

Two hours later, I stood chewing the inside of my cheek as an airline attendant reviewed the pets' travel documents. Joe stooped to place our passports in a red backpack, keeping the crossed fingers of my left hand in the periphery of his vision. Getting the pets prepped for the move had been a major accomplishment, requiring multiple trips to the vet, applications flying between the U.S. Department of Agriculture and Panama's *Ministerio de Agricultura,* and a flurry of FedEx packages between government agencies. The last hurdle was clearance by the airlines.

The fate of our entire move seemed to hang in the balance. *What would we possibly do if they say the pets can't fly today?*

Moments stretched into eons before the uniformed desk attendant lifted her gaze to us. "Well," the pleasant face said with a smile. "It looks like you guys are heading to Panama!"

I didn't realize until that moment that I had been holding my breath. I exhaled as relief washed over me and I turned to bury my face in Joe's Polartec vest.

~

In what seemed like years later, even though only a mere 14 hours had passed, my husband's sizable form cast a shadow on the tile floor from a bare light bulb behind his head. A sullen woman in a stained lab coat sat at a desk before him, shaking her head and muttering in Spanish as Lily and the cats were unloaded. Ana helped navigate what was quickly mounting into a full-blown crisis, and we had only just arrived.

"What is she saying, Ana?" Joe growled to the middle-aged woman on his right. The long day of travel had done little to soften our entry into the *tranquilo* country.

"*Momentito,* Mr. Joe," the black-eyed petite replied. "*Que pasa, doctora? Porque este proceso esta tomando tanto tiempo?*"

"Mr. Joe," Ana reported, narrowing her eyes at the other woman. "The *doctora* says that Lily is very sick, and she will not be able to release her. She is saying they'll have to keep her in quarantine for a few days."

"That is *not* going to happen!" I slammed my hand down on the chipped Formica. "You tell this *doctora,*" I shouted, shooting an accusing glance at the seated woman, "that we will *never* be leaving Lily here under *any* circumstances."

Ana put a hand out to each of us. "Can you come with me please?" she queried, her tone shrill. A moment later, we were standing just out of earshot down the hall.

"How much does she want, Ana?" Joe's voice ricocheted off the painted concrete walls as his hand patted his pocket. "I came prepared."

"Shhh!" Ana scrunched her face into a restrained rebuke, lifting a finger to her lips and glancing both ways down the empty corridor. "You can't just pull money out of your pocket, Mr. Joe. Now, I need you two to stay here." Her footsteps echoed down the hallway before she pulled open the sliding glass door covered in fingerprints.

My fingers grasped Joe's arm, my voice lowering to a hiss. "I don't care what it takes, Joe. But, if we don't get her out of here soon, I'm afraid she's not going to make it after those temperatures in the cargo hold. She didn't even lift her head when I peeked in the crate."

Joe nodded, his face grim. "Get back to her, Murph. What Lily needs most right now is her mom," he said as his hand cupped my cheek. I rushed back to find Lily.

The large kennel sat on the tiled floor, an island unto itself except for two smaller ones along the wall. I crouched outside the crate where Lily, a hulk of a Doberman, seemed shrunken into herself. Seeing my baby like this, the exhaustion of the weeks leading up to this move of a lifetime settled into my bones and I felt a tremor run down my spine. Kneeling down to the metal latticework, I covered my nose and mouth with my palm to stifle a gag.

"I'm here, baby girl. Your dad's doing his best." The pungent odor of feces and vomit hung in the air. I reached two fingers through the holes in the side of the kennel. "I need you to hang in there, Lily. We'll be out of here as soon as we can."

I looked at her there, her eyes turned toward me with only a question flickering in them, and I suddenly felt small like her, away from home, afraid and doubting myself for the first time in this entire relocation venture.

Cloudy eyes stared at me, though my dog didn't lift her head. Her sleek black fur was coated in puke. Fecal matter had splattered on all four corners of the crate's walls. I stroked a still paw with my fingers, my voice soft. "You are going to be *fine*, baby girl," I insisted. "I need you to hang on. We'll have you out of this horrible thing as soon as they let us."

Airport regulations prohibited a pet's crate to be opened until their paperwork was approved and inspected by Customs following the veterinarian's review. A stern-faced guard had been keeping his eye on us from the corner, shaking a finger in my direction an hour earlier when I began yanking apart the plastic ties on the crate.

Just then, Joe burst from the back office, Ana hot on his heels. "Let's go, Murph," he said, his long legs striding toward me. "We're all clear. Let's get them the hell out of this joint."

I jumped to my feet, emotion taking a back seat to survival, as I ran to a large stack of carry-on items leaning against our luggage. Tossing errant straps over my shoulders, I loaded up and headed toward the Customs desk, a few steps away.

Joe started dragging Lily's kennel toward the swinging double doors as Ana beckoned to three dark-skinned bellmen in faded uniforms from where they leaned against a wall. "*Vengan, vengan, vengan!*" she commanded, snapping her fingers. The men snapped to attention, rushing to relieve Joe of his heavy load, but the stench made them reel for a moment.

My voice propelled others in the noiseless room into motion, and a flurry of activity followed. Three dollies holding our **maletas** screeched to a stop in front of the lone scanner, as slender hands fed the pieces into the yawning mouth of the conveyor belt. Ana slammed forms down in front of the seated official who had been napping but pulled his glasses on before waving at the others to continue toward the door.

Then just like that, we scrambled toward the exit, sprinting as if their lives depended on it. And, in this case, one tall, black, four-legged one very much did.

~

An hour later, Joe burst through the wooden door Tomas held open for him, his arms straining under Lily's 65-pound weight. "Where's the shower?" he shouted. Ana led the way to a bedroom at the back of the small apartment. "Light! I need light!" Joe ordered in a way with which no one ever argued.

A row of halogens illuminated the small space as I ran in from behind. Forcing a curtain covered in mold to one side, Joe placed the motionless dog on her side in the tub as I turned on the water. Lily's eyes winced as lukewarm water sprayed from a rusty spigot above. My hand grasped for a half-used bar of soap on the tub's edge so that I could begin to lather the dark fur.

"That's my girl," Joe's voice cajoled. The dog's fearful eyes blinked open at the sound of his voice as our hands moved in synchronization and we scrubbed up and down the sides of her body.

"She's severely dehydrated," Joe snapped. "Let's get her out and make her a bed." I scrambled up, motioning to Tomas to help me yank a faded floral bedcover from the bed. Folding it, the two of us laid it in a square on the wood floor. Joe laid the quivering body on it.

"We've got to find Pedialyte or something," he said, before bringing his head down to look into the glazed eyes. "Hang in there, girl. I'm going to go find something to make you feel better." It took a lot to fluster Joe but in that moment, I could see in the set of his jaw that he was shaken to his core. To come all this way and lose our dog, our daughter? His whole body registered his love and affection for our baby girl in that moment.

"Is it even possible to find something like that at this hour?" I turned my gaze in Tomas' direction, as he stepped over Lily to follow Joe toward the front door. When our car had screeched through the city a few minutes before, the streets had been abandoned, the shop fronts dark. It was well past midnight.

Tomas nodded, his deep voice resounding down the hall, "Sí, Señora, es posible." He and Joe took to their heels, clattering out the front door.

Ana situated herself on the corner of the bed furthest from Lily's motionless body.

"You don't have to do anything," I said, as I propped open the heavy black metal door which led from the apartment to the exterior hallway to oversee the unloading of our luggage and boxes below. "Just watch her, Ana, will you?"

An hour later, Joe and Tomas returned as the last suitcase was being stuffed into the second bedroom of the small apartment. Ana had gone home, and Lily was finally sleeping. The crank-style windows had been forced open to let the nighttime breeze permeate the stale apartment air.

I stood in the kitchen, counting out 20-dollar bills, oblivious to the two workers watching me, their eyes wide as my digits separated 200 dollars from a much larger stack of money. Turning toward the door frame as Joe and Tomas entered, I asked, "Is this sufficient, Tomas?" as I fanned ten 20-dollar bills out in my hand like playing cards.

Tomas flashed his eyes toward me, as he pointed the workmen toward the front door. "*Esperan alli, por favor.*" Stepping close, he lowered his voice. "Miss JuliAnne," he murmured, "please no take your money out." From the very first day, my relationship with this hulk of a man was consistent: He was always looking out for me from the minute I'd touched down in Panama.

"Oh," I stepped back, confusion and fatigue crisscrossing my face as I relinquished the bills to his outstretched palm for him to pay the workers.

Joe turned bloodshot eyes toward me. "It took four stores, but we finally found it," he said, "Tomas was amazing." Measuring the precious liquid into a small syringe, he took my hand and pulled me toward the bedroom. "Now, let's go get our girl back in the game."

CHAPTER 13:
The Threat

As the six-panel security door swung inward, we were smacked in the face with waves of heat before we even stepped over the threshold. The clatter of the air conditioning unit we had grown accustomed to hearing over the past three nights was now silent. Our three pets barely stirred at our entry, a sure sign something was wrong.

Joe's hand felt the wall for the light switch. "Not good," he said. "The electricity's out."

I stepped in behind, weighed down with plastic bags. "Geez, it must be 120 degrees in here." I dropped my load in the tight foyer, crossing the diminutive space to crank open the old-fashioned windows. Sticking a hand through one of the panes, I prayed for a bit of breeze. But there was none.

The elevator bell dinged from the hall and a moment later, Tomas' large shadow fell through the doorway. "*Permiso.*" He hesitated before stepping over the pile of bags I had discarded as I'd rushed to get air in the room. Then, sensing the heat, "Wao."

"Tomas, can you please go down and talk to the guard to see if he knows anything?" Joe wiped his brow with a kitchen towel before he began to unload groceries onto the counter.

"*Sí, Señor.*" Tomas departed again.

"Honey, let's go ahead and call Ana, too."

Joe listened as I enunciated every syllable in Spanish over the phone, a request to speak to Ana. My voice reverberated down the hall from the tiny pink-tiled bathroom, where I was unloading toilet paper. "She's calling the owner."

Tomas returned 20 minutes later with the news that the building electricity was fine; only our apartment's electricity had been shut off.

Joe winked as he brushed past me in the hall. "Three days in Panama, and they're already shutting us down." Suddenly, the reality of what was happening felt very personal and more like a conspiracy against the gringos that had moved into the building. I felt trapped in a culture that seemed to be making it clear we were not wanted, although everyone seemed to welcome us when there was money involved. It was an untenable situation for our family of five and it was impacting our every move since we'd set foot on the tarmac.

"From the looks of this place, I'll bet it's because the owner didn't pay their bill." My eyes narrowed at the brown velvet throws atop a set of rectangular 1950s couches that were anything but the portrait of pragmatism. *Velvet in the tropics?*

Joe and I had spent an hour washing handprints from the windows and wiping what seemed like an inch of dust from the furniture the morning after we arrived, wondering how in the hell we had ended up in such a place after all the advance work we had done to make our transition a smooth one.

"We already know their cleaning standards are suspect at best." My good mood had dissolved with the heat.

"Be nice," Joe's voice warned, as we resumed sorting through the rest of the bags. "We're lucky to have a roof over our heads, remember? I'm sure it was just a mistake and they'll be able to rectify it soon."

"They fucking better," I returned, before jumping out of the way as a puddle of water streamed from the fridge when I opened the door. "I'm beginning to think that the biggest mistake we made was hiring Ana." Joe was the one who had asked me to get in touch with the real estate agent on Curt's glowing recommendation. I ducked the dishtowel that came flying at my head when my cell phone rang.

"Hi, Ana," I said, sticking my tongue out before turning my attention to the buzz of her voice. "Great, thanks so much. We really appreciate it." I set the phone down on the side table a moment later.

Joe looked up from the unpacking. "Well, what's the word?"

"Survey says we'll be live again by 3 p.m., according to Alex-a Trebec." I attempted a smile, fanning myself with my hand. "It's 1 p.m. now, so just a couple of hours to wait. I guess we'll survive."

"Come on, Vanna," Joe said, extending a hand to me on the floor. "Let me get you out of this disaster for some lunch." I returned a smile that could only convey one thing: Thank you for rescuing me from hell. But of course, I couldn't resist one more quip.

"Vanna is not the one who helps Alex Trebec," I scolded. "That's *Wheel of Fortune*, love." We both laughed, which broke the tension.

"Whatever," Joe smacked my rear as he pulled me upwards and we headed out the door. "Sorry, girls," he sang out in the direction of the napping animals. "You've got plenty of fresh water in the kitchen." I glanced back as Lily raised her pointy ears for a moment in response. My Lily, who just 72 hours previously had been precariously poised between life and death, with a load of water and lots of love, was now recovering and sleeping off the trials of what for her had been a crippling trip. It was a relief to see my girl, little by little, getting back to her feisty self.

In true Latin fashion, the electricity did come back on even though it was six hours later than promised. My phone calls to Ana turned from polite to insistent until the woman refused to answer at all. The lack of follow-ups did nothing to placate our rising exasperation.

"Has anyone in this country heard of customer service?" I seethed as I sat dripping on the edge of the building's pool. We had turned up our noses on the first day at the building's aging social area with its scattered, mismatched chairs and faded paint peeling off the pool walls.

"Desperate times call for desperate measures," Joe had announced after we'd spent hour after hour sweating in the airless apartment.

With a few more months under our belts in our new country, we would have known better; the lack of responsiveness to our quandary was due in part to the fact that this was Friday. And, on Friday in Panama, nothing ever happens after noon.

But, we didn't know. We were still green and most unappreciative of our proverbial luck when the electricity was restored that evening. Little did we know that this was just how it was on a daily basis in Panama. No harm, no foul. This was just Panama.

"Well, thank you, Union Fenosa," Joe said. He'd discovered the name of the electric company on a faded bill buried under a pile of plastic take-out silverware in one of the kitchen drawers.

Truth be told, our good fortune had nothing to do with the utility, but Joe and I didn't know that yet.

The following morning we were heading out to meet yet another real estate agent in search of a permanent place to live when my phone rang.

"Good morning, Ana." My clipped tone belied my lack of appreciation for the marked absence of attention we'd received the night before.

"Hello, Mizz JuliAnne." Ana's voice was bright. "*Como esta?* I need to come see you today. There's a problem with your apartment."

No shit. My tone dripped scorn as I ducked into the backseat of the dark gray sedan after Tomas opened my door. "You mean other than the ones we've already had?" *And, where is our apology, by the way, for turning off your phone last night, Mizz Ana?*

"No, it's something else." Ana's return was anything but apologetic. "The owner has asked that you move to another apartment."

"What? Why?" The treble in my voice rose to something akin to a shriek, audible among the sea of honks as we pulled out into a plethora of cars. "We paid in advance for that apartment and we've got another three nights to go on that contract."

"The owners want to make it up to you—the problem with the electricity," Ana continued, her tone turning smooth. "There's a nicer apartment upstairs, and he'd like you to move up there by this evening. You'll like it."

"Well, tell him thank you, Ana, but that's not necessary." I straightened up even though she couldn't see me. "Plus, the electricity came back on last night. We don't want to move—we've got stuff all over the place and all the animals are shell shocked from the travel. So, thank you, but no need. We have electricity which, at the moment, is all that matters."

"It came back on?" Ana's voice reflected her surprise.

"Yes, about nine o'clock." I raised an eyebrow at Joe in the front seat. *But, then you'd know that, if you hadn't turned your phone off!* "Anyway, tell the owner thank you, but we're fine now."

"But…" I heard the woman stutter, when my temper got the best of me. I cut her off.

"Goodbye, Ana. We're on our way to see some other apartments. I'll talk to you later," and I threw the handset back in my purse, leaving her hanging on the other end.

~

At 4 p.m. that afternoon, a pale man with medium brown hair and a slight paunch sat opposite Joe and me in the cramped living room. From his accent, it was obvious even to us that this man was not a Panamanian. While he was compact, his frame was made up of muscles formed in a gym except for his midsection, which implied a preference for fine scotch.

The man was speaking Spanish in a low tone, but something was off here; the hair on my neck stood on end as I looked into the unblinking eyes.

When he finished, our heads turned toward Ana in a game of ping-pong translation. She was seated on a chair across from us but was eluding any eye contact.

"What he says is, he wants you to move, please." Ana's voice repeated the same message that had already been delivered more than once that day. She had introduced the man as her brother and the apartment's owner, and though they sat opposite one another, I could see the resemblance.

I looked at Joe, who sat in silence observing the small man. His irritation could not be camouflaged any more than I could control what he wanted to say. The muscle in his jaw flexed. The air crackled with tension. I was beginning to regret my decision to let the two guests enter the apartment at all. Joe leaned forward, his gaze never leaving the smaller man's face.

"You tell this man that he already has our answer. We appreciate his offer, but we're only here three more nights and hopefully, by then, we'll have another apartment. We don't wish to move though we are very appreciative of his concern." He now directed his gaze toward Ana.

"And, I don't appreciate you and him showing up at our apartment unannounced, Ana. In our culture, that's considered very rude." Joe continued his unblinking stare at both intruders.

Ana averted her eyes as her tongue began to translate Joe's words into a flow of Spanish.

The small man flexed a powerful hand as she spoke, eyes flickering between Joe and me. As she finished, he stretched both arms skyward into a wide arc, then settled them along the back of the couch. Placing the heel of one cowboy boot across his opposite knee, he leaned back like he was settling in for the long haul. A loud exhale blew from his lips, as his eyes began a slow survey of the living area. He looked around, taking in the two sleeping cats on the floor, the bins in various states of disarray strewn across the room, luggage bursting from the second bedroom behind him.

A cold chill ran up my spine as my eyes followed his. *What is he doing, checking out all our stuff like that? What is he looking for?*

The long silence was broken by fevered barking on the other side of the wall. Lily had attempted to charge the man when he'd entered the apartment, snapping and barking at his waist. Her aggression had surprised us both, as this type of extreme behavior was typically reserved for other dogs, typically when the graceful animal was leashed. I had dragged her by the collar to the bedroom and closed the door, not wanting the guests to feel uncomfortable. Now I regretted that decision since her presence would have made this a very short conversation.

Calm eyes came back in our direction. The man said nothing. He just stared in a kind of standoff of defiance.

I could feel Joe contract beside me, like a drawn arrow ready to be fired. He put his elbows on his knees, leaning forward to return the stare.

My skin began to crawl. *What the hell is happening here?* I turned to Ana, eager to end the unexpected visit and the tension hanging in the air.

"Well," I said, forcing a smile. "Thank you for stopping by, but I believe we've concluded our conversation." I stood up, hoping that the two would get the message and usher themselves out of our cramped space.

A blank mask took over Ana's attractive features as she turned again toward the man to translate.

The man removed his heel from atop his knee. Stretching his arms skyward again, he stretched like a cat before coming to his feet. "*Muchas gracias,*" he said, though the tone coming from his thin lips was anything but thankful. He nodded at Ana, who followed him, and then headed down toward the door.

The heavy metal security door slammed behind them.

I turned nervous eyes to Joe. "What the hell was that?" I crossed the door to free Lily from the bedroom. She exited with loud barks, her long nose to the air as she bolted to the place the man had been sitting a moment before.

"I don't know," my husband replied, "but I think we need to find another apartment fast. I don't trust Ana after what just occurred here, and I don't like that guy." When Joe's sixth sense kicked in, he was almost always right, and with my own intuition telling me to bolt, we were on the same page.

My pupils were like platters and the alarms in my head were screeching bloody murder. I had learned long ago to listen to them and to act as soon as possible. "Let's get to work then." I crossed to my handbag and pulled out a stack of real estate flyers and a small notebook.

Twenty minutes later, Joe and I were perusing the details of what we'd seen that day versus what we had seen the day before, when we were interrupted by a loud *cra-a-a-a-ack*.

I jumped. "What was that?" I started to say, but before the words could leave my mouth, the bulb of the lamp snapped out, the light in the kitchen went dim, and the oscillating fan across from us began to slow. In that brief moment, it was clear: this was war.

Joe jumped up, heading for the switches on the wall. He flipped them one by one, before turning back, shaking his head. "Well, there you have it."

Rage began to burn down my throat through my stomach, as if a faucet holding pure, raw acid had been turned on and was coursing through my veins into my gut.

CHAPTER 14:
The Bribe

Buzzz. The intercom on the apartment wall woke me with insistence from the heat of the night. I sat straight up, my eyes straining to make sense of the small room.

Where am I?

Reaching out, I fumbled for the bedside lamp, but the turn of the switch yielded nothing. Then I remembered: we're in Panama. The electricity is out.

My feet stumbled down the hall to turn on my phone in the kitchen.

The intercom buzzed again.

I rubbed my eyes. *Surely, they have the wrong apartment.* I peered at the blue digits on the phone's face. *It's almost midnight.*

But the buzzing resumed.

I'll have to tell them they've made an error. I searched for my Spanish.

"Sí?" I answered in a hushed tone, so as not to wake Joe.

A voice crackled through, difficult to decipher in the haste of its delivery. "*Que?* What?" I strained to understand the string of words through the bad connection. "No, *usted necesita otro apartamento.* This is number 606."

The person on the other end continued their diatribe, but I couldn't understand, so I hung up.

There was a momentary pause before the phone began its incessant buzzing again. This time the deep baritone of Juan, the security guard, boomed through. The tenor of his voice belied his discomfort. "Señora, *disculpe*, sorry to bother you, but there are some men here to see you."

"We aren't expecting any visitors at this hour, Juan. Are you sure it's for us and not for someone else?"

"Sí, Señora, I am sure. There are three men here, asking for you and Mister Joe by name. They say they are here to evict you from the apartment," Juan's voice cracked.

"*Que?*" I stammered, as my anxiety hit the roof. *Evict us?* I glanced toward the couch where the small, cruel man had sat, hours before. A chill ran up my spine.

"Let me call you back." I hung up. Heart pounding, my bare feet left moist footprints on the tile as I rushed to the bedroom.

"Joe!" He had taken a sleeping pill. I wasn't sure I could wake him.

"Uhhh?" Joe roused at the sound of my frazzled voice, but only for a moment.

"Joe! Honey!" I put both hands on his shoulders, shook him hard. "Wake up!"

A bloodshot eye struggled to open. "Whaaaat?"

"Honey." I continued to shake him. "There are men downstairs— they're saying they're here to move us out of the apartment and it's fucking midnight."

The urgency in my voice connected with something in Joe's brain. "Huuhhh?" His hands grasped my wrists as he sat up in a panic. "Baby! What is it?"

I choked out the words. "They started calling 10 minutes ago. The guard says they won't leave. He says they're here to move us out." A vice grip was starting to close around my chest. "What are we going to do?"

The buzzing began again, piercing the quiet. I shook myself free of Joe's grip and jumped off the bed in search of clothes.

Out of the corner of Joe's eye, the light from an adjacent apartment clicked on and a face appeared inside a window pane across from our bedroom. "*Oye!*" a voice yelled. "Get your phone, for God's sake!"

Joe shook his head to clear the cobwebs, leaning down to search for the gym shorts he'd discarded an hour earlier. Pulling them on, he fumbled for a t-shirt from the top of the bureau and slid feet into flip-flops before shouting, "Honey, you stay here." Adrenaline was now hitting his blood stream. He whistled, "Come on, Lily, let's go." The Doberman ran to him as he put the pinch collar over her head. He looked at me, where I stood trembling. "This shit ends *right now*."

The incessant buzzing interrupted my strained voice. "But what do I do if you don't come back?" My eyes were wide with disbelief that this was even happening.

"Call the police! Call Juan Carlos! I don't know!" Joe threw the set of keys through the slats of the security door after he locked it from the outside. His voice was commanding. "Stay inside and don't come out for anyone but me."

Through the metal slats, I nodded.

Man and dog stormed down the hall.

The elevator bell dinged as Joe exited into the small lobby, Lily in tow. Descending the few steps to the landing, Joe burst through double glass doors that swung outward. One of them smashed into a small brown man standing at the building intercom. The man's finger held down the "call" button, his face covered in a sinister grin. But as Joe barreled through, he stumbled back, stunned.

In a glimpse, Joe noticed the baseball bat in the man's hand. Two other men stood behind him wearing wife beaters and carrying machetes. Joe approached, undaunted by what seemed like a scene out of a movie with subtitles.

"What is it you want?" Joe roared, thrusting his six-foot frame in their direction. "I'm Joe O'Malley, and I hear you're looking for me!" On cue, Lily snapped her ears erect and snarled, baring her canines.

The man with the bat tripped over his own feet in an effort to put more distance between himself and the large *gringo*. The surprise on the three faces melted into fear.

"*Well*?" Joe bellowed, taking another step toward them, throwing his arms wide. "What is it you *want*?"

In the background, the security guard cowered behind the open slats of the guardhouse shack. Lily strained at her leash toward the three men, teeth bared, emitting a series of sharp barks and growls.

The man with the baseball bat glanced at his two *compadres*. One of them nodded. Drawing himself up to his full five-six height, the man took a tentative step toward Joe, slapping the bat in an open palm for emphasis. "*Querimos el apartamento*. We are here to remove you."

The two assistants snapped to attention, rearranging their faces into dark scowls. Hands gripped the handles of their machetes, knuckles turning white, ready for action, though they watched Lily out of the corner of their eyes.

"I don't care what you want!" Joe yelled as he took another step toward them. "We're not going anywhere!" At this last word, Lily's muscular black and brown body erupted into more snaps and snarls lunging toward the man in front, who nearly fell backward.

The man with the bat raised his voice. "*Pero*, the boss said to get you out." He slapped the bat in his palm again. "So, we have to." Three pairs of beady eyes bore holes through Joe.

Joe stayed glued to the faces of his adversaries and then put his hand up in an assumed gesture of surrender. This was the last thing the men expected. "Okay," he said, but as his hand came up, he dropped the leash. Lily's muscular body lunged at the trio, teeth flashing. Joe made no effort to hide the wide grin that broke out on his face.

The three amigos jumped back as the dog ran back and forth in front of them, snarling and barking. This time, their hands came up in submission.

"*Sí, sí, sí, pero*, the boss man…he paid us to do it," said the spokesman, jumping again as Lily forced her snout into his crotch. He held the bat high above his head, fright washing over his slim features.

"Well, tell your boss to *fuck off*!" Joe snarled.

But, even in his fervor, Joe was a businessman, and his hand went digging in his pocket. His fingers found three crumpled bills. Without looking, he threw the sweaty money behind him, toward the street. "Now, take this and get out of here!" he yelled as the paper went flying through the air.

Three sets of feet exploded down the driveway, swerving past Lily, fingers grasping at the shower of money before it hit the ground. The dog gave chase, snapping at their tails and catching the fabric of one man's pant leg in her teeth. In a minute flat, the three men disappeared down the street.

The security guard emerged from his hiding place, eyes like platters. "Señor!" He put out a hand to shake Joe's sweaty palm, afterwards tipping his baseball hat and saluting.

Joe laughed as his hand clapped the uniformed man on the shoulder. "That's how we do it in the U.S., right, Lil?" he said, shaking a fist in the air. He whistled, "Come on, girl!" and the dog came running back to his side, panting, her ears sideways in a docile position. Joe motioned to the guard to buzz him back into the building's entry and ran for the elevator. "We've got to get upstairs before your mom has a fit!"

I lay waiting, huddled in a ball inside the front door of the apartment.

Seven minutes had never felt like such an eternity. When the elevator dinged and heavy steps sounded in the narrow hallway toward me, I jumped a few feet back until I heard Joe's urgent whisper.

"It's us, honey!" he said. "They've gone and we're okay! Let us in!"

My hands were trembling with such force that I could hardly function to untangle the locks. As I unbolted the interior door and caught sight of them, I stifled a shriek of relief. When the metal security door swung open a second later, my husband stepped inside, refastened the deadbolt, and grabbed me, all in one motion.

"Are you hurt?" I could not stop shaking. "Is everything all right? What happened? They're gone? You're sure?" My teeth started chattering as the questions flew out of my mouth.

Joe released a nervous laugh as he hugged me tighter and recounted the tale as Lily forced her way between us to stand between our legs.

When the story was done, I looked from Joe to the dog in disbelief. Joe was laughing. "How can you possibly laugh? And why does she look like she has a smile on her face?" The dog did, in fact, look like she had enjoyed the escapade, with her tongue lolling and her eyes shining.

Joe grinned at me in response before I covered my face with my hands as the shock cascaded into nervous giggles. As I grabbed him, we both collapsed to the floor, doubled over from tension at the unlikely tale, this most unwelcome entry into Panama and what had come our way in just five days! My teeth continued to chatter and my limbs continued to shake as Joe brought me close to him and held my head to his chest. I could smell the acrid sweat of his fear as it cascaded off his skin.

"Baby." Joe released me before he began stripping clothes from his body. "Lily played her role like a dream. She scared the living shit out of them."

I struggled to catch my breath, clutching the dog to me, while the tension continued to roll out of me with laugh after laugh. *It's okay now, they're gone, we are fine.* But my nervous system was having none of it.

"Do you think they'll come back?" I whispered. Joe reached out to hug me again and Lily nudged her muzzle between our necks.

"No, I don't!" Joe chuckled, pulling me up and heading for the bathroom. There, he bent over the sink to splash water on his face. "Lily chased those suckers halfway down the block."

I looked from Joe to the dog and back again, shaking my head, trying to make sense of it. "Is that why they left?" The whole thing had happened so fast, though the seven minutes for me alone in that apartment, waiting and helpless, had seemed like a lifetime.

"Well, not exactly." Joe straightened, wiping his face with a towel. "I told you…I paid them a bribe."

The fog of the moment dissolved and I realized that, as always, money was the hinge pin for just about everything. Panama was no different—just more blatant—and our lives were worth a mere few dollars and a growling dog to these men who'd just been bought off. My eyes widened, staring at my man who'd once turned the car around to return 35 cents in change to a cashier at Walmart. With everything I'd imagined about Panama, I had never imagined this. "How much?"

Joe took my hand and led me to the bed, putting his arm around me as he replied.

I jerked back, staring at him. "Seven dollars? Are you *serious*?"

A proud smile lit up my husband's handsome face as he grinned in the moonlight that was now streaming into the dingy apartment. He hugged me tighter. "Yep! A five and two ones. It's all I had, but it's all it took."

I shook my head. My body had stopped shaking, but my limbs felt like they were full of lead, tension turning to exhaustion.

Joe drew me back to lay with him on the pillows. "Don't worry." His tone was serious as he kissed my brow. "I'll get us out of here tomorrow, no matter what it takes." My skin began to shiver despite the fact the room was still blistering hot as I closed my eyes.

For all Joe's bravado, neither of us could sleep a wink the rest of the night. After playing my knight in shining armor, Joe tried to drown his inner tension by downing several shots of tequila before landing in bed. The adrenaline of the night coursed through him where he lay still, but vigilant, in case something else unexpected happened in our new country. But, true to his word, he made miracles happen, and we vacated the apartment in Punta Paitilla the following morning.

Once we were safe and sound in the new place that had been a real gift to find, and the eight prong locks in the security door had clicked shut, I dialed the phone to call Juan Carlos. For some reason, I felt the need to inform him. Joe was stacking all our belongings into a neat pile in one corner of the immense living room so we could sort things out at our leisure.

When he picked up the line, and after I had explained the previous day's events, the first words out of Juan Carlos' mouth were, "Who are these people?"

I almost dropped the phone. "What do you mean—*who are these people*?" I snapped. "How the heck would I know? This is *your* country!" I had no more bandwidth for anyone.

Juan Carlos then relayed his own story. He'd called the real estate agent two days earlier to demand a refund when the electricity had been cut off the first time. The agent had referred him to the property manager—the same beefy man who'd sat in our midst the previous afternoon, trying to get us to move.

But instead of responding to Juan Carlos' phone calls, the property manager had shown up at my company's high-rise office, unannounced. My boss' demands for a refund backfired when the intruder turned threatening: "Give me 1,000 dollars cash or some harm will come to your new hire and her husband."

My blood turned cold as I listened. Joe could sense that my demeanor had stiffened and looked over his shoulder at me, as if to say, "Crap, what now?"

"I didn't know what else to do," Juan Carlos' voice rattled. "So, I paid it. Honestly, I've never had this type of thing happen to me before, JuliAnne. This is not the norm in Panama, I can assure you."

But something did not ring true—or maybe my Spidey sense was way off after all we'd been through in such a short amount of time, and I was not comforted in the least by his assurance.

"What's not the norm: paying a bribe or being threatened?" It came out before I could stop myself, my voice flat, the words almost a challenge.

Silence hung on the line for a long moment. I wasn't sure where these random thoughts came from but clearly, I'd caught his attention.

Still no reply. Then, finally: "I'm sorry." The fatigue in Juan Carlos' voice was palpable. "I'll put the word out to have that Ana woman checked out. I think it's all these Colombians that are moving here these days— they're bringing all the crime with them."

I didn't say anything. I didn't know what to say at that point.

"In the meantime, please get settled in. Call me if you need anything else, and I'll see you in a week or so at the office," Juan Carlos finished in a more conciliatory tone.

I hung up not knowing much more than my intuition was telling me, but I did sense that Panama still held a few tricks up her sleeve for us.

Dinner that night was scrambled eggs and toast on paper plates. Joe, Lily, and the cats collapsed next to my weary body, falling into a deep sleep in the new bedroom. The air conditioning unit on the wall was cranked all the way up, all the lights were on, and the bedside clock read 8 p.m.

PART TWO

CHAPTER 15:
All That Glitters

I woke with the sunrise, a bleary eye forced open at the bright light beaming through bare bedroom windows.

"Ow!" I said, when a beam of light pierced my retina. I burrowed back under the covers, my left hand locating the warmth of Joe's sleeping form to snuggle in behind him, spooning his body with mine. Joe reached back a hand to draw me closer to him, patting the cool cotton around my curves. We breathed sighs of comfort.

But our slumber was short-lived. Billowing white clouds hovering above the horizon were pierced by sunrays that worked their magic on the floor-to-ceiling glass, spreading across the sky in glory. The AC unit kicked on with fury to combat the heat. The crank-crank-crank of its oscillation forced me back to wakefulness.

"Aarrgh," I said. I turned back to face the window as my brain kicked into full gear. The sunlight invaded my consciousness, transforming the spacious bedroom into a brilliant kaleidoscope of orange, yellow, and white. Kicking to free the tangle of covers from around my legs, I thrashed one way and then the other trying to get comfortable again, away from the intensity of the light.

My sigh was audible as I poked a hole from my cocoon to spy at the clock on the bedside table. 5:22 a.m. "Why does the sun come up here so damn early?" I threw back the covers and swung toward the tile. "And why don't apartments in Panama come with window coverings, like they do everywhere else on the planet? Bunch of fucking idiots!"

"Shut up!" A feather pillow accompanying Joe's voice sailed past my ear, missing my tousled head by an inch.

I grinned, rubbing the sleep from my eyes before reaching for brown-rimmed glasses. "Good morning, Blossom," I whispered. The white calico swatted at me when I attempted to pet her head. "Oh, you're still sleeping too, are you?" I swatted back.

Our new apartment faced due south with million-dollar views of the Pacific's jewel-toned, sapphire blue waters. Tiny lights dotted the dark water where fishing boats pulled in the morning's catch.

"Doesn't the sun rise in the east and set in the west?" I had posed the question to Joe one evening as we sat on the apartment's 25th-story balcony.

Rings of smoke from Joe's cigar hung in the humid air. "That's true in the U.S., but not in Panama," Joe replied. "Panama is shaped like this," he said, fashioning a sideways S with his hands. "Here in Panama City, we are in a bay along the top of this curve." His right index finger indicated the correct location. "But in the geography of where the country sits, it makes sense."

I smiled, knowing that his love of geography was something I could count on. At that moment, though, I was just feeling the pleasant lull of finally being someplace I could call home.

Pacific Sunrise sat in one of Panama's most prestigious neighborhoods, Punta Pacifica. It was considered to be the ritziest condominium complex in the city. The View, as locals referred to it, encompassed two high-rise towers, four low-rise towers, and a number of individual villas, all facing the ocean. A third high-rise within the cluster was under construction, immediately adjacent to our building.

The rent we had agreed to, at the ridiculous price of 5,000 dollars, was much higher than we'd budgeted and well beyond any amount we had ever paid, even for a mortgage. Even for *gringos* in Panama's hot real estate market in 2008, the fee was considered astronomical.

Joe's better judgment on the topic had surrendered to necessity to bring all of us to safety, given the instability of our "Colombian incident," as we had come to call it. "Yes, it's expensive," said my husband who was much more budget-conscious than me. "This may not be a permanent solution, but at least it got us out of that mess."

I hadn't argued. The fact that the owner had accepted our three fur babies without a fight or a deposit sealed the deal for me. Plus, the monstrous 3,800 square foot unit had been available for immediate move-in. It was either that or a few more nights of dealing with what we were sure had been a drug deal waiting to go bad.

And so, we had caved.

Months later, a friend informed us that we'd been victims of the local Panamanian custom, *Juega Vivo*.

"Ah, yes, you got hit with the Gringo Tax," he'd laughed one night after dinner. "They're all in on it. Every newcomer pays it on most everything they buy for the first few months they're in the country, until they get savvy." He chewed the end of a Cuban dangling from under a bushy moustache. "You can't blame the locals, really. When you're born into a country that's been conquered by foreigners for hundreds of years, and subjected to dictators for generations after that, it's hard not to resent the sizable gap between the haves and the have-nots. It's only just now starting to change, you know, in the last few years. But old habits like *Juega Vivo* die hard. Not everyone here does it, but many locals think it's the only way they can beat the system."

In the real estate realm, *Juega Vivo* was evident when foreigners were charged two to three times more for rent than a local would pay for the same unit. We were certainly getting an education that would have been nice to have had before we'd arrived.

While we were moving in, the leasing agent for the apartment arrived to deliver keys. He saw me staring at the naked floor-to-ceiling windows. "How soon will the light fixtures and window shades be installed?" I asked as I stood in the living room, gazing at the endless blue of the Pacific Ocean, which stretched to the horizon.

A long pause ensued as the broker's perpetual smile slid away. His brow furrowed. "Ehhhh, the owner doesn't provide these, Mizz Julian. That's for you."

"Whaaaat?" Joe's face shot up from where he'd been reviewing the rent receipt. "No, no, no, no. We don't. The owner does." The tone of his voice rose like a balloon. "We're *renting* the apartment, remember? We're not buying it."

"*Sí, sí, sí, Señor. Yo se*," the gray head nodded. "*Pero*, when you rent an apartment in Panama, it's up to you to purchase your own lights and your own coverings."

My heart skipped a beat as I took in the expanse of windows covering the entire length of the apartment facing the water. "You can't be serious!" Then I stopped, remembering what I had read online about Panamanian culture. I forced a breath into my tightening throat before walking back toward the broker. "That doesn't make any sense. Landlords always provide those things. They'll want to keep them after we're gone, of course. Plus, that would cost thousands of dollars."

The broker nodded but the confused expression on his face did not change.

"Why were we not informed of this on the first visit?" A storm rolled across my husband's handsome features.

"Well…," the sincere face began to turn bright red. "I don't know. This is the norm in Panama, so perhaps I assumed you knew. Did you ask me about this before?" The broker could not hold Joe's angry gaze.

"Well, no," Joe struggled to keep his voice from rising. "But something that costs this much is something people should be *told* about before they sign a contract!" He grasped the signed contract from the table in the middle of the room and shook it at the broker.

"Sí, Señor." The man's eyebrows remained furrowed. "I understand. *Pero no les preocupan,* don't worry." His face broke out into a hopeful smile as he lifted his index finger. "I have a friend I can refer to you that does blinds!"

As I spat what remained of my toothpaste into the sink, I had to smile. The broker's "friend" had given us a quote of more than 9,000 dollars for his "most affordable alternative." *As if anyone would invest that on a rental!*

My morning routine had never changed. *Pee. Brush teeth. Shower. Dry hair.* While my brain got going first, my body never fully awoke until the first stream of hot water hit my face.

Sleepy fingers hung my robe up on a hook behind the door before I stepped over a small threshold to enter the shower. *Who in the world needs a shower this big?* My mind queried as I turned on the tap and glanced around the large enclosure of glass and gold. *This thing is as big as my walk-in closet was in Denver.*

I took my time, working the soap into a lather on my skin, kneading the muscles of my neck and shoulders, knowing Joe would sleep for a while. *God knows, I need to unwind after the traumatic week of welcome we've had to this country.*

I adjusted the water to a midline temperature. *Even with the AC, hot water here feels too hot to me.* Reaching for Joe's shaving cream, I lathered my legs and bent over each with my razor and sighed. *How nice to finally have a morning where we don't have to be running out the door for something.* It was the first quiet moment I'd had since leaving Denver.

I prepared to face the day of odds and ends into a schedule that would be efficient. But efficiency is not a word that Panamanians know.

Processes in Panama seemed to take three times as long as the same ones in the States. We had spent the entirety of the past week getting new utilities ordered, cell phone accounts set up, and getting the apartment provisioned. Even finding all the household products we needed for the kitchen and the bath had entailed a full afternoon visiting four different stores in three various parts of town. The sweltering heat and the bump-n-grind traffic drained every ounce of positivity from our beings, leaving us perpetually wilted.

I turned off the water and swung the door open wide to feel for my towel on the hook outside, but my palm came up empty. *Whaaa?* I thought, before blinking as the water ran off the top of my head and streamed into my eyes. *Oh, damn!* The towel laid next to the sink, 10 feet away.

I stepped out onto the rug when something caught my attention out of the corner of my eye. As I turned, the glimpse of what I saw caused me to shriek as I dropped to all fours.

"Fuck!" I prayed my cry would be heard by my husband in the next room. "Joe!"

But the solid concrete walls blocked all sound.

I glanced back at the bathroom windows, which stretched from knee-height to the ceiling. At the moment, they still stood naked and unadorned, facing the steel frame of the high-rise that was going up next to us.

I had watched for the past two days as the workers poured concrete on the levels below us, creeping higher and higher by the hour. *And, now it's Monday….* I put my forehead against the hard marble floor. I lifted my gaze again in the direction of the steel structure, which was now giving construction workers a front row seat to my nakedness. Raising my head like a turtle, I pried open my eyelids to glance around. *I'm safe down here, but….* Then, a terrible thought hit me, and my neck snapped backwards toward the shower where I'd stood moments before.

"Nooooo!" The realization of what I'd just done slapped me in the face like a knuckle sandwich. The shower where I had just spent the last 15 minutes in relaxed bathing stood in full view of the naked window.

I popped my head up, scanning down a line of steel. "Maybe they were all working, and maybe…," but 18 smiling faces sat along the edge of the steel structure, staring back at me. And now, 18 mouths erupted into roars.

"Shit!" I ducked again as a number of hands lifted toward me in greeting.

My damp feet skidded on the tile as I raced for the countertop, grabbing my towel, throwing open the bedroom door and catapulting out.

The door slammed and I leaned against it, chest heaving. "Mother fucker!"

Then I collapsed, doing something I hadn't done in days. My body doubled over, hands clutching my belly, and I shook as peals of laughter cascaded from me, over and over and over again.

My husband's salt and pepper head poked up from beneath the covers. "JuliAnne?"

CHAPTER 16:
The Neighborhood

"Mizz JuliAnne," Tomas began as the car pulled up to the exit gate of the new building. The guard lifted a hand to wave the car through after raising the metal bar in front of us. "I have a little problem."

I raised my head from the backseat where I had been studying my Blackberry in one hand, a commuter cup of coffee in the other. "Yes, Tomas?" My eyebrows lifted, waiting. It was rare for my driver to share anything from his personal life with me. "What's that?"

"Mizz JuliAnne," Tomas hesitated, his eyes somber in the rearview mirror. "The guard told me that I can't park my taxi in your parking place anymore."

I started laughing. "Well, that's ridiculous. The guard can't tell you what to do. Our apartment comes with three parking spaces and we only have two cars. When you're driving me in my car, you are more than welcome to park your car in the other space. That's our right and I'm telling you that you can. So, you can park there, if we say so."

Tomas' face brightened. "Yes?" The deep creases around his eyes lessened as a smile returned. "I can still park there?"

"Of course." My eyes were curious, as I watched his face. "Why would you think otherwise?"

"Well, the guard says the building people don't like my taxi in the building." Tomas flitted his eyes toward me in the mirror before he returned them to the maze of traffic before him. I thought I saw shame.

"What?" The coffee in my mouth came spluttering out. "What difference does it make what kind of car you have?" I felt incredulous.

"Well," Tomas began, "they say a taxi can't park in *their* building. I have to park on the street."

My eyes narrowed. *Wouldn't this be discrimination anywhere else?* I wiped my mouth with a napkin, forming a reply.

"Tomas, you tell the guard or anyone else that asks that I said that's *malarkey*. The parking space is ours, no matter what anyone thinks of your car, and if they have a problem with me saying you can park in one of our spots, they can come talk to me or Mr. Joe."

Green eyes widened. "Okay, Mizz JuliAnne," he said, shoulders straightening in the driver's seat with pride, "I tell 'em that the *jefes* said it was okay. They listen to me now." He nodded as he spoke and seemed a little more confident.

I smiled as I turned my gaze out the window. I had a long way to go in understanding the idiosyncrasies of the separation of the classes in Panama and how it all worked. What we had seen so far didn't make sense to our North American brains. Joe and I would not abandon our democratic leanings just because we lived in a country where democracy was in its infancy. I strongly believed that every person had value and should have equal opportunity.

I recalled a conversation I'd had last week at a company dinner with Curt's wife. "I don't care what anyone else in Panama pays their maid." The words had flown out of my mouth with vehemence. "And, I don't *care* if I am overpaying. No one can survive—even in this country—on just 12 dollars a day for a full day's work. I'll pay what *I think* is fair." And yes, I was clearly the *gringa,* with an attitude, in a developing country that did not hold the same point of view that I thought should be universal.

I'd finished stating my firm opinion only to find Juan Carlos lifting an eyebrow at me from across the table.

Uh oh. I sent a smile his direction, before turning to nod at something else my dinner companion was saying. *And, what do you care anyway?* I couldn't resist another glance back at Juan Carlos, who had turned away. *You're one of Panama's elite, born into a prominent family, educated in the States, and now back to live high on the hog in one of the city's most elite neighborhoods. You're hardly among 'the people.'*

I didn't think I'd ever adjust to the way I saw many of the locals treat their help, working them 12 to 14 hours a day with no extra pay, six days a week. And their own labor laws didn't even protect them, at least not the maids. The household workers were considered the lowest of the low, with very few rights. *It just was not fair.*

Even so, the paltry sum of 15 dollars a day I paid my maid was still a pittance. *People here just don't get how good they have it: full-time maids, full-time drivers, full-time nannies.*

My mind flashed back again to several weeks ago, at one of our final going-away parties in Denver at the neighborhood bar. As the evening had waned, the men clustered at one end of the bar, the women at another.

"So, what's the first thing you're going to do, once you get there?" Five eager faces surrounded me, waiting for the exotic crumb I would drop next.

"Well," I blushed, "our driver is going to meet us at the airport...."

"Wait!" interrupted the cry. "Your *driver*?"

"You have a driver!" another cut in. "Holy shit, Miss Fancy Pants!"

"What?" shrieked another. "What *else* are you not telling us about this new exotic life of yours, JuliAnne?" This was accompanied by a finger shake.

"No, no, no, it's not like that," I stammered, color rising in my cheeks. "Yes, we'll have a driver because the traffic is horrendous, but that'll be our only luxury. I doubt we'll even have a maid."

"A maid?" One of the women was aghast. "You mean, like a full-time maid?"

"Well, yes, that's the norm down there," I took a gulp of my beer to hide my embarrassment. *Was this starting to sound like I was bragging?* "But we probably won't have one, since it's just the two of us...."

I grimaced as I came back to the present. My principled resolve had fallen within just a few weeks when Joe had insisted a full-time maid be hired. The combination of high humidity along with three pets' worth of hair in the heavy, tropical air became more than he could keep up with in the spacious, 3,800 square-foot apartment. And though our 25th-floor unit was high above five neighboring towers being built next to us, the thick red construction dust seemed to find its way in and coat everything.

Well, I'm not requiring my girl to live-in, I thought to myself, hoping no one could read my mind.

It was an option, of course, and in fact, it was the norm. The sizeable apartment we'd rented in our haste to escape Punta Paitilla had a reasonably sized room and bathroom off the laundry, designed for a live-in maid. *Reasonable that is, except for the fact that it's not piped for hot water, another thing the Panamanians don't think their help deserves.*

But, the decision to only have the girl come during the day was based on our desire to maintain our privacy.

"I don't want someone in our space all the time. It's just weird," I had said to Joe, so the tiny Indian girl we'd hired came Monday to Friday, from 7 a.m. to 4 p.m. Even so, I made sure not to write home about it.

~

"So, you take the leash like this." I had Lily's leash beside me, as I positioned the dog on my left. The maid watched from beside Tomas, pupils wide. "And you walk her like this." I took a few strides back and forth, showing the maid how to hold the leash in her hand.

"Tomas, can you translate please?"

Tomas nodded as a string of Spanish left his mouth, pointing to the various things I had explained.

I followed most of it—while I had studied Spanish in high school and college, the language had laid dormant in my brain for 16 years—and now Joe and I were taking turns on the computer doing 30 minutes a day of Rosetta Stone.

I waited until Tomas completed the instruction. "*Bien?*" I said.

"*Creo que sí,*" said the maid. "I think so."

"Okay, then. Tomas, please help her. Take her on the 30-minute loop." The maid's hands trembled as she took the leash from my outstretched hand.

"And, please, Tomas, don't let Lily get too close to anyone or any other dogs, especially children. The usual, just in case." Tomas and the maid looked more terrified when I mentioned children. Dobermans were not a dog found often in Panama so Lily was a very imposing presence everywhere she went.

Tomas nodded as he opened the front door and the two made their way to the elevator, with Lily leading the way.

I sighed as my heels clicked toward the expansive walk-in closet to change. *At least it will be nice to have another pair of hands to walk Lily when Tomas and I are running late getting home from the office.*

A pit of guilt formed in my stomach, as I hung up my jacket and removed my jewelry. *Joe is such a good guy. I don't blame him if his enthusiasm for being a house-husband is already getting old. What other husband would have given up a six-figure job to do this crazy thing?*

Joe's tennis shoes were absent from the closet floor. I pulled on spandex shorts and a top, lacing up my own shoes.

One of the best things about our new building was the two-story fitness center within the complex featuring racquetball, tennis, basketball, and a lap pool, plus the full-size gym with weights and machines.

Pounding away on the treadmill was one of my favorite ways to destress.

My treads squeaked down the hall when the front door burst open. Tomas and the maid stood panting, terrified looks on their faces. Lily's chest was heaving, and there was a dark piece of cloth hanging from her mouth.

"Tomas, I said 30 min…," I began, not having noticed the totality of the scene before me.

"Mizz JuliAnne!" Tomas' face was covered in drops of sweat. "Lily bit a man."

I felt the blood in my veins turn to ice. "What? Tomas, what happened?" I crossed over to my two employees. Fright mirrored in the dilated pupils of my new maid.

"A man ran by us, and she dropped the leash." He pointed to the maid. "Lily chased after him!"

"And, then?" I asked, looking from one to the other. The maid remained frozen, trembling, at the door.

"Then she ripped his shorts." Tomas' voice rose as he pointed to his rear end. "See?" he pointed at the dog's mouth and then to the piece of cloth.

"Shit!" I caught Lily by the collar, prying her jaws apart and examining the dark piece of cloth. Sure enough, it was lightweight material, just like my shorts. No blood. *Thank goodness!*

"Where is the man now?" I asked, adrenaline coursing through me as visions of lawsuits, angry fists, and eviction notices ran across the ticker tape of my mind. "Was he hurt? Did he say anything?"

"I don't know," Tomas panted, bending over at the waist to catch his breath. "We went to catch the dog and bring her back."

Better to take this bull by the horns and deal with whatever's coming, right off the bat, I thought, my face grim.

"Come on, let's go back down." I motioned to Tomas. "You," I pointed at the girl shivering in the corner, "stay here until we get back." The girl nodded, seeming relieved.

Tomas and I exited the building parking structure at a run, tracing the route. Outside, the sunset sky was ablaze in shades of orange and red.

Two men in white shorts and shirts were hitting a tennis ball on the single court. Three other maids were walking down the sidewalk with neatly groomed, gray schnauzers.

Tomas pointed to a place further down the lane where the sidewalk narrowed, beside the building. "Here, Miss JuliAnne. Right here!" A cluster of people had formed just past the spot, eyes focused on something in their midst.

Great, I thought. *Here we go. I'm sure it's a neighborhood committee ready to throw us out.* I squared my shoulders as we approached, ready for combat.

But, when we reached the crowd, two dark-haired children on new bicycles sprung from its midst. "*Vayan, vayan, vayan!*" sang two sets of proud parents. "Go! Go! Go!" The moms clapped their hands and the dads pumped their fists. A number of other children on bikes followed them, chubby legs pedaling as fast as they could.

I stopped in my tracks, looking around. Nothing seemed out of place. The sun was shining. The children were giggling. Parents were talking and laughing. Everything seemed normal…almost…serene.

"Tomas." My tone was suspicious. "Where did the man go after Lily tore his shorts?"

"*No se, Señora.* I didn't see him." Tomas was wide-eyed, innocent. "He just kept on running."

"He didn't stop?"

"No, Señora." Tomas shook his head.

I nodded, taking a last look around. But, there was no man, no HOA, no one waiting to pounce on the owners of the bad dog.

"Strange," I said, as we turned back to the apartment.

I kept an eye over my shoulder for weeks to come.

~

Beep! Beep! Beep! The semi's backup alarm pierced the quiet of the night before a diesel engine sputtered to life, its clatter ricocheting off the building walls.

I sat straight up in bed and fumbled for my glasses on the bedside table. The room was dark.

"Damn it!" Joe grumbled, pulling a feather pillow over his head.

"I can't believe they're allowed to start work this early." We had been in the new apartment six weeks now and the nighttime construction had begun two weeks before.

I looked at the digital readout on the ceiling, "It's 2 a.m." I snuggled up to my husband's back. "I thought construction couldn't start before 6 a.m."

"That's the way it is in the States." Joe's voice was muffled under the covers. "But quite obviously, no one is enforcing that shit down here, if those laws even exist at all." Joe dug in deeper under his pillow.

A spotlight swept past the windows, illuminating the bedroom like it was daytime. Lily looked up from her bed on the floor and blinked.

Rat-a-tat-tat! Rat-a-tat-tat! Rat-a-tat-tat!

The pressure began to build in my temples. I had been on enough construction sites to recognize the sound of the building's foundations being drilled. Since drills were expensive to operate, once they started up, the foreman normally kept them in operation for six to eight hours.

The prospect of either of us sleeping the rest of the night in peace was fading into oblivion. My bleary mind did the math. *Depending on the size of the building being built—and we know it's another high-rise from the looks of the billboard in front of the lot—drilling caissons will go on for several more weeks, if not months.*

"This could be just like living in paradise." The refrain from David Lee Roth's famous song from the 80s replayed in my memory, now an evil taunt. *Oh, you've got to be kidding me.* In times of stress, my brain often locks onto a song and plays it in my head 400 times in a row. That was happening a lot these days as the day-to-day stress of trying to get my new start-up position perfect was keeping me awake at night more than I wanted to admit.

I dug myself out of the covers to locate the pink foam earplugs I kept on the bedside table. Rolling them between my fingers, I stuffed them in my ears. *I hope these help. Otherwise, it's more like we're living in paradise lost.*

CHAPTER 17:
Club Union

A moment after my sleek coupe pulled up in front of the Club Union, a white gloved hand reached for the passenger door.

"*Buenas noches*," said the uniformed valet as he offered a second hand to help me. Horns blared from behind.

"*Muchas gracias*," I replied, as a thick fog of exhaust enveloped me when the car door opened. *Such service,* I thought, as I reached for my briefcase and swung a leg toward the pavement.

A second valet motioned my driver to pull forward and park in a roped-off lot ahead where a number of other chauffeurs congregated, recognizable in their Guayabera white linen shirts.

"*Bienvenida*, welcome." A third valet greeted me as I began to click down the marbled hall in search of the ladies' room. After the stressful day I'd had, I was expected to speak to the Rotary Club members at Panama's top social club this evening, and I wanted to tidy up first.

"Señora." A stern voice roused me from my focus on locating the ladies room. "Señora!" I swept my gaze backward to locate the source of the voice, almost colliding with a man in an impeccable black suit right on my heels.

"*A donde va?*" Black eyes pierced through me. "Where do you think you're going?"

"I have a meeting," I replied in halting Spanish, pointing to my briefcase. "*Un presentación con el Rotary.*"

The man's brow wrinkled as he struggled to make sense of me. He must have understood since he gestured toward a wide-paneled desk in the corner. "You need here," he told me.

I sighed when I saw three other people standing in front of the harried-looking clerk talking on a phone. *It's hardly security if they can't get people on their way any faster than this.*

Ten minutes later, I was ushered up the curved, marbled stairs behind the desk, past several open doors along a wide hallway strewn with Persian rugs. As I passed the other doorways on either side of the hall, my eyes were met with scene after scene of long-haired women in bejeweled evening gowns holding crystal champagne flutes alongside tuxedoed men with slick-backed hair.

What day is it? my brain asked. *Surely these couldn't all be weddings on a Thursday.*

The man in the suit I was following came to a stop in front of a paneled doorway. "*Mujeres,*" it read.

"*Le espero,*" he said. "I'll wait." I nodded, handing him my briefcase before pulling open the polished brass door handle.

Approaching a row of four marbled sinks, I crossed toward a wall of gold-gilded mirrors, reaching into my Gucci bag for powder and lipstick. I glanced around for a clock, but saw only a tiny woman in a gray and white uniform sitting on a foldout metal chair.

Raising a hand to smooth my hair, I brushed powder over my nose and under my eyes to hide the circles. I rubbed my lips together to moisten them with fresh color. *There. Better.*

Feeling curious eyes upon me, I smiled at the maid as I headed for the door. Crooked teeth and kind eyes smiled back. "*Buenas noches,*" we said, simultaneously.

I had learned the importance of the local custom of greeting everyone you meet. It stood in stark contrast to what I was accustomed to, but observing it dissolved much of the locals' intimidation at interacting with me as a *gringa*. It also broke down the language barrier, which was huge, since my Spanish was still taking shape.

A moment later I faced another six-paneled door which revealed a mid-sized ballroom with parquet floors and a number of round tables covered in mauve tablecloths. A sea of men in dark suits greeted my sight, many of whom turned my way, in interest, as I brushed through the double doors.

One of them, with a kind, wrinkled face, stepped forward with outstretched arms. "JuliAnne!"

My face broke into a relieved smile, thankful to locate my host so quickly; entry into crowded rooms and restaurants often felt more like an intrusion than a reception, with glances cast my direction turning into obvious stares.

Geraldo grasped my elbow to lean in and brush a leathery cheek against mine. "Welcome to Rotary!" He turned to introduce me to the circle of men with whom he'd been conversing.

Here we go, I thought, extending my hand with a wide smile toward each of the men, recalling what a Panamanian friend had told me months before as I tried to make sense of all the cultural norms. *Shake first, kiss second.*

"*Mucho gusto,*" I said as the cool skin of my palm was engulfed in the tepid dampness of the first man's fingers.

"*Placer.*" The 60-something-year-old man's tone was gruff. He scanned my face to see if I might cringe at his wet hand. When he saw I did not, he seemed to stand taller, regal, in his pinstripe three-piece suit.

Is this where all the vests in the world have gone? In these moments of formality, Snickety's humor often caused me to grin, before I could help it. *The bankers in Panama evidently never got the memo that vests became passé 20 years ago.*

I lifted my gaze to a second man with slicked white hair before I caught the flash of a white handkerchief being stuffed into his suit as his hand met mine.

My "*mucho gusto*" collided with his cleared throat, "*Placer.*"

The third man appeared my age or younger, a slender version of the man in the middle, but in a flashier suit. "This is Junior," Geraldo said. "He works in the family business, as well."

"I'll bet he does," Snickety hissed as the younger man scanned the length of my body as if he were undressing me from head to toe. His eyes swirled around the curve of my hips which amply filled out my skirt.

I extended my hand, as I watched him drag eyes up from my breasts, to my throat, and finally to my lips. His thin mouth curled into a smirk, as he clamped a wet hand over mine and his voice dripped thick with suggestion. "*A la orden.*"

I fought the inclination to gag as my skin began to crawl. Instead, I withdrew my hand naturally as I turned back to Geraldo.

"So, where do you have me on the agenda this evening?" I asked. "I brought an extra copy of my presentation, in case you want to test it."

Geraldo's face fell. "Oh, I...I'm so sorry." He took my elbow, steering me away from the group. "But, the national football team the Club supports just won the championship yesterday, and we asked them to stop by this evening to say a few words. We'll have to move you to the next meeting, next month."

I hoped my face did not betray my incredulity before I began to laugh. "Right, Geraldo," I said with a tired smile, "you're so funny!"

But Geraldo wasn't laughing. "I…I'm serious." Worried eyes scanned my face. "Is that okay?"

I rearranged my features into a look of surprise. "You're serious?" I stammered as my face began to redden. But, what may have seemed like a blush for those looking on was fueled by sheer anger at the absolute absurdity. *The football team?*

"Yes," Geraldo returned matter-of-factly, though his face had also turned bright red. "But I'd like to invite you to stay for dinner, so you can meet everyone and then they'll know you for next time."

My heart sank. With the day I'd had, I really didn't feel like socializing. However, neither did I want to appear rude. "All right," I said in a deflated tone.

Geraldo led me to one of the round tables, as the gavel pounded and the meeting was called to order.

Two hours later, I gathered my handbag and shook the hands of my tablemates before heading for the door. A glance at my watch told me it was well past 10 p.m., and I was exhausted.

But, before I could hightail it out, Geraldo's voice caught me. "JuliAnne, wait! There's one more person I want you to meet."

I bit the inside of my cheek before turning back. *Shit.*

Motioning from across the room, Geraldo's hand was beckoning me toward him. The last thing I wanted was to shake another sweaty hand.

But, all of this is the fruit of my own work, I guess. It was true my social dance card was full almost every weekday night with invitations from Panama's "who's who" as the launch of the redevelopment of the former military base had become headline news. And, with it, my company's interest to share the inside scoop on what was happening as the new project was fast becoming the hottest invitation in town.

Of course, it doesn't hurt that you have a pretty face, Snickety whispered in my ear.

Lighter hair makes me an anomaly, it's true, I grimaced before I arrived at the small group gathered around Geraldo. Panama's skin tones played out in a rainbow of shades: the indigenous butterscotch, the European pale (English, French, and Spanish, over the years), the West Indies black, the Chinese yellow, the *cholo* brown, and the *mezla* toffee. But it was the combination of my blue eyes with my lighter skin the Latin men seemed to find so tantalizing. In the States, I would have cried sexism, chauvinism, or something akin to the patriarchal norm, but in Panama, I had to learn to use this difference as an advantage and not take the attention to it as a personal affront.

"Here she is." Geraldo's eyes sparkled as if I were his own daughter. "JuliAnne, it's my honor to introduce you to Panama's Minister of Commerce, Señor Juan Hebron."

I pulled up all my stature and did my gender proud. "Your Excellency, Señor Hebron. *Mucho gusto*."

The man standing shorter than me had a hooknose. Suspicious eyes peered at me from under eyebrows that appeared not to have been trimmed in more than a month.

"Equally, Ms. Murphy," the minister replied, in flawless English. "I hear you are one of our new *extranjeros* in Panama to ensure the success of the new Panorama project."

"That's right," I started, but Geraldo had already stolen the words from my mouth.

"JuliAnne has years of experience in development, and she was hired to market the project all over the world! She will be presenting to us here in Rotary at the next meeting!"

I flushed at the effusive praise as my eyes met the minister's.

"I see." The minister arched an eyebrow as he gazed at me. "And how is Panama treating you so far?"

"Very well, sir," I lied. "The people here are lovely, and your country is beautiful." I kept my face neutral as I returned the minister's stare. I had learned months ago that particular question could be a minefield if not answered in a simple manner. Panamanians were very proud of their country.

"And, when did we start allowing women to attend Rotary meetings?" The minister's eyes continued their even stare at me as the words left his mouth before they flicked over to Geraldo to await his reply.

My mouth dropped open.

Geraldo didn't miss a beat. "About three years ago, Señor Ministro. There was a lawsuit in California about women wanting to attend, and we decided to follow suit."

I appreciated the instant reply from Geraldo and held my ground, though I could not conceal the shock that spread across my features as I looked from the minister to my host and back again. For the first time since I'd arrived in Panama, I was speechless. *Three years ago? This is 2008!*

"Fair enough." The minister drew his mouth into the semblance of a sneer, his eyes seeming to digest my discomfort with some satisfaction. He gave me a slight nod, "Ms. Murphy, I wish you the best of luck on your project."

"Señor Ministro," I recovered, inclining my head as the tiny Napoleon began to march toward the exit. His small entourage buzzed close behind.

I turned back to Geraldo, the circles under my eyes darkening from a weariness that suddenly gripped me. My lips parted to form words, but my brain came up empty. *What the hell just happened?*

"We'll look forward to seeing you next time," Geraldo said, leaning in to kiss my cheek again, as if nothing had happened. "Thanks for coming."

I stood like stone trying to process the situation, one that was not a part of my job description, nor part of any of my wildest ideas about what this job in a developing country would entail.

I nodded, mute, and forced a smile before pushing my leaden feet in the direction of the exit, which appeared in the distance, like a mirage.

CHAPTER 18:
Slam Bam, Thank You Ma'am

"How did you pick that *color*?" Curt's accusal hung in the air.

I fought to keep a sigh from escaping while patting my knee to counterbalance the urge to squirm. *Since when are any of you experts on color?*

He continued, "I don't think this website portrays our products the way we want them to be viewed."

"If you'll refer to page nine in your packets, there's a list of the characteristics we agreed we wanted to convey to our future clients about the project." I flipped there in the binder sitting in front of me on the table. "This new look and feel captures the top three of these, right off the bat. So, yes, Curt, to answer your question, a color on the website can always be changed, but a different color may not convey the same feeling we wish to achieve, in quite the same way." I lifted my eyes to find Curt staring at me. Unblinking, his eyes bored into mine.

Color rose to my cheeks. "What I mean to say is…."

"I don't *care* what we agreed upon last time." Curt's voice shot across the board room, finding its target in my chest. "I don't think you've captured what we asked you to do."

I attempted to look unruffled. Raising my chin, I stared back at Curt. *I am so sick of you changing your tune, you asshole.* But I kept my tone firm: "I'm sorry you feel that way, Curt. But what we agreed in our prior meetings sets the foundation for the creative direction we take. That's how this process works. If we wish to change the foundation for what we want to convey, we can certainly do that, but it will mean more time for the creative process. And, more time, as you know, means more investment required."

"Why do you always get defensive when I give my opinion?" Curt cut me off. "Can't you just fix it?"

"Fix…what, exactly?" I struggled to keep my voice even, clenching my fist under the conference room table. *Why are you always attacking me?*

"I don't think anything has to be fixed." Juan Carlos' soft baritone interjected from the end of the table. Four sets of eyes turned in his direction.

Finally, someone is speaking reason, other than me. I waited, watching the pen in Juan Carlos' hand work its way through his slender fingers, like a gymnast. I counted. *1…2…3…4…5.* Usually there was about a six-second pause between his initial words and the second piece of whatever the man had to say. Out of the corner of my eye, I watched as Curt huddled over his notebook, ripping out a piece of paper, crumpling it up and throwing it on the floor.

"I believe it's a matter of tweaking a few things," Juan Carlos finished, eyes focused over his reading glasses on the projected image on the wall. Then he cleared his throat. "I feel like we've given you the feedback you needed for your purposes, JuliAnne, yes? It's not necessary for us to regurgitate it any longer. It goes without saying that all of us participated in this process from the beginning and came to some conclusions at that time." His eyes settled on Curt's bent form.

Curt's fingers were flying across his Blackberry keyboard.

"Absolutely." My spine straightened, drawing myself up to an erect posture, the antithesis of the way Curt seemed to shrink into himself in these meetings. *Take that, you asshole.*

"We'll take all your comments into consideration and present the revised version in about 10 days." My eyes scanned the room. "Any other questions for me at this time?"

Three heads shook in unison. My eyes took in Curt's body language, his head caved over his spine and his frame leaning forward like a collapsing tent. He seemed to be in his own world.

"All right then." I rose from the table, signaling the meeting was over. "Thanks, all." I headed for the ladies' room to collect my frayed nerves, an experience that was now becoming an all too often occurrence whenever Curt and I were in the same room. I shouldn't take it personally since his erratic mood was talked about by everyone. But, weeks in, I already saw the handwriting on the wall: This job was taking everything I had and more.

~

I sighed as the door opened out on my side of the dark sedan. The proffered hand hung in the air, waiting: an invitation to the dance.

"Just a minute." Irritation and fatigue showed in my voice as I clicked on the ceiling light and adjusted my lipstick.

"Come on, girlfriend," Joe's voice cajoled, his fingers snapping. "Delaying our entry isn't going to change anything."

I closed my eyes, steeling myself for what was to come. "Just give me a second." I took a long inhale and blew it out between pursed lips before I put a cool palm in my husband's sweaty one. "You know I hate socializing with this prick."

"Hola!" Curt's voice bounced down the stairs like a children's ball as the restaurant door opened, and he clattered down the steps to the meet us.

Here we go. I felt my stomach clench as every ounce of my being screamed bloody murder, and I leaned in for an air kiss. I forced a perfunctory smile across my face. "Hi there."

"You look as beautiful as ever."

I fought a gag reflex as Curt's clammy hand squeezed the outside of my bicep. I breezed by him to hide my grimace. "Thanks."

Curt reached for Joe's outstretched hand. "Hey, buddy!" His hand went up and over my husband's shoulder to clasp it, as if the two were old pals.

"Good evening," I said as a small woman took my wrap, and Curt's wife looked up to greet me. "Good to see you, Anne."

"Heeeey…you!" The bleached blond woman slurred the words before she stood up swaying. Wine spilled over the edge of her glass as I leaned in to press a moist cheek to hers.

If I were married to your husband, I'd be a heavy drinker, too. I scanned the room to locate the seat furthest away from Curt. *"Buenas noches,"* I said as I pointed my heels toward dinner companions I hadn't yet been introduced to at the other end of the table. "Good evening."

But, Anne's hand on my elbow stopped me. "Sit down here with the girls." Anne's finger shook as she pointed to the chair across from her. "Please?" She stuck out her lower lip in a fake pout.

"I would love to," my hand went out to squeeze the woman's shoulder in mock affection, "but we have work to do, you know." I inclined my chin to the four people in power suits at the other end.

"All work and no play!" Anne said, a little too loud. "You and Curt are no fun these days. Well, come on then, Joe, you can sit with us, right? We'll have lots more fun down here. Can I get you a drink?" She patted the chair next to her.

"I'm always up for a drink, Anne, you know that." The look Joe shot above my head said, *You owe me*. "Of course, I'd love to join you lovely ladies."

I was just putting my clutch on the seat next to the clients when Curt returned from the men's room and pulled out the seat across from me. *Crap! I thought he was at the other end.* But moving away from him would be too obvious. I made my way around the end of the table, introducing myself.

"This woman is the genius in charge of our marketing." Curt's voice was bright.

Funny how the only time I get any praise from you is when you need something. My new tablemates acknowledged me with a nod.

Curt made a habit of summoning Joe and me to help schmooze potential Fortune 500 clients when they were in town. He was no dummy to the fact that my outreach into the business community was making me somewhat of a local celebrity. Plus, I was good at small talk; Curt was not.

The only thing you're good at is scaring the shit out of your staff, and getting people to sign on the dotted line. "So, when did you and your team get in?" I asked, turning to the woman on my left.

The night dragged on. I kept looking at my watch as the time seemed to crawl. Joe was on his fourth whiskey which told me he, too, had had enough of the evening's rhetoric. Suddenly, my husband pushed his chair back and excused himself saying that he didn't feel all that well and was going to call it a night. I hid a smile, feigning concern as he scooped me up along with my handbag and swept me away from the table, all the time whispering in my ear, "You owe me big time, Murph. And, I mean, big time, for this one."

I was happy to pay whatever he wanted.

~

During that first tumultuous week in the country, one of my top priorities had been to buy myself a car. I had started shopping during our house-hunting trip a month before, but when my kick-off meetings had stretched two days longer than they were supposed to, Joe had continued on without me. His new charcoal-colored Audi had been delivered the week after we'd arrived.

Now, it was my turn, and I was excited. Joe and I stood on the showroom floor of the dealership, admiring a shiny new model. I'd given it a lot of thought before I, too, had settled on a coup. *Classy, elegant, sleek*. This was how I wanted people to see me, and the Audi sedan was just the ticket.

"Isn't the point of having cars on the showroom floor so that people can sit inside them?" The door handle of the red model I jiggled was locked.

"Well, yes, my love," Joe smirked from the passenger door as he did the same, "but that would make sense, and I think we're learning that not much in Panama makes *sense* to the North American brain." He leaned over to peer through windows as dark as night. "Hmm. Maybe they don't want you to *see* inside either."

I cupped my hand next to my eyes and tried to look in from my side. "I've never understood the dark tint thing; it looks like the person is trying too hard, in my opinion."

Joe straightened to look toward a bank of glass front offices where several staff members were visible. A few were talking on the phone, but the majority were chatting away, oblivious to us. No one had approached us, even when the door had dinged and we entered 10 minutes earlier. "I guess we'll have to go find someone."

I followed his gaze. "God forbid they break up the party to help a prospective client." Astonishment was becoming a daily feeling that was not pleasant for someone like me who strived to have all her ducks in a row, at all times. I was faced with a dozen such moments a day, when the simple and logical solution or behavior in any other country seemed to either elude Panamanians or simply not interest them.

Ten minutes later, we sat side-by-side in one of the offices.

"You're sure you don't want to drive it first?" Joe looked at me.

"I'm sure," I replied, scrolling through my Blackberry. "There's no way I'm taking out a car that nice in this ridiculous traffic unless I actually own it. Plus, an Audi is an Audi. I like yours. I'm sure the ride on this one will be fine."

"Why are you looking at that thing?" Joe asked. "You don't start work for another week! Can't you just relax?" The seriousness in his tone got my attention.

"I know, I know. I can't help it." I dropped the device into my bag. Joe let out a sigh.

"Here we are," a thin man said as he entered. "I found the book of options for this car." A wide smile spread across his face as he sat. "It's the only one we have, so I had to get it from another *companero*."

I rubbed my palms together when he set the book down, and Joe smiled. I loved options.

The sales person pushed the book in front of Joe across the narrow desk. "Señor Joe, here's the color options for this model." His finger swirled above a palette of colors spanning two pages.

"Thank you, Juan," Joe said, pushing the book toward me. "But this is actually my wife's choice, as it will be her car."

As I leaned forward to get a better look, I pressed my fingers to the book crease to open it further. "I like this one," I said, tapping a platinum silver tone. "Juan, is the actual paint color more muted or shiny?"

Juan's hand snaked out to turn the book toward him again. "Ehm," he cleared his throat as he considered the colors on the page. "This one is more shiny, Señor Joe." He pulled the book from me and slid it in front of my husband again.

Joe's brow furrowed as he pushed the book toward me. "You can address my wife, Juan. Remember the car is for her not me."

Juan nodded, though his eyes did not look my direction.

What is his deal? "All right then." I sat up straighter. "I want this color. What interior options complement this exterior color then, Juan?"

Juan kept his eyes on the book as he took it a second time and turned it back around. Flipping through a few pages and examining each page heading, it became clear that Juan had no idea what he was doing.

"Aha!" Juan's face was triumphant, as he lifted eyes toward Joe once again. "And here are the interior colors that go with the platinum." He once again pushed the book in front of Joe.

I felt the color begin to rise in my face as I watched the book's trajectory toward my husband.

Joe's hand reached the book to redirect it toward me. "Juan." The impatience was now evident in his voice. "I *told* you. This is *her* car. Stop showing things to *me*, and show them to *her*."

Juan pursed his mouth, like he'd just taken a bite of a lemon. "*Sí, Señor.*"

The hair on the back of my neck bristled. I gazed toward the sales associate, who kept his eyes on the book. "That's right, *hermano*," I said. "And, I am *also* the one who will be writing you the *check* if we decide to do business with you." I waited for my words to register before I plunged forward. "And, right now, Señor Juan, you do not have a deal yet."

The man recoiled as if he'd been slapped. "*Sí, Señora. Vale pues.*" He forced a patronizing smile as he swiveled in my direction. "*Digame.* Tell me what you like." His eyes pierced into mine.

~

"That was a little harsh, don't you think, in the man's only book?" Joe glanced at me as we weaved through a myriad of parked Audis in the dealer's narrow parking lot.

"I was trying to make a point," I snapped. I could feel Joe bristle.

"Quite clearly you did just that," Joe said. "But...," he shook his head.

"But, *what*?" I stopped to stare at my husband. The muscle along my jaw line flexed as I gritted my teeth to keep from screaming. "The guy was being an asshole. I will not be treated like I am some little *mamasita*, even if that's how they treat their women down here."

Joe wrapped his arm around my shoulder, and pointed me toward his sedan. "It's cool. I get it. It's almost like they're stuck in the 1960s and don't know any better." Joe pulled open the passenger door and walked to the driver's side. "I just don't know that being mean will help." His voice softened in a way I could take in what he was trying to say.

"I don't care what they do or do not know!" My hand fumbled in my bag for a tissue when an errant tear escaped down my face. "I will *not* be treated like that, by him or anybody else, and you, Joe, should know that better than anyone." Suddenly, the stress of what seemed like another assault from this country cascaded over and down my cheeks in an unstoppable torrent. Joe pulled me to him, taking my tissue and dabbing my eyes and then my nose.

Joe watched as the stress of our first few days in Panama played across my features. He reached both hands toward me, pulling my shaking form closer. "Hey, baby, it's okay." He held me for a moment, rocking me like a child. Then, he leaned away and tipped my chin up to look in my red eyes.

I shrugged from the contact, sucking in all the ragged emotion into my body like a vacuum, shaking my head. "I'll be fine. Just give me a minute." I reached for the visor to take a look in the mirror. *Holy shit, I look terrible.* Suffice it to say the bleary eyes in the reflection were hardly those of the executive position I'd come to this country to take.

Snickety clucked her tongue, *You'd better come up with a new strategy for dealing with what surely seems to be commonplace in Panama if you're gonna survive here, darling.*

Joe turned the key in the ignition. "Let's get out of here and get you some food. I think you need it."

I nodded as my head began to pound. I felt a familiar migraine coming on and dug in my purse for some Advil. As I peered into the depth of my purse, digging for at least one left in my pillbox, I could hear familiar words along with the pounding in my head.

Quiet! my father's voice boomed. *I'll call on you when I'm ready to hear from you.*

Another tear slipped down my cheek, but I brushed it away along with the memory.

CHAPTER 19:
Super Star

Thunderous applause broke out as I stepped out beyond the podium to the center of the stage. I blinked as what seemed like millions of flash bulbs exploding on my retina.

Pop! Blam! Click!

Voices floated through from the other side of the spotlight, like ghosts in the mist. I could see the outline of shapes, but none of them were recognizable. Even so, I followed their direction.

"Queda, por favor!"

"Espere!"

"Momentito!"

Is this what it feels like to be famous?

I stood entranced for a moment, unsure. I was the last speaker in a long morning of presentations, which had run more than two hours late. *Am I supposed to do something else? Cross the stage?* No one had given me any direction for what would happen post-speech. Waiting for what seemed like an eternity, eventually I did what was instinctual and lifted a manicured hand in an unfamiliar wave.

The applause was deafening like the force of a thunderstorm echoing off a metal roof. My ears begin to ring.

Out of the corner of my eye, I saw movement. On either side of the stage, men were filing into formation before a set of stairs that ascended the riser on which I stood.

Good God, it's like this has been choreographed, though obviously someone forgot to give me any direction. I fought to keep my face straight as six pairs of feet marched toward me in perfect time.

My fellow speakers at this annual economic forum were adorned in full suit and tie, a mix of C-level business men with a sprinkle of Panama's dignitaries of some sort or other. In a jumble of feet and blinding light, each took turns to greet me, leaning in to kiss my right cheek. The applause began to die down.

A coordinator stepped into the limelight and placed the seven men standing on the riser in order. I stood on the outside edge of the small group centered around a white-haired gentleman in his mid-50s wearing an impeccable Gucci suit with a red sash across his belly. While the splash of color indicated his governmental stature, the dynamo stood shorter than me by several inches since I was wearing my four-inch heels.

The last time I saw a sash like that was in the Miss America contest. The wry thought caused my smile to deepen. I bit my tongue in an effort not to laugh.

"*Por favor,* move in," commanded the coordinator's face from just above the riser, as the woman's hands appeared and crunched the air toward one another, indicating the seven of us should get cozy.

Our faces stayed trained toward the cameras as bodies twisted and turned and feet took micro-steps inward.

My nasal passages began to protest as a wave of body odor mixed with spicy aftershave accosted my nostrils. The hair on the back of my neck rose to meet hot breath. The heat of several bodies rose to meet my own as the flash bulbs continued to burst, and I felt faint in what was a developing sauna.

Oh, please, no, I pleaded with my body as my nose began to twitch and a drip of liquid ran down the inside.

"*Uno más!*" One final photographer held up his finger.

One more minute. I sniffed. Wriggled my nose. Sniffed again. All without losing a dazzling smile.

"*Gracias!*" the voice rang out. The spotlights shut off as the audience jumped to its feet and bodies streamed toward the front of the room. The speakers scattered like thrown dice across the stage.

As if on cue, the man in the red sash extended his hand toward me as my sneeze exploded. My hand covered my mouth and nose as I turned my head backwards so that my trajectory would not spray him on his approach.

"*Pardon, Señor Presidente,*" I said as I ducked my chin in embarrassment and turned toward him.

"*No se preocupe.* Don't worry," he said. "It happens to me all the time."

His hand extended a monogrammed cotton handkerchief.

I smiled, taking it. "*Muchas gracias.*"

"*A la orden, señora.*" He bowed at the waist, eyes holding mine before sweeping his gaze down and across the stretch of my bust line.

The familiar flush rose to my cheeks as the prism of another flash exploded to our left. *Oh, shit, please don't have caught that on camera!* I was relieved for the moment to be interrupted by a cacophony of frantic voices, quickly approaching us.

"*Señor Presidente! Señor Presidente!*"

Then, we were pulled in separate directions as the crowd descended. It was half an hour later before I realized his handkerchief was still crumpled in my hand.

~

I squinted at the waves of heat rising up from the tarmac as sweat dripped down my neck and back. I resisted the urge to put a hand up to catch my hair as it whipped around my face.

I stood flanked by three other women along the blue carpet outside a tiny building adjacent to a private airport. Beyond us, the scene looked like a movie set: The airstrip lay in the valley of a jungled mountain range. On the hills around us, palm trees waved in the wind. On the blacktop between my colleagues and me, 35 private jets were stacked into three tidy lines.

I raised my eyes to the figures approaching from the most recently landed aircraft a hundred steps away. A middle-aged Latin man stepped ahead of an entourage of three women, four men, and five children toward our crew. Uniformed porters were pulling piece after piece of Gucci luggage from the jet's hold and setting them upon rusted carts.

Interesting, I thought as the family approached. Children in North America would be chomping at the bit to run ahead of the others, skipping, running, brimming over with glee or nervous energy. The children before me were the epitomy of my parents' ideals for how the young should be in public: seen, not heard, reserved. I watched as the five little ones filed into place behind their parents without making a sound. *Incredible.*

As the well-heeled crowd stepped toward us, I snapped my attention to meet the eyes of the man in front.

"*Bienvenidos a Panamá.*" My accompaniments called out in harmony as the family passed by them toward the glass doors.

"*Buenos dias, señores,*" I said, smiling. "*Bienvenido a Panorama.*"

"*Buenos dias.*"

"*Gracias.*"

"*Buen día.*"

Dark eyes met mine, taking in my light skin and hair with curiosity, scanning the gentle curves of my toned body, appraising the printed silk of my skirt and blouse.

Is it obvious these aren't designer? While my wardrobe was the envy of many back home, I didn't always shell out the big bucks. I had a knack for pairing lesser brands with the famous ones for a knockout look. But to these people…the crème de la crème of Latin American society, members of some of the wealthiest families on the continent arriving in this country for an exclusive economic summit… *I doubt they miss a beat. I imagine when you grow up in a private jet type of family, you can spot the top brand names in a millisecond.*

The family entered the building and our small crew relaxed before heading for the shade of a tree a few feet away.

So, if that's 35, I scanned the line up on the jetway, *then, we only have a handful left to go.*

Juan Carlos had informed me that our day-long welcoming committee to the former military base airport would entail welcoming up to 50 of these well-heeled guests. This seemed curious, given that we were months from beginning construction on the redevelopment; however, I was fast getting up to speed on the proclivity that Panama's elite had toward the ultimate in privacy. *Nothing gets more private and far from curious stares than landing in an abandoned air base,* I thought.

I turned to one of my counterparts. "*Que hora es?*" I tapped my wrist with my index finger as I said it to reiterate the international sign for time.

The woman, whose name was Maria Carmen, swept long dark hair back from where it was stuck to her forehead, fanning herself with a manicured hand. She turned a bejeweled wrist to reveal a diamond-encrusted Rolex.

"*Son la una y media de la tarde.* It's 1:30 p.m." The woman motioned to the other two Latin women before turning back to me. "*Quieren almorzar?* Do you want to eat lunch?"

The three of us nodded in unison and fell into file behind her back to the building. I had discerned hours before that this woman was the *jefa*, the highest-ranking staff member of the government's staff present. Everyone made a point of greeting her, kissing her, and informing her in advance of each jet's arrival.

Maria Carmen carried herself with an assured elegance, dressed in impeccable silk and patent sling-backs and dripping in diamonds and pearls. Her carriage testified to the fact that she had been born into Panama's *yeye* elite, a member of one of the lucky sperm club who had ruled the Isthmus for decades.

A blast of cool air hit us when the doors opened. *Whew.* I met the eyes of the guard on my left, a 30-something hottie with muscles bulging from beneath his shirt. A stern face appraised me. I smiled in return, "*Gracias.*"

His face broke into a smile, green eyes startling in contrast against brown skin. *Wow.* I couldn't help myself. *What a gorgeous color combination.* My eyes scanned the family who had entered a moment before where they were perched on overstuffed furniture in the adjoining room as the immigration official reviewed their documents in another.

This is definitely the way to do international travel, I thought as a uniformed official carried one woman's passport back to where she sat, munching on a finger sandwich. *Must be nice.*

Maria Carmen's four-inch heels clicked down a narrow hallway past a number of closed doors. Pausing at the last wooden door on the right, she knocked and then reached for the door handle.

"*Permiso,*" she said, breezing through. "Pardon me." I got a whiff of spicy Givenchy perfume as I followed her inside. Maria Carmen closed the door behind me and as she did, the cacophony of voices echoing off the block walls stopped.

Deep voices rang out from four men huddled around a narrow table. "*Buenas tardes,*" they said. Two women were stepping over a low bench to join them. An older woman in a polyester dress stood at a kitchen counter along one wall, removing plastic bags from Styrofoam containers of steaming food. My stomach growled as the smell of roasted chicken, fried plantains, and rice wafted to my nostrils.

Maria Carmen washed her hands in the antiquated sink. As she dried her hands on a towel, she muttered something to the woman preparing the food before motioning for me to join her at the table. Soles squeaked and plates squealed as everyone scooted down to make room for the two of us.

The older woman set the last of the food containers in front of Maria Carmen.

"*Momentito,*" I said as I walked around the table to where my handbag lay on the floor. I searched in it for a moment for the package of nuts I remembered buying the day before, but came up empty. *Drat.* No nuts meant I had no food.

I'd assumed—this being my very first day representing my new company and not knowing any better—that since the event was at an airport that at the very least there would be a vending machine or two. But of course, there wasn't. *Since this airstrip only accepts visitors, like today's VIPs, it makes sense there's not enough foot traffic to support a restaurant, I suppose.*

With my North American brain, I'd also assumed there might be a restaurant nearby, or even a small market. But quick surveillance of the deserted streets when Joe had dropped me off that morning had revealed otherwise.

Of course, Juan Carlos didn't tell me any details about today, other than saying I needed to show up, and that the PR company would have everything ready.

The gal from the PR company had informed me the jets would start arriving around 8 a.m., so I had shown up at 7:30, assuming I might need to help put the final touches on the lounge that was being prepared for the incoming VIPs with our fledging marketing materials about the new development.

But when Joe and I pulled up that morning, only one vehicle sat in the parking lot: an airport security truck.

"Did I misunderstand the date?" I clicked back through my Blackberry to check as Joe drove into the empty lot. "No, it's today. And the hour is correct too."

A man in a long-sleeved *guayabera* peered out the door of the tiny building as we pulled up. His face crinkled as he scanned our car.

"Why don't you double check with the guards to be sure before I leave you?" Joe suggested, glancing around at the ghost-like buildings standing sentry above vacant streets. *This place is a little eerie.*

Once I had shown my passport and the guard had checked it against his clipboard, his demeanor had changed from suspicion to reserved friendliness. "*Pase,*" he said with a shy grin, opening the glass door wide and ushering me into the lobby.

"*Donde está la habitacion para los VIPs?*" I struggled to remember to open my mouth wide so that the guard could understand my stilted Spanish. I'd already been told that I wasn't enunciating enough and to watch my pronounciation.

"*Aqui está.*" The guard pointed to the room we were standing in.

I scanned the fingerprinted windows as I took a few steps toward dusty black leather furniture. *Is this pleather?* Sweeping my finger across the top of a chair, I cringed as dust bunnies flew and cloud particles swirled in the air. A sneeze formed in my nose.

This is the VIP lounge? And, though it wasn't my party, nor my responsibility, I felt a wave of anxiety wash over me. *I wouldn't bring any VIPS here, much less the wealthiest families in Latin America!*

I turned to find the guard watching me. I rearranged my grimace into a smile. "*Y cuando viene la empresa de relaciones publicas?* When does the PR company arrive?"

The man consulted his clipboard. "*A las ocho de la mañana.*"

My shoulders relaxed. *Well, at least they will be here shortly,* I thought. *Surely, they are bringing some other type of setup for this place.* I glanced around at the two aging couches and one chair sitting in the middle of the room. Other than a side table and a mirrored coffee table, the room was devoid of any other furnishings. The walls were bare. I sank into the chair.

An hour later, I was still waiting. *How the hell are we going to get everything set up when the first plane is scheduled to be anytime?*

The Customs and immigration staff offices had arrived. No one had asked me about the PR company, nor seemed to be concerned that it was now past 9 o'clock and they hadn't shown up.

At 9:05 a.m., the caterers made an appearance. Since no one else was there to direct them, I decided to take the bull by the horns. "Put the food here, to one side," I instructed the two sleepy-looking delivery men. "And over here, the coffee and drinks."

As they finished, the clock read 9:30. Still no word from the PR company and the room was still a complete disaster. I approached the guards. "Do you have…?" I didn't know how to say rags or dusting solution, so I acted it out as if I were doing it.

"*Sí, sí, sí,*" said one as he disappeared into a back room, returning with a stained rag that looked like it had once been used to clean an airplane engine. No spray. I took the rag. *Better than nothing.*

"*Y una…?*" Again, I acted out the scene for sweeping the floor.

One of the guards struggled to keep a straight face, at my antics. "*Sí, pero el deposito está cerrado.*"

I shook my head. "*No entiendo.* I don't understand." I followed the guard to a closet that was locked, indicating he didn't have the keys.

Oh, good grief, I thought as I watched him jiggle the locked knob. *So, they have a broom, but it's locked, and there's no key? So much for preparation!*

Taking the rag, I wiped down the furniture. My hands turned gray by the time I finished the two couches, requiring me to wash them and the rag in between each piece of furniture. By the time I finished, my face was flushed and my brow glistened with sweat. As I stood up to take stock, my face flushed with color when I noticed a small crowd standing in the hall, watching me. I exhaled, wiping my hands on the rag and smiling at them. *What are they all staring at?*

At my acknowledgement, the crowd began to disassemble, clamoring over each other to get back to their respective posts as if they were embarrassed. I watched them for a moment before returning to take another look at the rearranged furniture and the clean windows. *Well, I guess this is as good as it gets for today.*

I was just returning from the bathroom with reapplied powder and lipstick when the first jet landed and the PR company arrived.

I surrendered to the hugs and kisses that are customary for greetings in Latin America, attempting to hide my irritation at the PR staff members. "Good to see you, too," I said, "but I thought you guys were arriving at eight, according to the guard's schedule."

The PR woman's eyes held mine for a moment, blank. "No," she said. "We told Juan Carlos we'd arrive around 8:45."

"I see." I twisted my wrist in the air to look at my watch. It was ten o'clock. I returned the woman's gaze, waiting for an explanation, or an apology. But none came.

~

Now I sat next to Maria Carmen at the lunch table, empty-handed.

Maria Carmen lifted a perfect eyebrow. "You don't have any food?" She looked critical.

My face flushed as I shook my head. "No, I didn't know there wouldn't be a restaurant or anything." My stomach growled as if on cue.

A condescending smile crept across her face.

Maria Carmen shook her head at me. "*Señora!*" she called out, motioning to the woman in the uniform to come close. "What other food do you have over there?"

"*A ver*, let me go take a look," the maid said. She returned a moment later. "*No hay nada, Señora Maria Carmen, lo siento.* There's nothing else, I'm sorry."

Maria Carmen snapped her fingers at the fellow tablemates. "*Oye, amigos. Esa gringa* did not know we didn't have a restaurant on-site, nor did she bring a lunch."

"No, no, no, it's not necessary," I protested. I grasped at Maria's arm. "I'll be fine."

Maria Carmen shook off my hand, shaking her head as 10 pairs of dark eyes appraised the empty space in front of me at the table.

"Can we please help her out and share some of our food so that she doesn't starve on her very first day with us?" Maria Carmen turned back to the maid and asked for an extra plate, cutlery, and a napkin. "*Por favor, Señora.*"

Two or three heads nodded, motioning for the plate to be passed their direction. The rest returned to their conversations.

I felt the emotion rise in my chest as a full plate of steaming chicken, rice, and plantains came back to rest in front of me a moment later. The maid set an iced tea alongside it. "Pardon me one moment, I need to wash my hands," I said, rising to hurry to the bathroom to catch the tears before the rest of my *compadres* saw them.

In the dim light of the bathroom, I wiped my eyes. *What is wrong with me? It's just a little lunch, for God's sake.*

As I stood there, I realized how grateful I was for my new work colleague's insistence. The waves of heat and hunger and overwhelm from all the cultural changes had made me dizzy a few minutes earlier. While I felt like I needed to go lie down, I acted like everything was fine.

Maria Carmen had seen right through it, and she had saved me. I knew in that moment that she and I were going to be friends.

My first friend in Panama, I thought as gratitude swept through me like sunshine, and I returned.

Maria Carmen's dark eyes raised to meet me with a smile. "*Bienvenida,*" she said.

And while I'd heard the word "welcome" many times before, this was the first time I felt anyone had actually meant it.

CHAPTER 20:
The Awakening

The smell of booze hit my nose long before I felt the hand clamp down on my left breast.

"Baby," he slurred.

The cold hand of fear gripped me as a chill ran down my spine. I pushed the hand away.

"Stop it," I mumbled. "I'm trying to sleep."

"But, I miss you." The teasing tone was one Joe used when we'd made love early on in our relationship, one I had once thought was cute.

"It's the middle of the night," I pleaded, squeezing my eyelids back together to block out the light streaming from his bedside lamp.

"But, baby…" The touch that was usually velvet now belonged to Paddington Bear, pawing down the side of my rib cage toward my groin.

"Shit, Joe!" Adrenaline poured into me as I shot up to a sitting position, fists clenched. "It's the middle of the night!" My fingers sought for my glasses on the bedside table. "It's 1:30 for fuck's sake, and I have to be up in four hours!"

"Sorry! Sorry!" The slur rose to counter my attack. "Didn't mean to offend you!" His hand waved. "Never mind, never mind!" He sank back into his pillow, reaching for the half-full tumbler of amber-colored liquor.

My pulse pounded in my ears as I glared toward his bent form. Glassy eyes avoided mine, as he pulled a Kindle from the drawer and placed the screen between the two of us.

"God, damn it," I muttered, as I turned my back and curled into the fetal position.

Joe's voice began to hum a faint tune.

"Stop it." If my voice had a temperature, we wouldn't have required air conditioning for the rest of the night.

"Stop what?" It was Joe's turn to protest. The e-reader slammed down atop the covers beside me. "What is your problem?"

"You were *singing*!" My fingers excavated a hole in the covers so the accusation could spew from my mouth.

"I was not!" Joe huffed. "Why are you being so sensitive?" The mattress heaved as he pushed himself up. "Why don't you just leave me alone?"

"Leave *you* alone?" I jerked the covers back to see his backside disappearing down the hall. "You're the one who woke me up!"

"Oh, shut up!" As the door slammed, it shook the room.

"Shit," I muttered before I stretched across to click off his lamp. Crawling back, I burrowed into a ball, pulling the covers back over my head. The rhythm of my heart continued to rattle my rib cage.

You have a choice, I told myself, feeling my chest balloon with a long inhale. *Now, count to 10 and breathe.* As the breath left my body, the tension began to dissipate. But my ears stayed on alert as cabinets began to slam open and shut in the kitchen.

Keep counting.

At eight, silent sobs began to slide out of me, one after the other after the other.

Let it out.

Somewhere after 35, I lost count.

~

When the alarm went off four hours later, I awoke with a Kleenex crumbled in my hand. Then I moved through all the rituals of the morning, preparing to leave for work, and as I got my coat I saw Joe passed out cold on the couch. Fury began pulsing through my body.

"*Buenos dias, Tomas,*" I said as I entered the car, knowing full well the tone in my voice echoed one my mother had used with me as a child when I was in big trouble. As evidence that body language trumps language barriers, Tomas stiffened beside me, the involuntary reflex of the student caught with candy in class, though he hadn't done anything. He cleared his throat, "*Buen dia, Señora.*"

Tomas maneuvered the car from the stillness of the parking garage into the cacophony that was early morning Panama: birds trumpeting, horns honking, dogs barking, maids chatting at the building entrance waiting for starting time. I bit my tongue in an effort to hold back my anger and counted to 10 in silence.

At seven, I opened my mouth again, attempting to mask the full-on fury that had overtaken me. But again, I caught myself. *It's not his fault*, I reminded myself. *Don't redirect your angst on him. That's not fair.*

I knew what it was to have anger descending on me that had nothing to do with me. I dealt with it every day at work. So, this morning, instead of speaking, I remained silent until the moment the car pulled up to the office.

CHAPTER 21:
The Board Meeting

"Ow." I had bitten down on my pen so hard that the inside of my cheek caught between my teeth. My tongue explored the injury. The sour taste of blood woke me from my trance where I had been staring out the window.

Through splotchy panes, my directionless gaze took in the sky, which was a listless color of pale. Vestiges of the morning's torrential rain rose in wave upon wave of steam outside, causing the rows upon rows of square military barracks to appear like a mirage.

But I could only wish this was a dream. *At least in my dreams, I always seem to come out on top,* I thought with a tinge of anger.

I turned back toward my desk in the small rectangular office. *Six months ago, today*, I thought, *and it already seems like six years.*

I rewound my memory back to November, nine months earlier, when Joe and I had visited Panama for the first time. Back then, it all felt like a dream come true to get this exotic job and all I had cared about was getting here. What I had envisioned in that dream come true was nothing like my reality now. It was as if the air had been let out of my bubble.

The three days of our interview trip had flown by in a flurry of information, activity, meetings, and viewings. I recalled standing outside the hotel as the final afternoon turned to early evening, waiting to be picked up by Joe, who had been out with the driver.

My face had welcomed the cloudless sky, my eyes closed, as I'd taken in the sounds and smells of the city. I could still hear the *beep beep beep* of car horns amidst the back-up alarms of delivery trucks and the sounds of construction. Motorcycles whizzed by, hustling and jiving through the frenzied traffic. Smells of urban life curled my nose in disgust and delight: rancid garbage decaying in the afternoon heat interspersed with notes of floral sweetness. That had been my first taste of Panama.

Chaos, I had thought, when my eyes had opened and I stared up at the patchwork quilt of Panama's haphazard architecture. Colorful laundry hung on drooping lines in front of unpainted hovels adjacent to glistening new skyscrapers, still under construction. *This place is utter, delicious chaos.*

I had never been a conformist. I adored adventure too much. Joe and I enjoyed vacationing in places so off the beaten path they were often hard to pinpoint on a map.

But, can I do it?

Snickety had piped up. *Amongst all this filth and craziness? You haven't seen the half of it yet. You'll never make it here. It's too much for you.*

"But it could be fun," I said aloud, interrupting her scolding voice. "Plus, I'll do it if it I *want* to," I mused. "Correction: If *Joe* and I want to," I added. The conversation continued in my head: *You know once I set my mind to something, I go after it with everything I've got. The question is, do I really want this?*

The knock on my office door jolted me back to the present.

"JuliAnne, are you there?" The British accent belied the visitor's identity.

"I'm here," I said as I walked over and gave the door a swift yank. The door had a habit of sticking, which was unsurprising given that my company had rehabbed the Army Police's former office space. The building, which had to be full of asbestos given its age, had been closed up for almost a decade prior to our arrival.

The man stood there before me, pushing up his glasses, as if he were nervous. "They're ready for you," he said in an apologetic tone, his eyes scanning my face.

"All right then, Seth," I said, turning for my notebook and pen. Tucking them under my arm, I closed my eyes for a moment and inhaled deeply, squaring my shoulders like a soldier being sent off to the front line.

Like a lamb to the slaughter. The thought scrolled across my mind as I turned to accompany Seth to the boardroom. I could almost see the word "slaughter" scrawled in red blood dripping down the hallway walls as we passed.

I reached the door handle first before tossing a glance back at Seth that may have screamed, "Help me! Please help!" He returned a silent thumbs up. Then, I pasted a pleasant look on my face and opened the door, bracing myself for what was to come.

~

Two hours later, I exploded from my office in such haste that my handbag ricocheted off the door facings as I headed for the entrance. My heels clattered down the stairs as I descended and the day's humidity enveloped me as the front door gave way.

I stumbled in an attempt to run, scrambling to keep my balance, not used to rapid movements in dress shoes, but my feet carried me forward, successful in delivering me around the side of the building and behind the parking garage before the dam of emotions I was carrying burst forth.

Tears began to course down my cheeks as I made it past the single-story parking structure, where I knew they couldn't hear me through triple-thick concrete block walls.

When I got there, I let it out. "Mother fucker!" I screamed as I doubled over, my knees buckling to the ground as the waves of emotion released in torrents. I pummeled fists into the warm earth. "Stupid fucking idiots! Holy shit! Fucking morons!"

The muscles of my shoulders clenched, bringing on a full tension headache, as my tears streamed into rivers, pouring down my face and into the dirt. Puddles formed as my body shook under the weight of the emotions I had held in for months.

The force of my crying swept through me with such intensity that my vision began to go black. I reached out a hand to steady myself against the side of the building. As my fingers touched wood, my cognition began to return.

This is no time to black out, I told myself. *Have your moment, and then we need to pull it together until the end of the day.* My breath came in short staccato rasps. *Breathe deep. Slow it down. You have to get it together.*

I began to count my inhales and exhales. "Calm," I whispered. "Calm down."

As the explosion abated, I became conscious again of my surroundings. I glanced around quickly. *Though I could care less if anyone sees me,* I thought. *I never lose my cool. And surely what I just went through warrants a fucking meltdown!* Even so, I breathed a sigh of relief that no one was in sight. I reached a leaden hand into my purse for a tissue and my compact.

My nose honked as I blew it and surveyed the damage in the tiny mirror. I wiped the residual moisture from my face. *I'd better take a walk and get something to drink,* I thought, grateful that my presentation had been the final one before the lunch break.

I took a few steps down the alley in the direction of Dell, whose largest call center in the world was located down the street behind our offices. Their canteen with snacks and sodas was open to the public. I had never felt as grateful for the tiny store as I did right now. Other than a gas station half a mile away, this was the only on-site option for sustenance on the project. After the scenario that had played itself out in the boardroom, I had very little appetite for sharing lunch there with any of my colleagues. The canteen now seemed like a blessing sent directly from God.

The crunch of gravel behind me made me turn. Seth waved at me to wait up.

Fuck.

"Hey." He was a little out of breath as he came up alongside me. "How are you holding up?" Seth seemed sincere enough, but I was not interested in talking to anyone.

"How am I doing?" My voice was incredulous, though his question had been kind. I felt the surge of rage again behind my eyes. Thank God I had my sunglasses on. "How am I *supposed* to be doing…," my voice cracked, "…after navigating something like that? How the hell do you *think* I am?"

Seth looked taken aback. He looked at me sideways. "Don't take it personally, JuliAnne," he said. "It does get easier."

I swallowed the biting remarks about the board members who had sat in that room and looked at him in disbelief. "This happened to you?" Maybe in fact I was not some personal punching bag for my colleagues. It would be a relief to think that this might just be the norm…for everyone.

I had witnessed, in my very first meeting with the company, that Seth was Ethan's guy: Ethan was always looking to him for the answer on something—for confirmation on financials, for the history on a vendor conversation, for the backup of the presentation. Whenever Seth spoke, his words carried significant weight with the ownership. Ethan and Julio always seemed to agree with him.

Seth nodded, though he kept his eyes straight ahead. "Yep. The first two years were pretty tough," he replied, "but it does get easier."

My memory scrolled back to a few minutes before.

When Ethan had begun pounding his fist on the table, I had jumped out of my chair. He had yelled at me—in a *raised* voice.

"This is shit!" he'd screamed. "Rubbish!" Later, "This looks like you don't know what you're doing!" The words had ricocheted off the boardroom walls. When he'd shoved the packet of papers I'd set in front of him a few minutes earlier sideways in his anger, they'd taken flight before fluttering one by one to the floor. No one else in the room had moved a muscle.

I was certain I would never become accustomed to this type of treatment. *Nor should anyone, for that matter,* I thought. *Nor do I want it to get any easier. Being treated like this in a professional environment—in any environment—is unacceptable.*

I said as much to Seth as we bought sodas and began the short walk back to the office. It was apparent neither of us felt much like eating.

"That's true," he said. "And, I agree. No one deserves that. But it's his money, and sometimes this is just the way he gets. He feels entitled."

It was true that Ethan was a majority partner in the project. So, there was no doubt that the "it's his money" argument rang true. But I didn't buy that this behavior was acceptable, no matter how much money anyone had; money did not buy anyone the right to abuse people.

I pondered Seth's response further. It was true that without Ethan and Julio, I wouldn't be in this job, much less this company, much less this country. The butterflies in my stomach re-engaged their familiar flight pattern as I pondered that.

I still don't think it's right. Snickety was indignant. *What gives someone the right to act like that—demeaning another—over something they didn't want to hear, or because they don't like something?* She wagged her finger in disapproval.

Agree to disagree, was one of my many mottos. *But, you always must find a way to work it out and move forward. That's real life. There's no reason for ugliness.*

My mind rewound again to the last day of my Panama interview. I was standing on the overlook high above the project with Juan Carlos. The tropical breeze blew through my hair as I gazed down at the landscape of the former military base. Palm trees lined either side of the abandoned main street, waving in the wind. Hundreds of small white blocks of concrete peeked from behind jungled hillsides. An airstrip faded into the distance on my left. Hawks and buzzards circled above the two of us.

The city of Panama was visible in the distance, and the Pacific Ocean lay sparkling at my back.

The opportunity to make my mark—from the very beginning of a project of this size—beckoned to me from the future. What adventure! What fun! What a challenge! I felt the sun on my face, and I knew right then and there: I was—we were—going to Panama. They would choose me for this job. This was what I had been waiting for.

Within the month, I had signed the two-year contract.

Two years had seemed like it would be a flash in the pan. Joe and I would come to Panama, have some fun, do a bunch of traveling, then return to the U.S. with lots of stories to tell.

Now, from where I stood, two years stretched before me like a life sentence. *I still have 18 months to go.* The realization sank like a stone in my stomach.

That heaviness activated the vice I had been fighting in my head all day. Now, the pressure tightened a notch as Ethan's voice raised itself once again in my mind.

It was the statement he'd closed with that had really stung. "Maybe we need to make a change." When his accusing gaze swung in my direction as the words left his mouth, I knew without a doubt exactly what he meant.

The change he was talking about was *me.*

~

I hid in my office until Ethan and Julio had departed the building. I hardly wanted to show my face, even in the hallway, with the shame that now covered my body like a blanket. I knew in my heart that I had absolutely nothing to be ashamed about and that the only shameful behavior was on the part of Ethan. But it was as if over the months, I had developed a kind of PTSD and my recoil from outrageous behavior on the part of either Ethan or Curt felt like a fresh assault.

I had *never* hidden from anyone in a professional setting, but as fear coursed through my body, my mind invented scenarios that had me returning in humiliation to the States after being fired on a whim. I was not going to let this take ahold of me. I tried to shake off the uncharacteristic paralysis when Snickety chimed in, right on cue.

How many rounds do you have left, Missy? You're letting these assholes overpower you and you have put your baby girl in the driver's seat, so what do you expect? Of course, you want to hide in your room, like you did as a kid. Kick their ass or just quit, for Christ's sake! You have all the power you need, but you keep forgetting that!

Snickety's positive spin caught me off guard. But, she had always pushed my face right into the matter at hand without hesitation, and this time she slapped me upside the head and I got it right away.

Is it possible that I allowed myself to be be treated like this? Have I really lost the means of protecting myself? Attack after attack from inside my own ranks left me feeling helpless and afraid. But was I? Is it—all of it—truly about them when they do this shit? Or is it really about me?

Fuck it! Snickety waved a hand as if my confusion could be so easily dispersed. *You have to get back to your own strength and either learn to stand up or leave.*

I bowed my head as exhaustion took over me. *But how?*

The rest of the day, I bounced back and forth between feelings of embarrassment and reason. *It's not my fault that four guys here don't get how marketing works in the rest of the world,* my ego screamed. *That hardly makes* me *the failure!* I worked overtime to remember the truth of the situation but got bogged down in familiar scenarios of fiasco.

The others in the room that held any clout—Julio, Juan Carlos, and Curt—had looked on, mute, while Ethan had held court with his bellowing. I would have expected someone to say something in response to what Ethan had to say. *I mean, Juan Carlos and Curt both saw and approved my work before I ever presented!*

Finally, my adult self kicked in with some needed outrage. Bile rose in my throat at the betrayal I felt from the lack of support I had received from anyone in the room today and on more occasions that I could count. I had once lived and worked in an environment where having your colleague's back was the status quo, hadn't I? I mean, maybe it hadn't been perfect, but when my boss had approved something in the past, I would expect them to stand up for me when it came under fire, or at the very minimum help defend it before it got shot down. Could it be that different here in Panama?

The truth was I had never really failed at this job or any job. I had always been the star, the student passing all the others with my ideas and my excellent grades, the executive who was always recognized for her integrity. So, why now? Why was I doubting myself for one second?

I had never failed like this. I never knew failure at any level, really, because I *always* did my homework and I *always* sought out solutions and I *always* delivered those solutions. I got out of my chair and paced the room sorting out the reality of my situation. The walls of my tiny office stood like prison walls I was trying to break out of, when all the while it was my own jail I was trying to escape: a penitentiary of belief.

Indignation rose in my chest. This was how I did business: I was a consummate professional; I never yelled, I never screamed, and I sure as hell never put people down. Nor, would that type of behavior be tolerated in the workplace in the U.S.

Had Ethan never heard of the hostile work environment?

My heart fell as I returned to reality of Panama, and Latin America. *You're not in Kansas anymore, Dorothy. And where the fuck are your ruby slippers?*

I could see why Latin America was stuck several generations back when it came to doing business. I was trying to give this experience the benefit of the doubt by adding my own brand of professionalism, my experience, my capability, my common *sense* to the entire equation. But none of that had helped me one fricking ounce in the scenario that had played itself out in the boardroom this morning. I was running out of strategies.

My mind kept looking at it from every angle—analyzing it, replaying every facet, listening to the tone that accompanied every word, over and over and over in my mind. My brain tried to make sense of it, to find fault, better yet to find a solution. Something. But my washing machine of a mind kept spinning.

It was a longstanding habit in this type of lengthy analysis that I always queried myself first. *Was I prepared? Did I do my research? Did I use industry best practices? Did I fulfill the task? Did I deliver what the leadership required?* Only after I'd exhausted this avenue would I turn to consider anyone else.

My office phone buzzed. I stretched my neck toward it to see the caller ID, then shrunk back in my chair at the name.

Fuck. There's no escaping. He knows I'm here. Staying holed up in my office with my door closed was not exactly my *modus operandus.* Mr. Attention-to-Detail had no doubt noticed.

I picked up, wary. "Hi, Curt. How are you?" I braced myself.

"Got a minute?" Curt ignored my question, his voice terse. My heart sped up.

"Sure, what's up?" The hair on the back of my neck stood to attention.

He interrupted. "Can you come down to my office?" Again, his tone dripped icicles.

Great, I thought as I hung up and gathered my things. Walking down the hall, my heart began to pound so intensely that I could feel its reverberations through the fabric of my shirt.

A moment later, I stood outside Curt's office, waiting like a school child at the principal's office.

"I need a sec," he'd said when I'd knocked and entered, holding up his palm toward me.

"Sure." I backed out and closed the door.

Five minutes passed. Sweat dripped down the middle of my spine.

Finally, a shout. "Yep!"

"Hey," I started before Curt interrupted.

"So, do you want to tell me what happened in there?" His words cut me off. "You were such a disappointment." These were words I had never heard anyone say to me before.

"Well...," I began again.

"Because what I saw was that, once again, you did not deliver what I asked for...and now you've got the entire ownership questioning not just you, but the entire management team about the direction we're headed." Curt's face writhed like a bull whose cinch has just been tightened.

"I don't think..."

"I'm not asking what you think!" His palm shot out at me again.

"Stop! So, what you need to do *right now, this week*...is find a way to deliver what we've all been asking for," the snarl snaked across his features, as his eyes pierced me. "And, if you don't, JuliAnne..." The pen in his hand began a rapid staccato against the side of his computer screen. "If you don't," here, my nemesis began to shake his head, "you're not going to be employed here much longer."

My face froze as I stared back at him. "You're threatening to fire me, after I presented work that both *you* and Juan Carlos had already approved?"

Curt threw down his pen before swiveling his chair back to face his laptop. "This is me doing you a favor," he sneered. "I'm telling you what was discussed after you left the room. It's up to you whether or not you want to do anything about it."

I stood up. "I've taken the feedback that was delivered today and I'll be incorporating it, as I said I would in the meeting, Curt."

Curt ignored me and started tapping away on his computer.

"Oh, and by the way, thanks for your support during the meeting," I shot back as I turned toward the door.

Curt cowered in his chair, pecking at his keyboard.

"Next time—if there is a next time—I'd appreciate *that* kind of favor instead of the one you gave me today. Because that's what decent bosses do, Curt. They support their people." I slammed the door as I departed.

My Blackberry buzzed. Juan Carlos. The text read. *If you're still here, please stop by before you leave.*

Fuck me. The blood in my temples pounded in my head like a freight train. *Did these guys have a meeting to coordinate their JuliAnne attacks today?*

"All right then, God damn it," I said to the empty hallway as I took to the stairs.

As I rounded the corner, Snickety held out a hand with a pink pair of boxing gloves. *I think you're going to need these*, she said.

"Indeed," I snarled, and headed for Juan Carlos' office.

~

When I exited the building an hour later, the sun had set and night had fallen. Though the streets of the area were lined with streetlights, most of them had been turned off years before when the base had been decommissioned.

Grateful for the blackness that enveloped me, I felt my way down the stairs toward the sidewalk, breathing in the cooler air that came with the night.

The headlamps of a car ignited across the parking light, flashing twice. My tired eyes glanced up, grateful that Tomas had seen me. *Good man,* I thought. *At least there's one guy who's looking out for me.*

As the Audi pulled up to the curb, Tomas reached back and pushed the backdoor open. Over the months on the commute to and from my office, I had found the backseat to be a welcome haven for me from the rest of the world's chaos. Though our high-rise apartment was a mere distance of 14 kilometers, the drives could last up to two hours due to Panama's perpetual snarl of traffic. Tonight, I prayed there would be traffic, so that I could shut out the day, the fear, and the self-analysis. I sank into the backseat with a heavy sigh.

"Hi, Miss JuliAnne. How are you?" Tomas' courteous and soft smile greeted me with the customary shine in his eyes via the rearview mirror, a blessing after being raked over the coals. The accent on *you* in the question felt sorely needed.

"*Mal*, Tomas," I said. "Very, very, very bad." I kept my eyes toward the floorboard.

"Oh," replied Tomas in a worried voice before he went silent.

I normally attempted to gloss over my irritation and my frustration from the office when I began the sojourn home. I had observed Tomas exchanging pleasantries with the other drivers in the parking lot over the months. I wasn't stupid; I knew that gossip was a local pastime, and that the *extranjero* executives were the most popular topic, so I kept most of my life to myself.

But tonight, I was too tired to care. My body felt like I had been run over by a Mack truck. After the follow-up meetings with Curt and Juan Carlos, my ego had been trampled to the floor, and my emotions had been wrung out like a sponge.

Tomas kept a nervous eye on me in the rearview mirror as he navigated through the twilight-lit streets. The business crowd had made it home by this hour, and the commute was condensed to an easy half-hour. I realized I had not even called Joe to say I would be this late. I didn't want him to ask me why. I didn't want one more negative about our time in Panama to become dinner conversation, especially since by now Joe had probably had a lot to drink and I simply had no more bandwidth for one more male acting out.

Even in my despair, I could sense Tomas' severe discomfort with my state. I could feel his eyes on me, doing a frenetic dance between the roadway and my bent form.

Panamanians were known to avoid uncomfortable situations like the plague. Normally, at the slightest hint of a conflict or the need to discuss bad news, the locals would vanish without a trace. I had never seen the likes of it, the manner in which an entire room could empty in a flash, when a cross word was spoken or an inquiry was voiced over who was responsible for something that had gone wrong.

When the car was safely in our parking spot at home, I noticed Tomas twitching with anxiety as he stood waiting for me to take the car key from his hand.

"What time tomorrow?" he asked, eyes jerking every which way in an effort to avoid the pain on my face.

"Seven, Tomas," I replied. The defeat in my voice was palpable.

"*Listo, Señora, buenas noches,*" he said as he stumbled backwards in an effort to escape any further contact with me, as if the depth of my emotion would infect him.

My heels echoed as I exited the garage and made contact with the marble floors of the lobby. Even their noise that had always felt like confidence marching down the hall felt grating. I took off my shoes and walked barefoot the rest of the way. Two security guards roused from a lively conversation to raise a hand to me as I crossed an expansive seating area with an enormous orange Persian rug toward the bank of glass elevators. Their "*Buenas noches, Señora*" were swallowed up as the elevator doors closed behind me.

I located my key and stood like stone at the front door, once again bracing myself for anything. I turned the ornate lock of the apartment's security door and heard the comforting pitter patter of Lily's nails on the tile, approaching from the other side.

"Who's that? Is that your mom?" Joe's playful voice said to the dog from the other side of the couch. He popped his head up from the movie he was watching, but the, "Hi, baby, welcome home!" faded from his lips when he saw me enter like a fighter who lost the match, shoes in hand.

Lily's exuberance turned to alarm as she turned tail and ran back to her dog bed.

"Honey," Joe exclaimed, coming my way. "What happened?" He rushed toward me with a tumbler of Scotch in his hand.

The notebook I had been carrying dropped to the floor with a clatter. My purse dropped off my shoulder and plopped down beside it.

"Okay," he said as he took the keys from my fingers. "Long day, huh? You're home now. Relax. I have dinner waiting for you."

I searched his eyes and felt comforted until he came in for a long kiss to calm me down and all I could smell was liquor. His words were slurred even if they had been meant to be supportive. I felt a heavy feeling come over me as he set down his drink and scooped me into his arms, his hand quickly descending to my ass to give it a squeeze.

"Hey babe, maybe a little one on one would be just the medicine for your hard day at the office." I pushed him away and headed for the bedroom without a word.

The floodgates of my mind opened with accusations as I collapsed on the bed, face down in my suit. Every bit of energy I'd summoned for the day and the big presentation now slid off and left me in a puddle. Joe stood in the door and observed my silence, uncertain what to do. He headed back to the kitchen for another drink to gird him up for whatever else might come.

Forty-five minutes later, I exited the large glass shower in the master bathroom. Joe stood mute as he handed me a towel and my nightgown. After I lifted the printed silk over my damp head, he led me to the bed where the sheets had been pulled down.

"Take these," he ordered, placing two Excedrin into the palm of the woman he knew so well. I swallowed around the hard lump in my throat before I lay back in the coolness of the fresh linens.

Joe sat next to me on the bed, and his palm stroked my face briefly before he began to reach for my skin underneath the sheets. He slipped a hand along the side of my breast under my nightgown, an invitation to intimacy, but I lurched away as he reached his mouth toward mine.

"Holy shit, Joe! Are you serious? I'm hardly in the mood for sex, for Christ's sake! Leave me alone." I pulled away and then pushed him off of me. Joe retreated like a wounded soldier as I fought to explain.

I shook my head in frustration. "I, I just need to sleep, honey. I'm sorry. I just don't want to have sex right now. I need to just get ahold of myself." The days of peeling off our clothes and diving into bed to forget our troubles had died with my skyrocketing stress level soon after we'd arrived in this country.

"Do you want to talk about it?" Joe slurred. He took my cue and went and sat next to the side of the bed in the easy chair and waited.

I swallowed and tried to catch my breath. Joe passed me his glass of Scotch. I stared down at it and looked at his face, which was rapidly descending into a kind of stupor. I grabbed the glass and drained it, but didn't hand the glass back to him.

"That's my girl!" He sat back down and waited for me once again. This time he didn't return first to the kitchen to replenish his drink.

The words began to form on my lips, about what had happened in that boardroom that day, at the horror of the indignities I had suffered. How Ethan had made the immediate transformation into a prehistoric monster at the conclusion of my presentation when he didn't like something I said. How my initial surprise had turned to horror when this previously friendly, super professional guy had given way to the indescribable beast who had attacked me verbally and torn my credibility limb from limb, literally exploding across the room. How the other three had sat there, stoic, without a word uttered in my defense, watching like voyeurs, as if they were at games in the Coliseum in Rome, watching a lion tear apart its prey.

Anguished heaving from deep within me choked the description I had begun. I rolled sideways into the fetal position as I felt again the piercing of Ethan's words into my breastplate, as he laid into me again. *Perhaps we need to make a change. Perhaps we need to make a change. Perhaps we need to make a change!* The threat rang in my ears over and over as I began to drift off to sleep. Just before I did I glanced at Joe, who had been silent for some time, only to see that he had fallen asleep. My heart nearly cracked as I buried my face in the pillow only to hear one more voice before I went into the darkness and safety of sleep.

Poor thing. Snickety crinkled up her nose at me with pity. *You just didn't know what you were getting into. Be careful what you wish for, dearie.*

CHAPTER 22:
The Home Invasion

Lily greeted us at the door, her body wagging from head to tail. Normally such enthusiasm was reserved for weekends when we went to the beach. This vacation had only lasted 10 days but it had delivered a much-needed dose of normalcy and sanity, back home in Denver.

"Baby girl!" our voices sang as we abandoned our roller bags in the foyer and bent our faces to greet her. "How are you? How are you? We missed you so much."

The dark tabby cat came running down the hallway to rub in between our legs while the smaller white one hung back with wide eyes.

"Elphaba, Blossom, how are you?" I scooped one into my arms for a quick head rub. "Oh, yes. We're back now." As Blossom pushed against me to jump to the floor, in classic stand-off form, I reached for Elphaba from between my legs. "Everybody good?"

Joe straightened up from where he'd been scratching Lily's hind end to rub Elphaba behind the ears as well. Our eyes met as we said in unison. "Swiss Family O'Malley." We laughed again, which was a welcomed place to find ourselves after all we had been through since our arrival in Panama. Even the animals had grown accustomed to the heat now, so Joe and I were finally allowing Panama to be what it was, as much as possible.

I made more of an effort to control my attitude that had developed since we arrived, though that continued to be a huge challenge. I snuggled Elphaba under my chin, relieved to be back with our furry family.

Lily danced down the hall and the cats followed. Joe wheeled his roller bag into the first bedroom as I pointed mine toward the closet in the master.

The refrigerator door opened. *Schmack.* Joe's voice came from around the corner. "Do you want a beer?" I paused a moment, noticing my breathing getting shallow and thin.

"No, thanks. I don't need anything." I waited for the inevitable pop off the top of the glass bottle of Corona.

I heaved my *maleta* onto our bed before sliding the patio door open. "Whew." I wiped sweat from my brow. "Let's get some fresh air in this place, girls." Warm breeze blew in, causing the curtains to billow as I crossed to the den to open the opposite facing door to the balcony.

My high-heeled boots clicked across the wood floor before I sank into the couch with a sigh. As I crossed one foot over my knee to remove my boot, a flash of light caught my eye from the floor.

"Huh," I said, leaning over to click on the lamp. Suddenly, the room came into view.

"Shit!" The light illuminated a thousand fragments of glass beneath the coffee table. "Joe!" I yelled as I bent toward the mess, trying to make sense of what I saw.

The space where a glass shelf had once hung below the coffee table was now empty.

"Check this out." Heavy steps brought Joe into my peripheral vision, brandishing a small bottle. His smile faded when he saw the incredulity splayed across my face. "Everything okay?"

I motioned downwards. "I'm not sure what happened here, but we're down one glass shelf. Looks like someone had an accident."

"Jesus." Joe bent down to examine the shards, setting the small jar in his hand on the wood above it. The glass lay sparkling in perfect formation of the shelf's original shape on the floor. "What the hell happened?"

"I don't know, but you'd think Tomas would have said something." My brain was working overtime, reviewing the past week's schedule of instructions we had left for Tomas during our absence.

"Maybe he didn't see it," Joe said.

"How could you not see this?" I asked, realizing as the question left my mouth that it was, indeed, rhetorical. We were talking about the man who neglected to wash the car and buy the newspaper if it wasn't hand written on his list every single week, though he'd been doing both for months now. This was not a country of critical thinkers. I shook my head, the enthusiasm I'd had on the plane for coming home wilting on the vine. "Oh, never mind." I pushed myself erect. "I'll get the broom and the dustpan."

As I stood, I noticed the small glass jar Joe had set down atop the table again. "What's this?" I asked, reaching for it. The cherub-like face of the Gerber baby smiled at me from the label.

"Baby food?" I winced.

"Bananas, to be exact," Joe nodded. "From the fridge. Top shelf."

"Really?" Bewilderment began to morph into suspicion. "Who do we *know* that has a baby?" My face betrayed my thoughts.

"Well, certainly the only people that were *supposed* to be in here don't have a baby." Joe's eyes crinkled as he surveyed the dismay on my face. "But then that list is pretty short."

"If either Tomas or Angela had a baby in here, I'm going to fire them," I said as anxiety began to bloom in my chest. The staccato of my boots reflected my anger as I stamped toward the utility closet. *Relaxed vacation, JuliAnne has left the building.* "They were specifically told that no one was allowed up here."

"Do you think there's a chance that either of them actually *listened* to what you were saying?"

The refrigerator door opened and closed again as Joe replaced the baby food jar and pulled out another Corona.

Lily followed me into the maid's room, pupils wide, to watch me yank the closet door open in search of cleaning utensils. Paws flailed on the slick tile as I turned back in haste.

Joe was scooting the ottoman away from the window to make a clear path for the clean-up, his face still scrunched up, a detective at the scene of the crime. "The only way this could have happened is if someone fell from this direction," he reported, pointing at the table leg closest to him. "This end collapsed, and someone had to set it back up to make the table stand." When he put a foot on the leg in question, the wooden piece wobbled.

"Jesus Christ." I shook my head as Joe began to sweep. "The thing weighs 400 pounds; I can't even move it by myself." My gaze scanned the area—the sofa beside the table, the love seat forming a parallel L to the sofa, the sliding glass door to the balcony a mere four feet away. "It's not possible that no one knew about this."

"No." He shook his head. "Completely not possible. But what is possible…," he pointed with his chin to the base of the glass door leading out to the balcony, where a three-inch shelf protruded up from the floor, "…is that our friend—whoever he was—was not familiar with our little trip hazard here."

My eyes crossed the distance between the lip on the floor and the table. I had stubbed my toe there many a time, causing me to curse Panamanian construction. I nodded, my mouth in a line. "Yep. I see it."

"If these doors were open all the way, and if someone not familiar with that lip stepped backwards, say, during a party…" Joe reenacted the potential pathway of the perpetrator's fall.

"Yep, got it. Unbelievable."

"Boom!" Joe smacked his hand on the top of the wood table, causing me to jump. "The coffee table folds, and if the person is large enough, the shelf below falls from the impact, causing it to shatter."

A large body appeared in my mind's eye, reenacting the scene Joe had just outlined. *Tomas tips 250 pounds, easy.* I gritted my teeth.

"So, no way it was Angela." Joe's words were a statement, not a question. The slim woman in her 50s that served us as a maid five days a week had only been scheduled to be in the apartment twice during our absence.

"Of course not." My head continued to shake. "She couldn't move the table either, not without help. But, why wouldn't they clean it up? Wouldn't it make sense to make it look like nothing happened? Maybe they would hope we wouldn't notice, at least for a while?"

"But, that would be *logical*, JuliAnne." Joe's voice was grim, as he began to push the fragments into the dustpan. "And, as you know, very little in this country is logical. Now grab me the trash can please, so none of this gets dropped on the way back to the kitchen."

My temper began to escalate. "Why would he do this to us?" My arms began to gesture in wild arcs, as if I were an evangelical preacher directing the choir. The relaxation of our 10 days away had now been forgotten. "We trusted him to take care of Lily and the apartment! And why would Angela cover for him? What's wrong with these people? Don't they understand the value of trust? We're their employers, for fuck sake!"

"We haven't even seen Angela yet, Murph." Joe's palm pushing the air in my direction was an unspoken directive to calm down. "We have to give each of them a chance to explain."

"You mean *I* have to give them a chance to explain." The edge in my voice belied my fatigue at being the only Spanish speaker in the family almost two years in. The task of translating instructions to our help sometimes had its downsides. These days, that task had been expanded to help Joe with contract proposals for his new consulting gigs.

Joe cut his eyes at me as he swept the last of the glass from the dustpan into the bin. "Yes, *darling*. I was talking about you." Wiping his brow, he set down the dustpan in exchange for his beer on the shelf, and turned the clear bottle up to take a swig. "But don't expect that you're going to get the truth. You know how it goes here; they always cover for each other."

"God, damn it!" I stamped my foot. "I guess we just can't trust anyone in this mother-fucking country." I crossed my arms to contain the rage that was beginning to roil behind my breast bone.

Joe just lifted his eyebrows. "Don't you think you're overreacting a little? It's a broken table and a can of baby food…"

"No, I don't!" I shouted, stamping off toward the bedroom. "I'm going to go unpack." Joe shook his head, draining the dregs from his beer, and carried the trashcan back to the kitchen.

Ka-ching. Bottle cap number three clattered to the counter as Joe let out a sigh. He looked at Lily, who sat watching him. "Anything else you want to share with us, girl?"

The elegant form wagged as she crossed over to lick his hand. Brown wavy hair bent down to meet the point of her black snout. "Oh, yes, I love you too."

"Aarrgh!!" I let out a yell from the master bedroom.

Joe straightened to see me catapulting from the bedroom door, holding my hair dryer in front of me.

"What now?" Joe chugged half the bottle as he braced for the worst.

"They used my fucking hair dryer!" I screamed. "Look at this!" I pointed at the machine's vent.

Joe motioned for me to come closer to the bar. He eyed the offending strand of long black hair hanging from the hair dryer's grate, before shrugging his shoulders and lifting his beer once again. "Well, at least they had a good time," he grinned.

"I'm going to mother fucking call Tomas right now!" I shrieked, storming off to find my cell phone.

Joe put his palm in the air, a silent *Stop*. "Hang on, JuliAnne. We don't know for sure it was him. You can't just call and accuse. You know that. That will only backfire."

"Then what the fuck am I supposed to do? I don't even want to stay here now!" I spun around to face the large dining room table, six chairs lined up like children ready for church. "Who the heck knows what else they did here?" I walked to the second bedroom, pointing at the made-up bed. "Or here?" I turned on my heels toward the sofa. "Or anywhere?"

"All right, JuliAnne," Joe's deep baritone interrupted. "I think you need some air. Why don't you go change your shoes and take Lily out?" And with that, he came out of the kitchen, brushing past me towards the second bedroom.

I stood there for a moment, feeling his departure like a slap in the face. *What?* I thought. *How is it a problem that I'm upset? Someone we trusted has wronged us here, for God's sake!* Trailing his footsteps into the other room, my shadow graced the door before I crossed the threshold. My husband's attention had been redirected to his suitcase, where his hands were sorting dirty clothes from clean. "What just happened?" I looked concerned.

"What just happened is what always happens, JuliAnne." Joe kept his back to me as he continued sorting.

I shook my head to clear the cobwebs. "What is that supposed to mean? You aren't making any sense! Why is it a problem that I'm upset that Tomas—or whoever it was—betrayed us?"

It was Joe's turn to shake his head, though he kept his back to me. He stilled for a moment before he turned my way. "Never mind. We've had this conversation before. You can't hear me, so it's not even worth it."

A rock sank in my stomach. "What conversation? What are you talking about?"

Joe's brown eyes pierced mine, and for a moment behind the anger, I glimpsed something akin to an ache. "The one where I remind you that you can't blame everyone else for our move to Panama. We're the ones who decided to move here. You're always so bitter about everything, so angry."

Heat poured like fire out of my belly, threatened to consume me as I heard his words. "What the *fuck* does this situation have to with our move to Panama? This…," I stuttered, turning back toward the living room and our audience of cats and dog that had gathered at my feet, "…This…," I waved my arms to encompass the space and everything in it, "This… is about us being be…be…betrayed by someone we trusted to take care of our stuff and our animals while we were gone. And as *usual*, they took advantage of us, and acted like everything is just fine and couldn't just tell us the bad news or didn't say anything about it but left us to discover it and, and, yes, *yes*! It's yet another fucking example of why *I hate* this country!"

As the last words left my mouth, a strong sense of *déjà vu* hit me, and the oxygen sucked from my lungs like helium from a balloon. I swayed on my feet as the truth of what Joe had said hit me.

He's right. I stumbled to the couch to sit, the shock of this truth sinking into every pore in my body. *He's right. This is not just about a broken table and a party in our house. I do hate this country.*

I was so consumed in my reverie that I didn't feel Joe come to sit beside me. Only when he took my hand in his own, my consciousness returned to the present.

"I'm sorry," said the voice of the man I loved. "But it's true. You're so angry all the time. Nothing makes you happy. Where is the girl I fell in love with? The one that wanted to embark on this crazy adventure together? The one who loves to have fun?" His hand squeezed mine before it lifted to stroke a strand of hair behind my ear. "I miss my JuliAnne. I really do." I didn't look up but I could sense the soft smile crossing his face.

I lifted my eyes to take in the kindness in his eyes. And just like that, the spring of sadness and regret and the pressure and the fear and the stress and the unhappiness I'd been holding in my chest for months and months and months came crashing down. I collapsed into a puddle in his arms. The howls of pain and hurt that ensued were those of an animal, not of a woman. And for the first time in months, I threw off the mask of perfection and having it all together, and I let the torrent of irritation and frustration overcome me.

He sat there, stroking my hair, rubbing my back while I allowed myself to feel the full impact of what I was just now realizing. When the weird noises finally stopped coming, I lifted my hand toward him in search of a Kleenex, and he complied. It was a sign of support, one we'd forged over the years.

After a considerable amount of nose blowing and face wiping, I stood up and turned to look at my husband. The words stuck in my throat as I met his eyes, regret rising in my chest that I had taken my angst out on him.

"I'm s...s...sorry," I said, my face crinkling with more tears.

"Hey," he said, turning my bent chin up toward him, so that I could not hide. "All I want is for you to find happiness. That's it." His tone turned juvenile, and he shrugged his shoulders in jest.

"That's all. That's all I want. Just a happy wife."

I couldn't help the relief that broke across my face. I nodded, forcing a smile to emerge.

"And, all this shit." It was his turn to wave a hand above his head and around the room, and I knew he was talking about all the chaos in the country. "It is what it is. We'll get through it. But, we gotta get you to a place where you can find some happiness, Murph. Or none of this is worth it."

The stream of silent tears continued down my face. I nodded again, mute.

"And in the meantime, let's have some fun with this little mystery of ours." The mischievous gleam in his eye invited me to come out and play. "We know we're not going to get the truth or real answers from anyone, so let's have fun with it."

I wiped the snot from my face again before it dripped onto my lap. "What do you have in mind?"

"Well, for starters, let's leave the baby food in the fridge and see what happens."

I chuckled. "Baby food!" I shook my head. "How the hell could anyone be so stupid as to forget the baby food? Don't you think they got home and the baby got hungry?"

Now the tears were streaming down Joe's face as he laughed with me. "Right? I'm sure they were so busy breaking the table—" Joe's eyebrows shot straight up his face, "—that they kind of forgot about the baby. I guess we're lucky they didn't leave the baby here too."

A laugh burst from my chest.

He patted my leg. "Okay? Now let's go get unpacked and get to bed." He leaned over to peck me on the mouth. "We've both got busy schedules this next week, starting tomorrow."

"All right," I sighed, returning his kiss. My eyes turned serious for a moment, as I grasped his hand. "Hey. I love you."

"I love you too, Murphy."

And with that, Elphaba jumped down from her perch to follow him into the second bedroom, and Lily and Blossom followed me into the master.

CHAPTER 23:
Tomas Busts Himself

"Where do you go today?" Tomas asked without his customary glimpse in the rearview mirror.

Posed in the familiar soft, accented baritone, the question had become such the norm for me that it was a comfort. Other people had their water cooler gossip and their Starbucks; I had Tomas.

I set the plastic thermal glass in the cup holder, the requisite paper towel wrapped around the bottom of it. The fight to keep the car free of humidity was a constant battle.

"*Vamos a la oficina primero y despúes a la ciudad para un par de reuñiones.*" Though I had some knowledge of Spanish before we moved, my vocabulary and my ease of speech had improved via the four hours of study I did every week with a private tutor. Tomas filled the gaps.

"*Muy bien,*" Tomas' green eyes flashed with approval. "Very, very nice."

I grinned. "Tomas," I began, taking a copy of *La Prensa* from the designer handbag that lay at my feet as the car moved down the ridge that separated our neighborhood from the main road below. "*Esta bien si yo lay-o un po-kee-toe mee-in-tras estamos en cai-yay a la off-ee-cee-na?*"

"*Claro.*" Tomas' head continued to bob, though he never took his eyes from the road. "Of course, Miss JuliAnne. Go ahead."

The soft paper snapped to attention as I unfolded it to its full breadth. "*A ver,*" I said. "Let's see." A photo of two familiar faces smiled from above the fold back at me: a man with slick-backed hair in a crisp black and white tuxedo and a petite blond in turquoise sequins that grazed her high heels were two of Panama's elite I knew.

"A-ha." I pointed to the attractive couple, reading the caption aloud, slowly pronunciating the words before me. "*El Presidente y la Primera*

Dama lay dawn la been-va-need-a a el Doo-kay day York day el Reh-ee-do Ooh-nee-do, Prin-cee-pay Andrew."

"*RAY-ee-do*," Tomas corrected me.

"*RAY-ee-do.*" I pulled my lips back from my teeth to allow for the second syllable to expand. "Ray, Ray, Ray," I continued. "*El doo-kay been-dra manana al pro-jek-too…*"

"*Pro-YEK-toe*," Tomas corrected again. "*Es pro-YEK-toe*, Miss JuliAnne."

"*Pro-YEK-toe*," I repeated. "*Pero*, Tomas, why is the 'huh' sound used sometimes for double L and other times with J in Spanish?"

"*Bueno, pues.* That is a good question." Tomas cleared his throat, shifting in his seat.

On certain days, I found it amusing the way his chest swelled when I asked him these kinds of questions. Since Tomas' mother had taught English in his younger years, he considered himself a bit of an expert.

"My English is very good, Miss JuliAnne," he often reminded me, as his head dipped like a bobble head doll.

"You speak English very well, Tomas. It's true." I returned his nod. "And you are getting better every day. I am your English teacher and you are my Spanish teacher."

Such was our amusement in these shared moments that we would burst out laughing at the irony of those statements. *If people only knew*, I mused. *The gringa executive and her Panameño.*

A week had passed since our return from vacation and our discovery that a baby, a woman with long black hair, and a mystery guest who had broken our table had invaded our apartment. After several days of covert interrogation passed off as casual conversation with my household employees, the scoreboard for the discovery process read "Staff 1, Gringos 0." As usual, the locals weren't giving anything up.

Joe and I briefed each other on our collective efforts every night over an after-work cocktail.

"I don't have any idea what happened with the table." I mimicked my latest conversation with Tomas as I lifted my wine glass to my lips. "At least that's the translation." I rearranged my features into the famous blank look that Panamanians were known to give at the smallest hint of confrontation. It was as if a curtain had fallen down over the face, taking all semblance of expression with it. "Maybe Lily was playing with the cat and jumped on it?"

"Now it's Lily's fault?" Joe snickered as cigar smoke rose in a circle above his head. "And, Angela?"

At the maid's name, my lips pursed as if I'd been sucking on a sour *limon*. "It wasn't like that when I left on Tuesday, *pero*…" I shot my eyes left and right to see if anyone else was in the room. "*Pero, Señora*, Tomas is not the man he presents himself to be."

"What the hell is that supposed to mean?" Joe took a dreg from the crystal snifter of tequila in front of him.

"Basically, she said that Tomas is not faithful to Maria, he has a lot of women on the side, *and*…," I lifted the wine glass as if making an important announcement, "*and*…that Maria is not even his *wife*."

"Whaaaat?" Joe leaned forward as tequila spurted from the sides of his mouth. "I have a hard time believing that. We've known Maria for two years now. Tomas brought her to the office months ago to introduce her, and even gave her my phone number for emergencies." His finger wagged back and forth, a local gesture we'd both adopted. "Plus, Maria's the one who calls in when Tomas is sick!"

I recalled Angela's sincere face: skin glistening under a bright-colored do-rag, her forehead dotted with beads of sweat.

I lifted my palms toward the ceiling. "I'm just the messenger here. I asked Angela how she came by that information, and she said Tomas had admitted it to her."

"Well, if he's not married to Maria, then who *is* his wife?" Joe studied me from across the table.

I drained the last of my wine with a shrug. "She didn't give me a name, only referred to her as the 'other woman in the house.'"

"Wow." Joe took another puff on his cigar. "So, was it her insinuation that Tomas is our culprit for the broken table?"

"Pretty much." I rubbed my temples. "Though she didn't come right out and say it. As you know, they rarely bust each other."

Joe set the stub of his cigar on the ceramic ashtray I'd bought him for Father's Day. "So, I guess it's settled then. Our faithful driver is a lady's man who brought a woman who is not his wife up to cavort in our apartment while we were gone, in addition to somebody's baby, and in so doing, broke our coffee table."

"Case closed," I said, bending down to loosen the straps of my sling-backs.

"I'd sure like to know for sure how it happened though. Wouldn't you?" I glanced toward the coffee table which stood bandaged like a wounded soldier. "What did Tomas ever say about the baby food?"

"You and your inquiring mind." The smirk ran away from Joe's face as he stepped to the kitchen counter to pour himself another shot. "That's right, I forgot to tell you. The mystery of the Gerber baby bananas."

Earlier that week, the jar in question had disappeared from the fridge. The mysterious disappearance narrowed our list of suspects to a list of one, since Angela hadn't come to work that day.

"Well." Joe paused to down a second tequila with little effort. "I asked him on Tuesday morning before Angela arrived, when he came back with the paper."

My eyes followed him, hanging on his every word like a reporter getting the scoop. "And?"

"He said it was his," Joe finished, his feet heading back toward me.

"He admitted it?" I sputtered.

Joe held up a hand in my direction to silence me before lowering himself to the couch. "Stop! He didn't admit to anything, except that the baby food was his."

"Did you ask him whose baby…"

"Still talking!" Condescension flashed across my husband's features. "You're not at work anymore, Murph. Can you just shut up and let me finish? I had a long day with my clients, too."

My eyes narrowed as I braced myself for our customary fight. I leaned back against the seat cushion with a scowl, crossing my arms.

Joe shook the ice in his glass. "He *said* that the baby food was part of his new diet for his workout regime."

My eyes rolled skyward. "And I assume his workouts commenced when we left town?" Tomas' tank-like physique belied his daily intake of the working man's staple, rice and beans.

"Right." Joe brought his smoldering cigar to his lips.

I swatted the air as a hoard of mosquitos dive-bombed, heralding sunset. "So really, as usual, we know nothing more than we did before."

"Bingo." Joe motioned for me to lean toward him as he exhaled puffs of blue smoke my way. We'd read that cigar smoke acted as a natural mosquito repellant.

"But, that said, let's give our man a day or two. You know he always busts himself without even knowing it." Joe dragged hard on the cigar and then washed down the smoke with his last gulp of tequila.

"Oh, what's the use?" Forcing a sigh from my lips, I headed back inside. "It's not like anything I do is going to make any difference."

Are you talking about Tomas or Joe? Snickety mocked as I crossed the threshold. *Because it doesn't seem like you're having much success with either.*

My husband's gaze followed my backside as I disappeared into the bedroom and slammed the door. He turned back toward the cats, who were sprawled across the loveseat from where I'd departed. "Your mother needs to work on her ability to let go of the things she can't control," he whispered.

The white cat batted an eye.

"Oh, yes, I love you too," he slurred as he reached over to scratch her under the chin.

~

The following morning, Tomas and I were driving out of the parking garage when he broke the silence. "Miss JuliAnne," he asked. "How's Lily?"

"*Muy bien*, Tomas," I replied, taking a sip from my travel mug. "She's happy now that we're back."

"Yes," Tomas nodded. "I was a little worried while you were gone because she did not eat."

I stopped tapping on my Blackberry midstream. "Really?"

"Well." Tomas recounted as the car made its ubiquitous U-turn among towering palm trees toward the Bridge of the Americas. "I am not sure, *pero* she did not eat much for several days after you left."

"Hmm." My ears perked up though I kept my eyes straight ahead, a trick I'd learned when my stepsons were teenagers. A tingling ran up my spine, the sure sign that breaking news was imminent. "So, what did you do?"

"One day, she didn't eat at breakfast or at dinner." Tomas' words tumbled from his mouth, one after the other like a confession. "So, when I came back to walk her before bed, Maria and I fed her some McDonald's."

"McDonald's?" I bit the inside of my cheek. "But, Tomas, did you remember Lily is allergic to beef?"

"Oh, yes," Tomas nodded. "We brought her some Chicken McNuggets."

I reached for my cup to take a swig and stifle the chuckle rising in my throat. *Just like a teenager.* "I see. Well, that was very nice of the two of you, Tomas. And, did she eat them?"

"Not at first." Tomas puffed out his chest. "But, then we fed them to her by hand and she ate all of them."

"That was really thoughtful of you, Tomas," I said, though the wide smile on my face had nothing to do with kindness. "Thank you so much for taking such good care of Lily while we were gone."

"Yes, Señora." The big head bobbed.

"And for telling me about it," I continued. "I'll be sure to share this with Mr. Joe. I'm sure he'll be *very* interested to hear this," I said, keeping my face straight ahead so that the laugh did not burst from my chest.

A smile the size of Texas blazed across Tomas' face though the sun was rising behind us in the opposite direction. There was no higher compliment in Panama than reporting a job well done back to the *jefe*.

So, that's it, case closed. I thought, recalling the yellow hardback covers of my favorite childhood spy series, Nancy Drew. *The mystery of Lily and the Chicken McNuggets.*

We never found out what happened to the coffee table, though the story made for entertaining dinner conversation for years to come.

CHAPTER 24:
The Sting

I hated these nights with a fervor, the ones when sleep avoided me like the plague. When the creatures from my days haunted me in every dark shadow of my dreams. And, I hated it more that this disturbance held a familiar rhythm: sleepless night, next day exhaustion, and the adrenaline overload from a daylong battle at the office as evening turned to night. The pattern was never-ending.

I tossed and turned in the damp sheets, my mind refusing to simmer down. It was a cruel eventuality that I would surrender to the fight: pupils constricting to focus on the green readout of the digital numbers my alarm clock cast above on the ceiling.

You're becoming an insomniac.

This accusation bothered me, though I wished it didn't. The shady character projected there, on the movie screen of my mind's eye, showed a silhouette of a woman in a trench coat, her collar pulled up tight against the cold. A cigarette smoldered in her hand as she stood in a dim-lit alley behind a dumpster.

Insomnia is God's way of visiting justice on the guilty. My stomach clenched at the voice. *Is there something you need to confess before the Lord?* I could imagine the familiar words spitting from my mother's pursed mouth.

Well, you must have done something wrong, my father's deep baritone chimed in. *Or they wouldn't be treating you this way.*

Don't be ridiculous. My left-brain kicked in with a vengeance. *These guys are just a bunch of stupid assholes. This has everything to do with* them, *not you, JuliAnne.*

Does it? My father, always the judge and jury, leaned back in his chair at the dinner table, chewing on a toothpick. *Did you listen and consider every possible angle?*

The phrase appeared in cursive on the Sunday School chalkboard, written by a stooped woman in a floral dress and crimped hair. *Shortcuts are like sins; they always find you out.* "Repeat after me, children."

A choir of childish voices recited back in singsong unison: "Your sins will find you out."

God, damn it, I did consider everything! My hands began to shake as the relentless questioning began anew in my head. I was never *anything,* if not fully prepared. But, the back and forth of the day's disaster in the office kept repeating like a frustrating scene in Groundhog's Day, over and over and over again.

Two men sat with scowls in the chairs opposite my desk. The hair on my arms stood at attention as the energy in the room crackled between the three of us.

My voice rang out, firm and clear. "Look, Curt, Juan Carlos. I'm not sure what you want me to do here, but I'm sick and tired of being the pawn in your games." My stomach leaped at my courage.

Had those words really left my mouth?

Of course not, my perfect older sister sniped. *Though they certainly should have. When are you ever going to speak up and defend yourself?* I began to deflate under the pressure of so many naysayers both in me and outside of me.

In my mind, a pair of faceless hands waved a poster with the letters "DE" and a picture of a fence painted on it in red. "De-FENSE!" the crowd roared, cheering on my resolve from the sidelines, though this particular game had been over hours before.

Aren't you sick of them treating you like a child? Snickety joined the conversation.

*Well, yes, but…*my vision returned to the scene.

Beady eyes bore a hole in me. Curt's anger was palpable, his voice accusing. "This is not what I told you to do, JuliAnne. I told you *exactly* what I wanted, and this…whatever *this* is." Spittle sprayed from his lower lip. "This…shows me your head is not really in the game. That, and the fact that *this* ad is not going to get us any customers." He flicked the paper in front of him like it was a gnat.

My eyes narrowed to slits. *As if* you *know the first thing about marketing, you fucking asshole!* I had to bite my tongue to keep from shrieking. Curt was my boss, after all, and I was wise to hold my tongue. The jerk had admitted he didn't understand a thing about my trade the first week I'd been on the job, however, that had been back when he was still attempting to play nice in the sandbox, and God knew those days were long gone. Even so, I clung to that admission when these ridiculous antics played out time and time again.

I blew a long exhale before I replied. "What I *attempted* to explain earlier, Curt, is that your approach will not work. It doesn't answer the questions the clients need to know about Panama. We have to convince them that Panama is the right country, first, before we get into details about building heights and corridor widths. In my experience, this..."

"I don't give a *shit* about your *experience*." Curt's voice echoed off the painted concrete walls, ricocheting down the hall and causing everyone in the building to quiver in their seats. "I told you what I wanted, and you are giving me everything *other* than exactly what I asked for!" Curt's face twisted into angry contortions, reminding me of the Transformer figurines my nephews had unwrapped at Christmas a few weeks earlier.

Is this behavior befitting of the number two guy on the project? The blatant disgust on my face showed my opinion of Curt's childish outburst. I reshuffled my features into a neutral state before swiveling my chair toward Juan Carlos.

"Juan Carlos." My eyes pleaded for the smaller man to interject some sanity into the meeting. "Perhaps you'd like to update Curt on the different direction you asked me to take, following the last meeting between the three of us?"

Juan Carlos had his arms folded across his chest like a shield, one hand gripping his chin. His eyes were cast downward at the storyboard in question.

Having learned over the months that Juan Carlos' deliberation required more time than mine ever did, I waited as my breath wheezed down my throat in an attempt to open the thick tension in my chest. *I think I need more than a bulletproof vest to stave off the grenades these two keep launching at each other and now at me.*

Juan Carlos' tentative voice broke the silence. "Ehm," he said, which always reminded me of a music teacher calling out the correct musical key for his choir to follow.

Go ahead, Juan Carlos. Put this asshole in his place. I bit the inside of my cheek to keep an evil grin from spreading.

"In this case, I think Curt is right." He glanced away from me toward Curt.

My mouth dropped open as the familiar *zing!* of the arrow of betrayal found its target in the center of my heart. "What?" I spluttered. "But, Juan Carlos, you told me last week you wanted to see this advertisement more in line with our brand messaging, not from a product perspective." I paused, realizing my voice now sounded desperate, weak. I took a deep breath, dialing it back a notch before I continued. "Do you recall that conversation two weeks ago? You said you'd bring Curt up to speed on your line of thinking?" I paused and held my breath, waiting for Juan Carlos to do the right thing.

Juan Carlos swung cold eyes back at me. "I don't recall that at all, JuliAnne." His face was awash in that familiar neutral mask. He shook his head. "You must have misunderstood."

I opened my mouth to say something, but no words came. My eyes probed, urging him to recall the conversation we'd had in the hall that day. It had been such a relief to hear him come in line with my opinion. I'd actually felt the man *saw* me that day, the way his eyes smiled into mine after he acquiesced to the original direction I had recommended we take. It had been such a successful moment that my feet had almost floated on a cloud back to my office.

But there was nothing there. No recognition, nothing. *Why are you lying?* I winced at the weight of duplicity I felt in my gut. The words I knew to be true never made it to my lips, though I felt them in every ounce of my being, like Shakespeare. *Et tu, Brute?* I could never ask that question aloud and expect to stay employed here. Once Juan Carlos made up his mind, he clung to it like a battleship. Sink or swim, he was loyal to his opinions when it served him and even Curt, even though they despised each other. The boys club was unmistakable.

The room began to spin. "All right then, gentlemen." I felt like Alice in Wonderland having drug-laced tea with the rabbit and two mad hatters. My survival instincts kicked in as I came to my feet. "Apparently, there was a misunderstanding." Though, in fact, there was nothing further from the truth. "If you'll give me a day or two, I'll have another draft in front of each of you as soon as I can."

"The sooner, the better," Curt snarled. His chair screeched as he pushed himself up. "And, next time, take better notes." He stormed from the office.

As if in an alternate universe, I watched as Curt's insult hurled toward me. When I ducked, it bounced off the wall and landed in my trash can.

The cell phone on Juan Carlos' lap shrilled. "*Sí?*" he said, bringing it to his shoulder, grabbing his things and heading for the door, eyes never meeting mine.

Coward!

A moment later, a face framed with shoulder-length dark curls appeared in my doorway. "Everything okay?" The woman's English was accented, a look of nervous anxiety splayed across her broad features.

I forced a wan smile in her direction. "I'm fine, Ana Christina, thank you. Just the usual." But my body betrayed the truth that the impact of the meeting had me nauseous. I clasped the desk to keep my knees from buckling. I straightened my shoulders from the weight of the experience and tossed a smile toward Ana Christina. She returned a knowing smile. Her time in the company had been short, but she already knew the affect Curt had on just about everyone.

Ana Christina's smile disappeared as the door closed. My forehead found its familiar place on the desk as the acid in my stomach began to churn more. *Will I ever win? Is it even possible?* Being the only woman on a project of this size had felt like such an opportunity, but now I was seeing it for what it was: them against me. The gender issues in this country were playing themselves out in the boardroom every week, and Curt was not even a Panamanian. I had been unprepared for this reality.

It was the glimpses of sanity—like that conversation in the hall with Juan Carlos last week—that kept me going. These semblances of someone seeing how hard I was trying to make a difference in this country, on this project, despite the fact that Curt treated me like a punching bag; despite the fact I was performing near-miracles to overcome the daily inefficiencies and meet unrealistic timelines the leadership insisted upon; and despite the vendors' local custom of disappearing when shipments or services were going to be delayed.

It was me who was the one keeping it all together, in the midst of being tossed back and forth like a tiny *lancha* on the waves created by the ticking time bomb that threatened to explode between Juan Carlos and Curt on any given day. Their bitter competition was bleeding into every aspect of my dream job and I was a casualty of their anger all too often.

Surely, at some point, I thought, *someone will recognize that I am doing everything I can. Surely, at some point, someone will save me from this madness. Surely, at some point, I will get the accolades I so justly deserve for staying afloat between the two mad hatters. Right?*

Somewhere in a distant part of myself, Snickety broke through. *Wishful thinking, girl. The real rub is that the only one to save you from this mad-as-a-hatter situation you are in…is…you. Don't depend on any of these knuckle-heads to throw you a life raft.*

I lifted my gaze to stare with red-rimmed eyes at the three black frames I'd hung with care above my desk. Each of them celebrated some aspect of the prior big wins in my career: a photo with the former governor of Colorado at a groundbreaking in 2005; my long hair flying along with the American flag as fireworks burst behind me at the opening ceremonies of the new Denver Broncos stadium in 2001; a group shot of my team receiving an award for the best marketing campaign in the nation for a new Denver community in 2007. The awards and the accolades and the past successes all seemed like a distant memory.

None of this is helping you now.

"Thanks for the support." My voice, dull with fatigue, brought me back to where I now sat at 2 a.m., staring into the darkness of the ocean off our 25th-story balcony. My mind was a washing machine spinning with second guesses, self-judgment, and a big dose of resentment.

Where did I go wrong? The question was rhetorical, but it was the one that haunted me most, the one I always asked first. *Because with results this bad…* Curt's angry face rose in my conscience, alongside Juan Carlos' blank one. *Surely there was something else I could have done differently, something else I should have fixed. So, that means it's them.* My hand went to my lower belly, an instinct to protect this truth, like an unborn child. I knew this, in my heart. *It has to be them, right? I've tried everything, every way I know how to—all the ways and styles and business practices I know of to dispel tension, to reach accord, to reach resolution.*

None of it had worked.

So, if I know that I am a pawn in a war that is not mine, can I let myself off the hook, even a little? Can I cling to my reputation of producing excellence even when my work is torn to bits?

I found my way to the bathroom as nausea continued to plunder me.

A haggard face stared back at me in the mirror. My fingers traced the dark shadows under my eyes. What had once been tiny lines were now mapping out into noticeable wrinkles around my eyes, my mouth.

What had happened to the happy-go-lucky, balls-to-the-wall, in-your-face, kick-ass-and-take-names executive who had descended from the U.S. into Panama? Where had she gone?

The truth was, I didn't know. The hollow face continued to stare back at me.

I dropped my head to my hands. *The truth is I don't really know much of anything anymore.*

CHAPTER 25:
The Morning After

The sound of breaking glass woke me from a deep sleep, followed by a tremor that shook the floor beneath the bed.

A cold sweat swept over me as I jerked upwards. I tuned in to the sounds of the night. *Another earthquake?* We'd had two the year before. I patted the pillow beside me for Joe, but the bed was empty.

Garbled sounds came from the direction of the kitchen. "Joe?" I called out as I grabbed for my robe. "Joe?"

No answer. Lily was already at the bedroom door, whining. My heartbeat thumped in my chest. *Something isn't right.* I could feel a cold certainty in my stomach.

As I came through the door to the kitchen, I called again. "Joe?"

Out of the corner of my eye, my husband's size 13 feet stuck out next to the TV. "Joe!"

I raced to him, Lily hot on my heels. She reached Joe first, standing over his form where he lay sprawled out, naked and motionless. She dropped her nose down to his face, sniffing.

"Joe!" My feet skidded on the tile as I hit some sort of liquid. I grabbed a chair to catch myself. In a split second, my eyes scanned the scene: Lily's ceramic water bowl on its side, my husband sprawled next to the kitchen counter, his body convulsing. Blood spurted from a golf ball sized protrusion on his temple.

"Joe!" I screamed in what suddenly seemed like slow motion. His body continued to contort as I knelt beside him. Blood was pooling around his head as his head jerked side to side. "Fuck! What do I do? What do I do?"

The emergency training I had taken years ago surfaced. *Assess the situation: Fall with impact to the head. Broken glass. Body seizing. Danger of broken neck? Secure the head.* I was taking deep breaths to stabilize my overwhelmed thoughts when some semblance of sanity took over and I was able to do a reasonable assessment.

Is the victim conscious? "Joe." I patted his cheek. "Joe, can you hear me?" I grabbed his jaw in my other hand to stop the jerking, careful not to stress his neck. "Can you hear me, Joe?" The heat of the night mixed with the fact that the fans seemed to be off produced cascading sweat that dripped off my face onto Joe's.

"Uhhhh." A jerk of his head indicated he did, though his eyes were rolling. I held his head so that he would not wrench his neck as he came to.

"Help me!" The shrill voice was mine. *Place pillows on and around his head.* I scurried sideways on my knees to lift three from the couch. "Stay there, Joe," I said. "Don't move, whatever you do. Please don't move. You might have broken your neck."

I grabbed a clean kitchen towel to mop up the blood spreading across the floor. A second one wasn't enough. I wet the third to dab Joe's forehead to see if I could get a better look at the wound. The stream of blood was turning into a gush. My heart rate was increasing by the second. *Fuck! Fuck! Fuck!*

My hand shook as I reached for the phone on the wall, punching in four digits. "Come on, come on, come on!"

A faint voice picked up. *"Alo?"*

"Buenas noches!" I shouted. *"Ayudame! Le habla la Señora JuliAnne en apartamento 304. El señor se cayó. Necesito una ambulancia!"*

"Como?" The voice was thick from sleep, confused.

"Apartamento 304!" I forced myself to slow down, enunciate. *"Llama… una…ambulancia, por favor! El señor…tuvo…un accidente."*

"Ay!" The voice on the other end snapped to attention. *"Sí, sí, sí. Listo."*

"Me explico?" Did you get it? This was no time for bad translation.

"Sí, sí, sí." Slamming the receiver down, I raced for the bedroom, yanking on the gym suit and tennis shoes I'd worn earlier that evening.

"Passports, passports, passports," I chanted. I ran back to where Joe lay groaning on the floor. The jerking had stilled; his body was quiet and his eyes were closed and his breathing was irregular. "Hang on, Joe. I've called an ambulance."

Not waiting for a response, I pounded back to the closet. Clothes for him. Clothes that will be easy to put on him. Underwear, pajama pants, a t-shirt, his house shoes. I dropped the clothes and his passport on the floor in a pile where I could pick them up all at once.

Lily stood in the hallway, watching me dart from one place to the other, sorting, gathering, collecting in a frenzy.

As I came back to the living room, the reality hit me like a ton of bricks. *We live on the edge of town. How long will it take an ambulance to get here? With this much blood, I don't think I can wait. Is his life in danger? I have to take him in myself.*

Then: *But how do I get him down to the car?* Joe was a looming 6 feet 4 inches and a solid 210 pounds. There was no way I could maneuver him myself.

My brain was in overdrive as I grasped for my house keys and sprinted for the front door. *I need a man. I need a man. I need a man. Someone who will be strong enough to help me get him down to the car.*

Looking back as I put the key in the lock, it hit me that Joe was still naked. The split-second question: *Should I dress him first?* Life or decency? Lily's face was the last thing I saw as I shut the door behind me.

First I knocked on the doors on our floor. "Help! Help!" I cried as I pounded on the three other doors in our hallway, all home to able-bodied men. I went from one to the next, calling out the names of their inhabitants. "Help! Barry! Rusty! Help!"

No one answered.

I flew down the stairs to the next level. My fists pummeled the wood of one door after another there, desperation climbing with the realization that it was almost midnight.

"Help!" I cried. "I need help!"

My brain computed that the front door in these apartments was the farthest point from the master bedrooms. With air conditioning or fans, my shrieks from the front door would be muffled at best.

Repeating another round of pounding on each door did not lead to any response. I descended the stairs again. Here I began anew, pounding, then ringing the bell for a neighbor named Paul. He was a big, strong guy. He could help me. I pounded again, yelling. "Paul! Help me!" My finger pressed the bell, once, twice, three times. I put my ear to the door, waiting.

Footsteps! I banged again. "Paul!" I felt the hesitation on the other side, the pause as he looked at me through the peephole. The door opened.

"JuliAnne?" Paul's eyes widened as he took me in.

"Paul!" I almost jumped on him in my fervor. "Help me! Joe has fallen and I need to get him to the hospital, but I can't get him to the car by myself. Can you please come?"

"Of course, of course!" His face blanched as he nodded. "Give me a second. I'll be right up."

I left the apartment door open so Paul could get in as I began to dress Joe's still body the best I could. Dressing a sack of potatoes and getting limbs into the appropriate places while making sure not to disturb Joe's neck was akin to a miracle at this point.

Paul arrived just as I pulled Joe's underwear up his legs to cover his privates. "Oh, boy," I heard him say as he entered, before he knelt beside me. Lily didn't bark when he entered, sensing the emergency. She paced in the background around the three of us.

As Paul and I finished dressing him and pulled him up off the floor, Joe began to rouse. "What's going on?" he slurred.

"Hang on," I told him. "You've had an accident. Paul's here to help us get you to the car." Unfocused eyes told me my husband was not fully conscious.

Against all odds, we got Joe up and out the door and down to the landing. Paul stayed with him, propped up against the front door as I screamed around the corner with the truck. As I'd grabbed for car keys a moment before, my brain had said, "Truck." It was the only car we could get him into, as tall as he was, especially in this condition.

"Will you be okay going by yourself?" Paul asked as we pushed and pulled Joe's frame into the front seat and secured his seatbelt.

"Yes, yes, yes! Thank you so much." I put the truck in gear, though I wasn't really sure.

The diesel engine roared as we sped off.

Joe began to come out of his shock. Barely lucid amidst the cloud of tequila and sleep meds in his system, his neck rolled toward me from where I had him strapped in.

"And just wheeeere are we going?" Joe was disoriented and drunk.

"You fell and cut your head." I glanced his direction as I navigated the two-ton beast through the dark streets. "Do you remember?" A second glance revealed a glaze over his eyes that held the truth. "I need to have the cut on your head checked out." Now that Joe was semi-alert, my voice took a less sympathetic tone.

Joe's nightly drinking had increased and had become the source of most of our arguments. Joe would protest, with one disclaimer after another, that, in fact, he had everything under control.

As for me, my life showed the strain of his drinking and losing himself to a bottle of tequila or Scotch, with a pronounced lack of memory around what went on in our household almost every evening. Our home life was fast becoming a minefield which often resulted in unwanted advances, coarse words, name-calling, and a wicked anger inside him that had turned this man I adored into some version of a monster. I often slept alone while he passed out on the couch to some TV show. Tonight was no exception, but the ante had just gone up: The man I loved was a danger to himself, and to me, when he drank.

A clumsy hand reached my direction, surprising me. "Nooo..." Garbled words floundered out of his mouth. "I'm fine." His breath filled the car with the rank odor of alcohol. I turned away from him as I sped through the less crowded streets due to the hour. I was relieved not to be tied up in some traffic jam amidst a sea of cars.

The stench of tequila emanating from my husband's body took my breath away. I turned my head back toward the road as anger billowed in my chest. "You are definitely *not* fine," I snapped. My tone was unmistakable; I was fed up.

In his stupor, Joe slurred on in some sort of incoherent rant.

As the tires screeched down one street to another, I balanced my cell on the steering wheel. Thinking ahead, I realized I might need some help once we got to the hospital with language. I dialed my best friend from work, Jackson. By the grace of God, he answered.

Surprise echoed in his voice. "Well, you're up late..."

"Jack," I shouted. "Listen! This is important. Joe's had an accident and we're on our way to the hospital at Paitilla. Can you come?"

Jackson and his boyfriend were on their way home from a late movie. "Of course, we'll meet you there."

At the hospital, tires squealed as I zoomed into the ER entrance. I jumped out and ran inside, where a lone woman sat behind a desk. "Help me, please!" I screamed.

She lifted her eyes from a computer screen, blinking, before she stood up. "*Que?*"

I waved my arms toward the truck. "*Necesito ayuda!* My husband fell.

He's in the car."

Not waiting on her response, I grabbed a wheelchair from beside the entry and bumped it over the uneven surface of the parking lot to where the truck was parked. As I opened the passenger door, an orderly in a white uniform ran to meet me.

"I don't need that," Joe bellowed as I unhooked the seatbelt. But his feet failed him as he got out and he fell into the orderly's arms. Relief overwhelmed me as the orderly took over.

Joe was taken in and put into a hospital bed until the ER doctor could get to him. A nurse came to examine and clean his wound. The minutes crawled by. As we waited, I realized just how tired I was.

As he came out of his stupor, Joe became more and more vocal and belligerent.

"I don't need to be here, JuliAnne," he hissed. "It's just a scratch. I want to go home. I have projects I need to visit in the morning." Joe was anxious and would hardly let anyone attend to him without a fight.

"I don't care what you think," I shot back. "You needed to see a doctor, so we're here and we are staying here until you are okay and you are... cleaned up." It was the truth that I had avoided speaking aloud in our many fights. Joe needed to get sober.

The doctor on call appeared. He spoke English, though none of his staff did. I gave him the condensed version, no details.

As the doctor examined Joe's head, he eyed me. "Tell me what meds he's taking. And by that, I mean other than alcohol?"

Despite his haze, Joe's eyes pierced mine. The shake of his head was almost imperceptible beneath the doctor's fingers, but I saw it. "No," he mouthed as the doctor turned to the nurse for the stitching materials.

I paused, looking sharply at his face, not knowing exactly why Joe did not want to tell the doctor the whole truth and nothing but the truth.

I shook my head back, my eyes hardening as I returned his stare. "Something to sleep and something for pain. Is that right, honey?" I shot a tentative look at Joe, who slumped down into himself with a kind of defeat I had not seen in him before. But his expression didn't stop the torrent of my honesty.

"He takes them every night and has been drinking far more than usual," I said in a kind of hush.

There it was, my Judas moment. Speaking those words aloud filled me with such relief, but at the same time they filled me with the cold clamp of fear. *What would Joe say when we got home?*

"Aha," the doctor said. "That's the reason you're doing as well as you are, then, Mr. Joe."

I looked at the doctor. "What do you mean?" The utter shock on my face made the doctor pause. He could see my confusion.

"If he'd been sober, his body would have tensed up before the impact." The doctor pierced my husband's forehead with a long needle as I cringed. "The substance interactions kept him relaxed, probably saving his life in the end."

A chill ran down my spine, as his words settled into the fog of my brain. I looked at Joe, who was just as speechless as I was.

"I'd like a CAT scan and an MRI before you go home," the doctor said as he tied the final knots. "You'll need to stay here for a while longer," he told Joe.

As my husband's body came out of the trauma and the drug cocktail, his mental stupor also began to wane. And with it, so did his Irish temper. "I don't need a fucking CAT scan, I'm fine!" he thundered. "I want to go home." Joe clamored to get up off the table, though he was barely able to coordinate his intentions.

The doctor and I tried to calm him. "You need to stay still," the man insisted. "You've experienced a major trauma to the head."

But try as we might, Joe refused to stay still. "I want to go *home!*" My normally rational husband was anything but in this instance. His limbs flailed as he continued to yell.

After a few minutes and repeated attempts to subdue him, the doctor threw up his hands before turning to me. "Well, Señora, you'll just have to keep an eye on him then since he won't cooperate." Annoyance played across his features.

My cheeks flushed red as I apologized to the doctor and thanked him for his help. He ticked off the things to watch for, and then Jackson and I loaded Joe up in the truck to go home.

As we crested the hill below our building, the sun broke over the horizon. It was 5 a.m.

By the time I got Joe back upstairs and put to bed, it was 5:30. Once I had wiped up the fragments of the accident scene, I sank into bed beside him and fell asleep even before my head hit the pillow.

Two and a half hours later, my hand screamed out from under the covers to hit the snooze button. *Shit.*

My hand explored the table top in search of my glasses. Settling them on my face, I pried my eyelids open to squint at the clock. An instant headache flooded my temples. The numbers were fuzzy around the edges. *Not a good sign.*

Forcing aching limbs upwards, fatigue hit me like a truck. The room spun for a moment. My feet stumbled over Lily's bed as I made my way toward the closet.

Lily groaned at the disruption before putting her head back on her pillow. *Of course, she's exhausted too.*

When we'd returned a few hours earlier from the hospital, our loyal pup had been sleeping sentry by the front door, waiting.

Moments later, I sat huddled in the living room in last night's gym suit, my hair pulled back from my forehead in a headband, eyes puffy from crying. The wheeze at the back of my throat was the only audible sound in the still air. Muffled noises outside indicated the day had begun for the rest of the world: the piercing calls of the black birds, the dull roar of a neighbor's sports car as it left the garage, the deep baritone of the guard greeting the maids as they arrived one-by-one.

My mind scrolled through the week. *What day is this? Wednesday? Thursday?*

After what seemed an eternity, I turned my head to look at the microwave. *8:10 a.m.*

Tardiness, for Tomas, was unusual. His normal arrival at 8 a.m. on the button came day in, day out like clockwork, an endearing habit unusual in a country of latecomers. It was something I admired most about him.

Tomas' key scraped in the lock. I waited until his hulking form came around the corner, the familiar soft-sided blue lunch bag underneath his arm.

He gave a start when he saw me sitting there. "*Buen dia,* Miss JuliAnne." He recovered before he saw the finger on my lips and redirected into a whisper. "Miss JuliAnne?"

Hugging my arms tight around my body, tears began to cascade down my cheeks. I waved a hand for him to follow me to the balcony.

Lunch bag still in hand, he followed me through the glass doors. Lily squeezed in between his legs as he turned his body sideways to cross the threshold.

Sliding the door closed without a sound, I sank onto the nearest wicker chair. Tomas' eyes followed me in silence, his eyes wide with worry. In any other situation, I knew he would be wondering, *What have I done?*

But my tears were signal to something else, since I rarely let him see them. My face crumbled as I attempted words.

"Tomas," I managed to squeak, though that was squelched by the sounds of my sobs slipping from me one after the other a moment later. My body trembled as my hand reached out for the Kleenex box on the table.

"Miss JuliAnne, what happened to you?" The stilted phrase would have made me smile in any other circumstance.

My hand went out for another Kleenex. "Joe had an accident." The voice past my sobs did not sound like mine. "He fell and cut his head open."

Tomas started toward me. "Miss JuliAnne! Is he alright?"

"No, Tomas." My head shook. "He's definitely not. I mean, we're back from the hospital but…" I struggled to inhale, feeling the pressure in my chest release into another wave of sobs.

Tomas raised his hand to chest level, then pulled it up and down, like he was pumping the brakes. "*Tranquila*, Miss JuliAnne. *Tranquila*. Take your time." Tomas had a soft and very compassionate side despite his sheer bulk. His eyes were warm and comforting as I slowly unraveled.

My hands shook as they covered my face, and the torrents of fear and terror that I'd held inside from the past few hours took over. The put-together executive woman Tomas was accustomed to seeing dissolved. But in those next few moments, somehow, it didn't matter.

Even so, I could feel his discomfort, sense the air moving as he shifted in his chair. While he was doing his best to support me in the moment, it was clear that he was out of his depth.

When the storm of emotion passed, I wiped the rivers from my cheeks. I was touched to see only extreme care reflected in those green eyes.

"Where is Mr. Joe now?"

"He's sleeping. We just returned from the hospital a few hours ago." I grabbed another Kleenex and that all but emptied the entire box of tissues.

Tomas' eyes widened again. "And he is fine, Miss JuliAnne?"

"Not really, Tomas. He had to get stitches in his head." I drew a line across my brow under the hairline, to show him where.

"Oh, man."

Oh, man, indeed. Scenes from the night before played out in my brain like a bad movie. I didn't focus on details, just the high points, though the reality of my husband's drinking habits was no secret to the man in front of me. Indeed, it was Tomas who bought the liquor every week. Even so, I felt embarrassed as if this truth would stain what he must think of us.

Tomas' hands remained clasped in front of him as I concluded the story, his eyes grave. "I am here for you, Miss JuliAnne. What do you need?"

My chest heaved with fatigue. "I'm not going to work today, Tomas. I need to keep an eye on Mr. Joe. Can you take care of Lily, and I'll call you when I need you?"

"Stand by me," Tomas said, coming to his feet as I stood up.

"Thank you, Tomas." I looked into his green eyes and nodded, though his words didn't really make sense. "Thank you."

"Come on, Lily," he said, heading back inside.

I watched as Lily pranced around him to get to where her leash hung. A moment later, the front door opened and closed and they were gone. I stood in the room alone, feeling the weight of the crisis seep into my body, leaving me weak and exhausted. But exhaustion was now my staple emotion since having moved to Panama. The work with men who seemed to have little respect for me, and now my disintegrating marriage, was taking a toll that would lead me to understand more about myself than I ever wanted to know. I would have to tackle Joe's drinking another day. But after the episode the night before, it needed to be sooner rather than later.

I slid the glass door closed with a sigh, sank back into the couch, and covered my face with my hands.

CHAPTER 26:
Turmoil

I slammed down the phone with the force of a tsunami. The crash of the receiver bounced off the handset and ricocheted down the hall. My staff jumped, looking at one another in dismay.

A moment later, I threw open my door, high heels screaming down the hall toward the main entrance as fast as my legs could carry me. Ana Maria and Pedro stared after me, open-mouthed. Ana Maria got up to follow, but Pedro motioned for her to sit down. She gave him a look to remember and then ran after me anyway.

"Did she take an umbrella?" The receptionist was frozen to her seat, eyes like platters. She'd never seen my composed, smoother-than-glass-exterior unruffled in 18 months, much less however one would describe the tornado that had just swept past her desk. "*Oye, muchacha!*" Ana Maria snapped her fingers in front of the girl's face as she repeated the question. "Did she take an umbrella or not?"

The girl shook her head.

Setting her face into a thin line, the Panamanian woman grabbed two of the umbrellas kept by the front door in an elegant stand for visitors, and opened the door.

The force of the incoming storm blew into the office. Ana Maria struggled to keep her balance as she fought one umbrella open into the wind and she began to descend the stairs. Rain fell in torrents, so thick she couldn't see the sidewalk below. "Here goes," she muttered as she stepped off the bottom step and her four-inch heels were submerged.

Meanwhile, I sat shivering inside my car in the executive's parking area. In my haste to escape, I hadn't even noticed the rain until it was too late. Now, my hair was plastered to my head, my skin soaked to the bone. I reached out a shaking hand to turn the air conditioning to a higher setting. Within moments, the windows of the sedan frosted over, creating a cocoon. I welcomed the moment.

It was one of the few days that I had driven myself to the office. Tomas had called in sick, a rare occurrence. I had grimaced at the thought of traversing the city in the morning's heavy traffic, but now, in retrospect, I saw there had been a reason.

"A reason, a season, a lifetime…," I repeated. "Wasn't that what you always said, Mom?"

My fists pounded the leather steering wheel as Curt's voice emerged again in my ear, screaming across the telephone line, even though he'd only been sitting one floor below me. I shook my head back and forth, trying to rid my ears of his voice. "No, no, no, no no!" Through all my best efforts to rise above and consider the source, there was something about this man that had started to erode my sense of self. With the knack this guy had for making me doubt myself almost daily, it was no wonder I felt I was losing the battle on all fronts…and perhaps, my mind.

A sharp rapping rang out on the passenger window.

I nearly jumped out of my skin. *Shit! Did someone hear me? Could it be Curt himself?* I leaned over and rubbed the humidity away from the window.

Ana Maria peered through. "I brought you this," she said, waving the umbrella and jiggling the door handle. I scrambled to unlock the door.

The thunder of the torrential downpour stilled all conversation as she jumped in and closed the door behind her. I grabbed the umbrellas from her outstretched hand.

"You didn't have to do that," I said, though my eyes shone with appreciation.

Ana Maria wiped her hand over her long locks and slung the water onto the floorboard before looking at me. "Oh, yes I did." She plucked a Kleenex from the box in the console between us.

"You scared the shit out of us, running out like that." She lifted her gaze to my rain-streaked face. "Kind of like you're doing to me now. You look scary!"

My eyes went wide before I burst out laughing as we looked at one another and then simultaneously pulled down the mirrors above us to look at our rain-soaked selves: not a stitch of makeup left, moisture streaming down our faces, hair plastered to our heads. Ana Maria's mirth matched my own. We belly laughed so hard that we could hardly breathe for a few moments.

"Yeah," I stuttered in between the last few giggles. "Sorry about that. I just had to get the hell out of there."

Ana Maria understood. She rolled her eyes skyward. "I know that feeling. Especially when Curt is involved." Her eyes grew somber, regarding me. She reached out to touch my arm. "Is everything alright? Pablo and I…we're really worried about you."

I glanced sideways before lowering my gaze to my hands. My fingers began a nervous dance between my hands: rubbing together, interweaving, separating, then repeating.

Don't do it. Don't confide in her. She loves you, but can she be trusted? Snickety hissed.

But no one ever asks how I'm doing. My jaw began to shake as I struggled to stem the rising tide of emotion. My chin dropped toward my chest as my head shook.

Ana Maria reached her hand over to touch my shoulder. "It's okay. Let it out. And, if you don't want to talk, it's okay. But please know, your secrets are safe with me. But if not with me, I think you need to talk to someone."

My head shot up, my pupils wide.

"Yes," Ana Maria continued, nodding. "I don't know if anyone else can see it behind the veneer you have up most of the time, but I can. And, if you don't start taking better care of yourself, they'll see it too. You don't want that, JuliAnne."

It was my greatest fear: to be seen as vulnerable. *Because then they might think of me as weak and incapable.* With the exception of the day my grandmother had died, I had never cried in front of a subordinate before. I lifted both hands to cover my face, as my shoulders began to shake.

Ana Maria's manicured hand patted my back as if she were comforting a child. "There you go. It's alright."

In that moment I said nothing more about the specifics of that day's battle, but I did let go of all my armor as her kindness touched through to my heart. I felt the weight of the entire experience in Panama cave in on top of me, without worrying about what anyone else would think. The pretense I kept up with my staff…with everyone…came crashing down.

Ana Maria kept her hand on my back until my silent shaking subsided. Though, even if there had been noise, the sound would have been drowned out by the pounding of the rain on the roof. In that single moment, the younger woman became my mother, my confessor, and my friend.

I sensed the ebbing of the emotional tide and raised wet eyes to Ana Maria's serious ones. "Thank you."

She nodded. "Of course."

"No, Ana Maria. I mean it. Thank you. So much." I mustered a sincere smile.

"*De nada*," Ana Maria returned, nodding again. Then, she cocked her head to the right, listening. "The rain is lifting," she said. "I'm going to make a run for the bathroom to get cleaned up."

"Sounds good." I sat back in my seat. Exhaustion was fast replacing the grief on my features.

"Hey," Ana Maria said.

When she didn't say more, I looked up.

"Maybe it's a good idea for you to go home and get some rest." When I opened my mouth to protest, Ana Maria put up a hand. "I'm just saying. Think about it." Her eyes flickered toward the office. "He can wait. In fact, the man *deserves* to wait."

I gave her a wan smile.

The latch on the car door clicked open, then closed, and she was gone.

I exhaled, pondering Ana Maria's parting words. I never left the office unless I was really sick.

But, you are sick.

I shook my head to get the voice out of my head. My mind was relentless in its search of confirmation. *Granted, nothing has been right since I came to Panama and took this job. Everything that was presented to me was a lie. The men I work for are assholes. But, it's my responsibility to do my best and to deliver on what I said I could do.* The familiar rush of my own power surged back into my core at the word "responsibility." For a moment, I returned to the confident, self-assured version of myself I used to know. Yet, the voices of family and culture and experience worked overtime to bring me back in line, back into submission.

Will it ever be enough? Despite the humiliation, the threats, the ping-pong game between the men and Curt's assholeness, will they ever see what a good job I am really doing? Or will it just keep on being the same demands, and never any credit or kudos? Will I ever even hear a thank you?

Curt's voice rang out in my ear, buzzing across my inner telephone line. "I don't care what you think. Just do what I say and get it done by tomorrow." The reality of such control on the part of one man trying to intimidate me suddenly brought me back into my right mind. *Where is the logic in this? This can't be just about me. It's about him! His need to control—to be forceful—to dominate, and I can't control it, much less combat it. Can I? And even if I can, am I up to the task of weathering the storm when the rules of the game are never fully apparen*t?

I didn't have the answers.

I picked up my Blackberry. My fingers flew across the tiny keyboard, buttons clicking under the speed of my delivery. When I finished, I paused for a millisecond, as anxiety churned in my stomach.

"Am I really doing this?" Then my eyes narrowed, and my thumb hit…send.

The next button I pushed was the one that turned the phone off. Then, I leaned forward and started the car. In the silence, a still, quiet strength poured into me. In my head, I knew that I was the captain of my own fate in Panama and by God, I was going to steer my own ship no matter what. But at the moment, this captain needed some rest.

A moment later, my sedan was flying down the highway, back toward the city and our apartment.

CHAPTER 27:
A Walk in the Park

My eyes popped open in the darkness, waiting for my alarm.

It's Saturday.

I knew the time before my eyes read the clock. Fatigue clutched at my body as my mind started to race. *Would it be too much to ask my brain to take a break on weekends?*

When I got up, Lily rose to follow me into the closet. I shut the door behind us, reaching down to scratch behind the dog's clipped ears.

"You ready to go for a walk, Lil?" I asked as I pulled on jogging shorts and tennis shoes.

We exited the bedroom in dim light, crossing dark wooden floors down a long hallway across a dining room. I glanced to the glass facing the patio, with a view to the Panama Canal. Clouds hung low over the park in front of the building.

"Let's see if we can beat the rain, baby girl." I reached for a red leash hanging on the back of the door in a tiny room off the kitchen. "If there's no one else around this morning, we can play catch." I grabbed a couple of new tennis balls and put one of them in my shorts pocket. Lily opened her mouth to take the second, her hind end exploding in wriggles of pleasure.

A moment later, Lily and I were descending a curved staircase down four flights of stairs. The steps were carved out of black granite with brocade accents in white marble, and while beautiful, they were an extravagant design for a building of this size. "*Altos de Amador*," the sign read, as we entered the lobby. It was our third apartment in less than two years.

"*Buenos dias!*" My voice rang out toward the guard as I pulled open a heavy wrought iron door between the lobby and the building's exterior.

"*Buenos dias, Señora.*" A portly guard looked up from his newspaper, his hand raising in a wave. "*Como están?*"

"*Bien, gracias, Señor Roberto. Y usted?*" I liked to call people by their proper names, no matter what job titles they possessed. I didn't adhere to the local custom of treating the help like servants. "People are people," was my motto. "Everyone deserves respect."

Lily and I stepped out into a fine mist. Thunder rolled in the distance. The dog paused and looked up at me.

"Well, I don't care, if you don't care." And off we went.

On most days, we would encounter a few other people jogging or walking on our morning route. But today was Saturday, the first in a series of Panama's annual *Dias Patrias* independence holidays, which took place every November.

"Looks like we'll have the park all to ourselves, baby girl!" I unhooked Lily's leash as we crossed over to a large expanse of green known as the Amador Causeway.

Lily bounded ahead a few steps before turning back to me with expectant eyes.

"Not yet. Let mommy get her exercise and we'll play ball on the other side, once we loop back." I always talked to Lily like she heard and understood every nuance.

I placed the ear bud of my headphones into one ear, winding the other around the strap of my t-shirt. Since we had moved to Panama, I rarely used both buds at the same time—in part because I loved to hear the cacophony of birdcalls as the sun rose above the Pacific, and in part for safety's sake. While Joe didn't like it, I insisted on walking in the early morning before the sun rose. The dim light of these sunrise walks often obscured characters lurking along the periphery of the Causeway, which made me a little nervous. While I'd never had a real problem, other than a little drunken heckling here and there, Panama was known for its propensity for all-nighters and this area was famed for its end-of-the-line party spots.

If someone was coming my way, I wanted to be prepared. This level of hyper-vigilance was one of the survival mechanisms I'd adopted for life in a foreign country. *Though no one ever seems to bother me once they see the stout Doberman by my side.*

I walked in the direction of where Lily had taken a sizeable dump.

"Though no one else in this country seems to get the importance of picking up their own shit, we still do our part, don't we, Lily?" I leaned over and did my duty. Without missing a beat, my hand scooped the pile, tying it within the small black plastic bag. *Now that I think of it, I've gotten pretty darn good at picking up other people's refuse too. Like every day with Curt and Juan Carlos.* I chuckled to myself at the truth in this statement.

"Let's leave the work shit at the office for the holidays, shall we?" Joe's voice rang into my memory from the conversation we had the night before, when we'd been relaying shared war stories at dinner. As usual, most of mine had been about Juan Carlos and Curt and were tinged with rage.

My voice caught in my throat when I saw the fatigue in his eyes. "Of course, baby. I'm sorry." I'd reached out a hand to touch his. A pang of regret flooded me. *When did I get so jaded? So negative? I never used to be like this.* I let go of his hand and sank into the reality of how Panama and this perfect, amazing job I had taken was turning me into a pessimistic naysayer. If Joe was not liking me, I was not liking who I had become even more.

Joe's fingers grasped mine. Brown eyes gazed back into blue. "It's okay. I just wish you could find a way to be happy."

All the vigor of my intense emotion drained away as I reached for my glass of wine. "I'm glad you've found some projects you enjoy, O'Malley, but I'm still just barely keeping my head above water with these guys most days, ya know?"

Joe's work had him intertwined with the same men I worked with—but as a consultant, he could walk away at any time. It was a luxury I did not have as an employee and was fast becoming a point of contention in our conversations.

"All right, all right. Let's just drop it." Joe knew that enough was enough and that he needed to help me find my way back to the opportunity of this moment, the opportunity of this move to a foreign country that had been so inhospitable to me that it made my head spin. He was helpless in making my time with this company better than it was turning out to be, but he knew that he had one magic bullet: loving me, no matter what. He looked up and grabbed my eyes and pulled them toward the smile emerging from his own.

But the pressure in my chest refused to give. I pushed back from the table, escaping to the guest bathroom in the hall for a few minutes. Sitting on the toilet, I'd latched the door, creating a quiet sanctuary for myself.

I'd started putting up a front with Joe the first few months after we had arrived. *It's not fair that he always has to put up with such an unhappy person for a wife. What did he do to deserve this?* As always, I was harder on myself than anyone.

Now, the lump in my throat began to rise again as the first rays of the sunrise began to glitter off the steel of the Bridge of the Americas and rain drops began to fall. *How could such amazing beauty be swallowed up by small-minded, competitive men?* I thought.

No! My feet picked up the pace. *I will not let another moment of my free time be eaten up with this bullshit. Focus, JuliAnne! Back to the present! Seize the moment!*

Lily ran ahead of me, tennis ball still protruding from her mouth, prancing from one side of the street to the other, her nose on a perpetual train of discovery.

"Come on, girl," I called her. "Let's play some ball."

The canine circled back, following me into the center of a large expanse of green as we clomped through puddles with an inch of standing water. It was the rainy season so rain was falling and accumulating every day, sometimes into the night.

At least in these games, I'm the one in charge. "Go!" I yelled—partly at the voice in my head and partly at Lily as the tennis ball left my hand and sailed through the air. Lily sprang into action.

As she retrieved, I turned to throw the other ball beyond me in the opposite direction. She came back at me full-force, paws pounding through the puddles like a horse out of the gate. But as she approached, a strange sound at the last second caused me to look back. My mouth opened in protest, but it was too late. Her massive form slid through the mud like a linebacker, colliding with the back of my knees.

The impact threw me backwards in an aerial somersault. Everything went topsy-turvy as I tumbled skyward and came crashing down, landing on the side of my neck. The crackling sound of electricity pierced through me as my vision went black.

Lily collected the ball 50 yards away before she ran back. Her head went still as her nose surveyed the scene. When I didn't move, she nudged my body. A high-pitched whine left her throat when I didn't move. After several more nudges, she lay down beside me in the mud.

The minutes ticked by as the rain fell. I have no idea how long I laid there, unconscious and alone.

"Lily!" I croaked as I came to, although my voice emerged as a whisper. I raised my matted head to see the dog's form approach me. A warm tongue caressed my cheek.

I reached for the shape of my glasses as if they were on the bedside table at home, but my fingers were met with cold, wet mud. The previous moments began to unfurl in my brain as consciousness returned and adrenaline hit my bloodstream.

I pulled myself up to my elbows, hands exploring the grass around me. *There they are.* The frames of my glasses were bent to one side, but the lenses were intact. Shaking, I placed them on my nose to survey what was going on around me.

The park remained abandoned, a heavy mist hanging low over the grass. My vision began to spin. I realized there was no one to help, anywhere, and I began to panic.

"Lily, my girl." I reached for my dog, who stood beside me, panting. The leash lay coiled a few feet away from me. I retrieved it on hands and knees, wincing at a sharp pain down my back and side. *I have to get home.* Blood rushed to my head as I stood, my vision threatening to go black. Swaying on my feet as my vision began to swim, I bent over to place my hands on my knees. My throat began to tighten as the reality hit me. *I'm losing consciousness.*

Breathe! a voice in my head screamed. *Focus on your breath, JuliAnne.*

I cast my eyes upward, scanning the landscape for the hill where we lived in the distance. *There.* My brain computed. Recognition. *Home. You have to get there. Safe.*

Adrenaline coursed through my veins as an electrical whine buzzed in my ears. I fought the inclination to double over again as sharp jolts of pain stabbed at my neck and my ribs. *I'm not sure I can make it.*

The voice again. *You have to. Focus. Get home.*

The force of my vulnerability hit me as our building in the distance blurred in my vision.

I tugged at Lily's leash. "Baby girl, I need your help," I cried. "Mommy's hurt. You have to get us home."

Lily pulled forward, and I stumbled to follow.

Joe roused from a deep sleep when the front door slammed. He sat up in bed, straining at the sound of feet shuffling down the hall.

Strange. I was always the epitome of quiet.

Lily burst through the closed bedroom door a moment later, her leash dragging behind. Her cold nose assaulted Joe's arm.

"Hey, girl." His hand went out to free her from the leash, but recoiled when it met the wet mud caked around her neck. "What the hell?"

My bent form appeared in the doorway like a shadow. "Joe?" My hair was slicked back with mud. Grass streaked down one side of my face. My clothes were soaked through. My gaze turned in his direction, but my eyes were searching, unfocused.

Joe rushed to me. "Honey!"

All the resolve I had mustered in order to find my way home crumbled when I heard my husband's voice. My body followed suit as I crashed to the floor.

Joe's muscular arms captured my limbs as I collapsed. He drew me onto the end of the bed.

As my skin made contact with the cool sheets, my face contorted with pain.

"Baby, what happened?" His hand cupped my face. "Are you hurt?" Gentle fingers probed me, investigating the bruises and the scrapes on my knees, thighs, and back.

My body began to shake as shock took over. "Lily and I were playing ball in the park."

"Were you attacked?" Joe clenched his jaw.

I struggled to breathe, but the pain in my side cut me short. I shook my head as my hand reached for my ribs and my neck. Joe's hand met mine.

"Honey? Did someone hit you?" I winced as his fingers examined my wounds before lifting my wet shirt to investigate. A deep red bruise splayed across my left side.

My voice quivered. "No, but Lily ran into me in the rain. It flipped me on my head. I blacked out."

"Blacked out?" Joe switched on the bedside lamp, grasping in the drawer for a small flashlight.

"Let me see your pupils." He clicked on the flashlight, focusing the beam in my eyes.

"Honey, you have a concussion." Joe had raised two boys through contact sports. "Your pupils aren't contracting like they should. We need to get you to the hospital. But first, let's get you cleaned up."

Joe pulled me to my feet to guide me to the bathroom, but nausea overtook me. Here we were, again, faced with a hospital visit, but this time it was my turn. "I don't want to go." Joe turned at the sound of my cry. "I'm scared."

"I know, baby. I'm scared too," he said, swabbing my face clean. "But we need to make sure you're all right." He doubled the washcloth over to wipe at my matted hair. "I would never forgive myself if you needed more than I could provide, and I didn't try to get it for you. You know how you felt when you found me on the floor in my own stupor, my head bleeding. You felt helpless and you knew you needed some help. Well, so do I. I need you to come to the hospital with me. Murphy, please."

I heard every word until the end. I started to say something but the room started to spin. The last thing I felt was Joe's hand grabbing me as I hit the floor.

~

My vision blurred as I came to, to the beep-beep-beep of the heart monitor and the smell of antiseptic.

Joe's face appeared in my periphery as if in a cloud, his face clear in the middle and fuzzy around the edges. "Hey." He smoothed the damp hair back from my forehead.

I tried to form the words to ask what had happened, but Joe put a finger to my lips. "Relax. The doctor said it's best if you not try to talk."

"But..." I struggled to sit up as the pain in my left side brought me to a swift halt.

"Whoa there, Nelly." Joe helped me recline in the bed again. "That's bound to hurt, given your injuries, but I'm glad to see you brought your patience with you."

My eyebrows furrowed as my memory scrolled back, full of questions. But as hard as I focused, nothing was coming.

Joe rubbed his thumb across my hairline, chuckling. "I can see your mind computing in there, Nancy Drew. But don't worry, I got this one covered. The doc says you're lucky you only sustained a concussion and some bruised ribs. That was quite a fall you took. You blacked out again after Lily got you home."

Flashes of memory began to explode across my vision like firecrackers, accompanied by a sinking feeling of panic. Our apartment building in the distance. Me trying to walk but feeling my feet drag. Fumbling with my key at the front door of the building. The guard rising to his feet as Lily and I passed, face aghast. The elevator ding as the doors closed behind us. The sign inside: "Dogs are prohibited in the elevator." The images tumbled in, one after another.

I winced as I came back to the present and the pain everywhere in my body.

Joe gave my hand a squeeze. "I brought you to the hospital to be checked out from stem to stern. You're going to be fine."

I closed my eyes at the comfort of his touch. *I'm going to be fine, but are we?* Visions of our fight the night before began to click through my mind like a slide show. Raised voices. The clink of ice cubes as Joe raised one glass after another of tequila to his lips. My protests when he'd roused me in search of intimacy after I'd already gone to sleep. Him crawling into bed in the wee hours after he'd passed out on the couch. A stone landed in my stomach as I turned my eyes back to him now. "And, Lily?"

Joe's eyes softened at our daughter dog's name. "She's fine. Just very worried about you. She's at home."

I tried to smile, but even that hurt. "When can we leave?"

Joe ran his fingers through his unruly locks, still fresh from bed. "They want to keep you the rest of today and tonight for observation."

I opened my mouth to protest, as Joe raised his hand. "I know, I know. But it's what you get for continuing to walk when it's still dark outside. I've told you time and time again, but you just won't listen, will you?"

My face contorted into a frown.

"Murph. I'm sorry." Joe squeezed my fingers. "But, you scared the living shit out of me." A crocodile tear slipped down his cheek. "I know I can't protect you from everything out there," the words caught in his throat before he cleared it. "And, I'm very sorry this happened. You know how much I love you. But sometimes you just gotta listen to me. I listen to you once in a while, ya know." The jest in his voice returned in an attempt to hide the quiver.

I stilled, looking at him.

He did listen to you, Snickety had taken up residence atop the heart machine. *Remember? When he listened to you, and you ended up here in Panama?*

I batted the guilt away. *This is all my fault, isn't it?*

Joe reached back, pulling tissue from the bedside table. He handed one to me and kept one for himself, blowing his nose into it like a trumpet.

A giggle bubbled up from my chest at the noise as I reached my hand for his. He tossed the Kleenex into the trash and came back to my side.

Fingers intertwined, I looked up at my husband and said the only thing that made any sense to me at that moment. "Thank you," I whispered.

Joe's nod was almost imperceptible.

"I'm serious." I squeezed his hand, watching the emotions roll across his grizzled face. "Thank you. For everything."

He nodded again.

"I mean it." Time stood still as we stared, exploring one another's faces like we hadn't seen each other in a very long while.

And in that moment, I felt he understood me. He understood what I was saying. Because my gratitude extended beyond the escapade we had traversed that morning. This was not just about the accident. I was talking about everything. I was talking about Panama.

CHAPTER 28:
The Lullaby

My mouth was moving, though I wasn't aware of it. The tune of a melody was faint upon my lips. Singing in a director's meeting was hardly my *modus operandi*, but the voices of my male counterparts droned on around me, evidence, as usual, that I might as well have been invisible.

How could anyone ever tell you, you are anything less than beautiful? my quiet lips sang.

My eyes appeared to be trained on a spreadsheet opened on my laptop in front of me.

How could anyone ever tell you are less than whole?

Though this was not a song that had been sung to me as a child, Shaina Noll's lyrics reminded me of seeing my infant sister fall asleep in my mother's arms to the soft *click-click-click* of the rocking chair. That glider had been a fixture in the bedroom I shared with my sister when I was 14 years old.

How could anyone fail to notice that your loving is a miracle?

As contentment washed over me in waves, a hot tear splayed down my cheek.

How deeply you're connected to my soul.

"JuliAnne!" Juan Carlos' voice screeched like a needle coming to the end of a record.

My hand came up to cover my mouth in a pretend cough as my pupils brought the big boss into focus. "Yes?"

"Thought we'd lost you for a moment." Juan Carlos' eyes bored into mine. "Where do we stand on this issue?"

"Sorry," I stammered, clicking the pen in my right hand as I straightened up. *Where the hell was I?* "I didn't catch the last part of what you said."

"We were *talking* about the need to amp up our presence at the big trade show next month." Curt's voice lunged out at me from across the table.

The muscles in my neck tensed as I nodded, though I made it a point not to make eye contact with Curt. I turned my chin toward Juan Carlos.

"I presented a strategy to do just that in the board meeting last month as part of this quarter's marketing plan." I fought to keep the anger out of my tone. "In our booth, we just completed new interactive iPad kiosks which will allow attendees to explore our products at their leisure."

Juan Carlos started shaking his head before my sentence was complete. "No, no, no, no, *no*." He wagged a finger in my direction. "Stop."

Acid poured into my stomach as I steeled myself. *Here we go.* "Juan Carlos?"

"I think what Juan Carlos is trying to say…"

It was my turn to put a finger up toward Curt. It was bold, but I didn't care. "Just a second, Curt. I'd really like to hear what Juan Carlos has to say."

Curt's mouth clamped shut as all eyes turned toward Juan Carlos.

Juan Carlos' eyebrow lifted at my offending finger before he peered over his reading glasses.

I used to find this particular habit of his kind of endearing, Snickety nodded toward Juan Carlos from my shoulder. *But now I know it's yet another way for him to deflect and attack.* Throwing me a wink, she uncrossed her legs from where she sat on my shoulder and leaned toward him, beckoning. *We're no longer fooled, Mr. Juan Carlos.*

My face didn't move a muscle as I held Juan Carlos' gaze. *That's right, you mother fucker. Go ahead. Give it to me.*

Juan Carlos blinked, uncertainty flashing across his face for a millisecond before he plunged forward. "Did the board approve the budget for the iPads?"

"They did." My index finger scrolled to the third tab marked "Budget" in the three-ring notebook on the table in front of me. "Would you like to see it?"

Juan Carlos' fingers gestured toward the book. "*Sí*, please."

I pointed at the correct tab as I slid it his way, fighting the urge to shove it. "It's the third one," I said before turning my shoulders back toward my boss. "What was it you had to say, Curt?"

Curt's voice shot out like a serpent, though his eyes never left the screen of the Blackberry in his hands. *Tapping out one of his infamous three word rebuttals, no doubt.* "I'm not sure iPads are going to cut it."

"Cut what exactly, Curt?" My face returned to my computer screen as I tried to hide my contempt.

Curt tossed the Blackberry aside. "Interest people!" he roared. "Get them to sign up for our lists. Buy our products! You know, *sell real estate* which is the reason we're all employed here, JuliAnne, though your staff often seems to forget that." He lifted his head to shoot arrows at me.

"Well, Curt." It was my turn to raise an eyebrow, though my expression remained neutral.

"The statistics from our participation in the last *five* trade shows has indicated an increased amount of traffic in our booth each time. But, as I explained in the last board meeting, unless we're offering an *incentive*, trade shows are not where people actually *purchase*—it's where they discover us, sometimes for the very first time. At trade shows, we're *educating* our future clients to look us up further—perhaps with a visit to the website or the Visitor Center..."

Curt exploded like a volcano. "If we can't get people to buy or lease at a trade show, then why the hell are we doing it?"

My stomach gave a lurch. "Trade shows are another part of our marketing strategy, Curt. It's another place for people to discover and get to know our brand, which will eventually lead to a purchase decision. In marketing terms, we call this process *layering*."

"I don't give a shit about layering!" Spittle flew from Curt's mouth, as his face turned purple.

"I want marketing that results in sales *now*! Not tomorrow, not next week, not next month, not next year. *Now!!!!!*" His fist crashed down on the table, spilling his coffee.

I bit the end of my tongue as I suppressed a smile. *You can lead a horse to water, but you can't make him drink.*

Don't say anything. Snickety's eyes never left Curt's twisted face. *Just inhale and count to five.* She flicked the ash off her cigarette before taking a puff.

I sucked in, feeling the muscles of my chest expand.

The snap of the three-ring binder at Juan Carlos' end of the table interrupted our standoff.

"It seems to me," Juan Carlos removed his glasses and rubbed the bridge of his nose, "that we need something else to really cause people to want to stop by and have a chat. But, JuliAnne's right, Curt, you must market in a number of areas before people really get what you're even selling. The average person has to encounter your brand about 12 times before they even recognize it. Isn't that what the article you showed me said?" he said, turning weary eyes my way. "Wasn't it 12?"

"Yes, 12." My eyes reflected gratitude as relief flooded me, though Snickety's head began to shake. *Beware! Just because he's coming to bat for you at the moment doesn't mean he won't turn on you in two more.*

"I have an idea," the director from our residential department piped up from further down the table. "Why don't we just get some of those models in tight-fitting mini-dresses like everyone else has, and have them be the ones handing out our brochures?"

Y tú, Aurelio? Hope sank like a stone in my stomach. *You're normally the voice of reason at this table.* My head had already started to shake. "That's a bad idea," I replied. "And, here's why." I began to tick off my fingers as I spoke. "A, Everyone else in Panama employs that strategy so we'd be copying them instead of standing on our own two feet; B, having sexy girls in hot little dresses doesn't really have anything to do with being a credible real estate developer; and C, that type of activity doesn't fit with our sophisticated brand."

"But, if it gets people into our booth, then doesn't that achieve what we want?" The deep voice of our CFO rang out from the other end of the table. "Don't we just want to get them in to take our brochures?"

My sigh was audible. *I guess we're going back to the 1980s.* "No, Sebastian, it's not just about how many brochures we give out, because the men at the show who stop by are probably just coming to talk to the girls, and that's not doing anything for us. Plus, statistics show that 85 percent of residential real estate purchases are made by *women* these days, and I for one, don't feel having sexy *chicas* in our booth will be relevant to *them*." I lifted my chin in defiance. "In fact, if anything, those women could find it offensive. We're not selling auto parts."

The fifth man at the table had been quiet until now. "I don't think we have to recreate the wheel. If it's something other developers are doing and it's working for them, we should give it a try."

I snapped my head around as rage unfurled in me. "Gentlemen!" The volume of my voice rose, though my tone was beginning to sound like a plea. "With all due respect, I don't even know why we're talking about this. Having curvy models in skimpy outfits as a way to drive traffic is blatant sexism! And it goes against *everything* we've worked so hard to establish in this market."

Sexism! The word hung in the air like a rebuke. Suddenly, my counterparts could look anywhere but at me.

Whoever speaks first, loses. I held my breath, counting the seconds.

Juan Carlos cleared his throat. "What I'm hearing is that the team thinks it's something you should consider, that's all," he said, his tone almost apologetic. "Of course, no one is saying you absolutely have to do it."

If my gaze had been poison darts, Juan Carlos would have been dead. I bit my tongue to keep myself from responding.

Juan Carlos' day-timer smacked as it closed. "Well, I guess that wraps it up for today," he said.

Notebooks slammed, laptops closed, and papers shuffled as the men in the room scurried out the door like rats in a race. In 30 seconds flat, I was sitting alone.

My ears perked up in the stillness at an unfamiliar sound. *What is that?* It sounded like an old man, gasping and wheezing. I inclined my ear, listening, and then realized—it was *me*. The sound of my breath was coming in sharp, fast rasps. My hand reached up to grasp the middle of my blouse as tension took hold in my chest. I doubled over as pain gripped me, but not before catching a glimpse of the woman in the mirror at the far end of the conference table.

The figure in the reflection caused me to stare, even as I gasped for air. The woman there resembled me but her eyes were vacant, her face thin.

Is this what I've become? I blinked at the mirror as the voices of my mother and Snickety began to cascade, one on top of the other.

Well, what do you expect? For her to look like the Queen of Sheba? She's stressed to the max, for God's sake.

She's the one who wanted to come to this Godforsaken place! Now she has to finish it! But, look at what this place is doing to her! She's aged 10 years in the past 18 months! Her hair has thinned and she's skinny. Look at that valley between her eyes! She doesn't even look like herself!

My hand went up to the pressure building at the center of my temple. "Stop!" I muttered. But I was interrupted as my body sent up a warning flare of its own.

"Oww!"

A sharp pain from the middle of my palm began to emanate up my arm. I looked down at the offending hand to see my knuckles were clenched, the fingers pressed into a fist, throbbing.

As I pried open my fingers, a stream of blood dribbled off my hand, narrowly missing my pant leg. I jumped up as two droplets splashed onto the tile. "What the...?"

I leaned in to take a closer look and there it was: a puncture wound in the shape of a half-moon at the center of my palm.

I grabbed the napkin next to my water bottle and pressed it into the wound to stop the bleeding as my mind started to race. *What happened? Why didn't I feel it?* My eyes darted around the room in search of the culprit before I dropped to my knees in search of a sharp object. *Maybe there's a loose edge or something...I did adjust my chair during the meeting.* I slid fingers along the sides to examine the edges before tucking my head underneath to survey the tile.

But nothing was out of place.

My mind sped up, searching for an answer as I knelt down and brought my eye to the table's edge. *Maybe a metal splinter?*

Nothing.

I came back up, eye-level with my binder, which still lay splayed open to the approved budget. My head began to pound as my hand began to throb. *My notebook?*

I investigated every piece of metal, every edge, every hard surface. Again, nothing.

I returned to my hand. Lifting the tissue, I peered in to examine the pulsing red slash, wiping away the blood to trace the wound with my fingertip. *In the shape of a half-moon...what could possibly...?*

Then, the truth hit me like a ton of bricks as my gaze rested on my fingertips. *Could it...?* As I extended my digits, a rock sank in my stomach. For there it was: a crimson stain beneath the edge of my own ring finger.

I sank back in my chair, still as death, to stare at the reflection in the mirror as the realities flooded in.

The gaunt woman returned my stare.

My hands began a nervous dance as my mind struggled to comprehend. *I did this to myself?*

When you don't respect yourself, there is always a price to pay.

In all areas of my life, the tolls resulting from this move were stacked against me like a house of cards. At any moment, I felt the pressure of them encroaching, ready to fall, threatening to bury me. My throat began to constrict as the slide show of angry faces—Curt, Juan Carlos, Joe—cascaded across my vision.

"No!" I shut my eyes and shook my head. From somewhere deep within my soul, a plea emerged. *If you give me a ticket and a "get out of jail free" card, I can be at the airport in an hour. Please.*

"It's not that simple, JuliAnne." My voice sounded more like my father's than my own. "To give up is to lose." I gritted my teeth as I sprung out of my chair and came to my feet. Gathering my things, I headed for the door. "And, we will never, ever, ever do that, unless it kills us."

CHAPTER 29:
The Advances

Two days later, hinges squealed as I threw my weight against the back door of our advertising agency's office, juggling handbag, briefcase, and a water bottle smudged with lipstick. *Anyone in this country ever heard of WD-40?*

Catapulting from the stairwell like a cannon, I scrambled to move beyond the doorway, knowing Ana Maria would make her exit any moment.

"*Sí, por eso.*" The Latina's voice preceded her before her body was spit out, like Jonah from the whale.

We stood for a moment, blinded by the blaze of sunlight before the heavy door slammed behind us. The force of it caused Ana Maria to teeter on her high heels.

Another reason to wear flats, I thought as I pried my sunglasses open with my teeth, observing my counterpart with the Blackberry glued to her ear. *Panamanian women and their fuck-me shoes. City-goers wear them everywhere except the beach.*

A giant purse dropped to the concrete as Ana Maria took the phone from her ear and pushed end. "Geez," she said, craning her neck in either direction. "Where are we?"

Two lanes strewn with bottles and candy wrappers down the narrow alley resembled the trailer parks in Arkansas I'd known as a kid, and not the backside of the flashy advertising office we'd just left.

"I'm not sure." I tiptoed onto a patch of grass where a stair should have joined the blacktop but didn't. My attempts to peer around the parking garage were unsuccessful. "I think we're over there." I pointed with my chin since my arms were full of binders.

It was on rare occasions that I drove myself into the city, but Tomas' girlfriend had reported him ill that morning, so I'd gritted my teeth and gotten behind the wheel.

"One sec." I placed a manila folder between my lips, juggling three large binders in one hand as I searched for my keys with the other. As I plundered my handbag, a convertible peeled around the corner, blaring Don Henley's "Boys of Summer."

Beep beep! The horn shrilled as the driver swung the car wide into the intersection.

"Watch out!" shrieked Ana Maria as I looked up a millisecond before the chrome bumper came within inches of our knees. We jumped back.

"Jesus!" I wobbled under the weight of my burden, struggling to catch my balance. The car slid past, the driver giving us a one-handed salute as he sailed past. Our surprised reflections reflected in his dark sunglasses. "What nerve!"

"Some people!" The smooth skin on Ana Maria's brow crinkled as the car zoomed down the lane. "But even so, what a ride!" She smoothed her hair as she stared after the disappearing coupe. "Wait…was that David from Alta Vista?"

"Oh, Lord, I hope not," I shuddered. David was the gregarious owner of another vendor of ours, whose office was on the same street. The tenor of my voice rose an octave. "But just in case, let's step on it!" I clattered across the street. "Come on!"

As if on cue, brakes squealed.

"Hurry!" I pointed my shoes toward the side street as gravel splattered and the Porsche whipped into a U-turn.

Ana Maria stood motionless, fiddling with her sunglasses.

"Come on, come on!" I hissed over my shoulder as the car barreled back toward us.

"Are we in high school or something?" Ana Maria grinned as the driver slammed to a stop in the street between us.

"*Buenos dias, señoritas,*" David shouted above the din of the music, white teeth gleaming against a perfect tan. His hand touched his forehead in a mock salute before he reached for the radio dial.

"*Hola,* David." Ana Maria leaned over the door of the convertible to offer him her cheek.

I struggled to keep the grimace off my face as David turned my way, expectant.

"*Buenas*, David." I fought the urge to lunge at him, though my tone could have frozen ice cream. *The last thing you'll be getting from me is a kiss, you mother fucker.*

"Hello, Ju-lee-ann-ee," David said in a sing-song voice as he tugged his sunglasses from his forehead.

I watched as his eyes roamed up and down the length of my body. "I was struck by your beauty as I passed," he leered. "So, I had to come back and say *hola*."

Bile rose in my throat as Ana Maria purred. "Oh, that's so nice. Gracias, David. It's good to see you, too."

I interrupted her coos by clearing my throat. "Ana Maria, we've got to go."

"Of course, of course." David extended a hand in my direction, smiling. "I'm looking forward to our lunch real soon, Ju-lee-ann-ee."

The only move I made was to turn my back and start walking.

He withdrew his hand before lowering his sunglasses. His gloved hand caressed the gear shaft before he shoved the car into reverse and he peeled away.

Ana Maria scowled as she caught up to me. "What was all that about?"

"The guy's a fucking asshole," I retorted, my thumb pressing the remote to unlock the Audi. *And a sexual predator that's getting away with it because you haven't said anything,* Snickety accused as a clamp suddenly seemed to tighten around my chest. I stumbled as the breath left my body, wincing as I doubled over. Opening the back door was a perfect cover for the hand I clutched to my chest. I shoved my bags into the floorboard before pausing, hands on my knees, panting. *Breathe, JuliAnne, breathe.*

"Really?" Ana Maria dropped her load, piece by piece into the backseat on the other side. "It seems to me he just has a thing for you." Fingers smoothed the length of her hair and the seat of her dress before her head disappeared into the front seat.

I felt the gag reflex rise in my throat as I fought to regain my composure. *It was certainly more than that.* With it, the pressure in my chest alleviated a touch. I shook my head to make the cough sound like a chuckle. Sinking into the front seat, I unscrewed the bottle cap on my water, hoping Ana Maria wouldn't notice my hands were shaking. I lifted the bottle to my lips and drank. "Well." I cast my eyes toward her, though I would not meet her gaze. "That may be, but he is very aggressive in the way he shows it."

"I'll say," she snorted.

I gave her a sideways glance as the engine roared to life. "What's so funny?"

Ana Maria's giggle rose in her throat. "Oh, don't worry. I'm not laughing at you." She shook her head. "No, definitely, not at *you*. It's *him*." Her torso shook as she pulled the door closed. "That idiot acted like he was 17 back there...whipping his car around to zoom back and ask you to the prom or something. What a sight!" Tears rolled down her cheeks.

I tried looking attentive to her humor but I was too focused on my breathing and regaining some composure. A shudder ran up my spine as I eased the car out of the parking slip. "I hope I never see him again."

Ana Maria stopped laughing. "Really, JuliAnne?" The smile left her face. "Was it that bad?"

A pit formed in my stomach as I rewound to the previous week's experience in David's office.

A cold wave of fear washed over me as the scene rolled.

"Yes," I said, my eyes never leaving the road. "It was."

~

"*Buenas.*" A voice crackled through the small box that had been stuccoed to the side of the building. The audio was so faint, I had to lean in to hear it.

"*La Señora* JuliAnne Murphy," I said, smoothing the back of my hair where the humidity had been messing with me all morning.

"*Disculpe?* What's that?" My sigh was audible, as I leaned in closer. *Do any of these stupid things ever work?* "*La Señora* JuliAnne Murphy," I shouted. "*Para un reunión con el jefe!*"

A buzz followed by the sound of metal on metal signaled the door had unlocked.

"Previously on Law & Order," I chuckled before yanking on the steel door. In Panama in 2009, this level of security was the norm; every office had it. The clank of metal on metal always made me feel like I was walking into a maximum-security facility.

My bangs blew backwards as a blast of ice cold air greeted me, and my vision was assaulted by large block letters on the floor in various shades of pink and blue. *Bienvenidos a The gency*.

Gency? The editor in me did a double take. *Of course.* An empty space at the beginning of the word "gency" looked like an A. *A-gency.* Turning the corner, I batted away my internal banter about the importance of first impressions.

"*Buenas.*" I had adopted the local custom of announcing myself every time I entered a room. In Panama, it didn't seem to matter if anyone else was present.

"*Buenas.*" The high-pitched whine from the intercom took shape in the form of a young female face behind a glass façade.

"I'm here for an eight o'clock with David and Mario," I said as I approached. My voice faltered, however, when an enormous set of breasts accosted my vision. *Jesus.* The young, nubile skin squeezed into orange nylon made it virtually impossible to look elsewhere. I pulled my business card from its monogrammed silver case and extended it toward the boobs.

"JuliAnne Murphy," I said, forcing myself to meet her eyes. The prevalence of near-nudity of the upper halves of female bodies in offices all over Panama never failed to surprise me.

"*Sí.*" She picked up a handset before waving a purple manicured nail and motioning toward some leather chairs. "*Momentito.*"

I crossed over, parking myself on the chair closest to the inner hallway. *Ana Maria must be late*, I thought, stealing a glance at my watch.

"Ju-lee-ann-ee." Footsteps pounded the hallway. Though I couldn't see him, I knew the sing-song voice belonged to David, who owned and operated the firm.

My face broke into a grin. David was one of the few people I'd met in Panama with whom I'd felt an instant affinity: he was sophisticated, educated, and engaging. Our rapport had been almost instantaneous. David had worked in Los Angeles for years with heavy-hitting professionals in the entertainment industry. His use of the English language rivaled mine, though he was humble enough to admit that he hadn't used it in years.

David's experience, having lived in the U.S. for many years, gave him the pedigree many others in Panama claimed they had and it didn't hurt that David was—as my grandmother used to say—easy on the eyes. His once blonde hair had long turned white, but he wore it with pride. He eschewed the all-too-common slicked back Latino look and allowed his natural curls to wave around the nape of his collar. Here was a man who reveled in his experience instead of trying to hide behind hair color and tight pants. Talking to him was a tall drink of water in this land of big-titted secretaries and loud-talking assholes.

"David," I said as he took ahold of my biceps and kissed both my cheeks. "How are you?"

"How are *you?*" Blue eyes beamed from behind horn-rimmed glasses. "Please." With a slight bow, he presented the hallway as if it were a red carpet.

My cheeks stained with the slightest hint of rose. The physical familiarity in this country caused me pause, especially with men. Coming from a culture where the handshake was the rule, this habit of kissing strangers was a big stretch. And, as the line of "appropriate" varied from person to person, the demarcation between chivalry and impropriety was often hard to delineate. *Relax*, I constantly reminded myself. *Don't be so uptight.*

Still, cultural upbringing died hard.

I fought the urge to stiffen as David's palm came to rest at the small of my back. "Ana Maria should be here any moment," I stammered, attempting to walk faster and lose the man's hand. *This does not feel normal.* "We're looking forward to seeing what you guys have for us."

"Of course, of course." David's voice washed over me like velvet as he followed me down a long hallway to his office. "Come in, come in, welcome!"

My pupils widened as he opened the door to reveal a room the size of an Olympic swimming pool with a multitude of sitting areas created by the way the furniture was placed. In one, a mahogany desk took center stage in front of a bank of windows facing into the treetops. In another, floral brocade adorned three overstuffed couches circa a country club in 1990. In yet another, a monstrous pirate's chest served as a coffee table. Windows and walls on all sides were draped in heavy velvet curtains that hung to the floor.

"Wow." The word slipped out before I could bite my tongue.

Don't act like the girl from Arkansas, Snickety reminded. *You're a high-ranking executive, for God's sake.*

David pretended not to notice. "Sit down, sit down," he said with a gentle push in the direction of the couch before he turned to close the door.

Uncertainty flashed across my face as I looked around. *Most appropriate place to sit: on the couch? Leather chair facing his desk? How many others are coming?*

"I like your gargoyles." I ducked my chin to cover a smile. I settled my things into the corner of one of the immense floral couches before sinking into it myself.

"Oh, yes, those are from Italy…Rome, in fact." David's chest swelled before a quiet knock caused him to do a U-turn. "*Sí?*"

"Would you like something?" David inquired as a woman in a polyester pants suit stepped in, balancing crystal glasses atop a polished silver tray.

I nodded. "*Cappuchino, por favor.*" I smiled at the woman. "*Gracias, Señora.*"

The woman gave a silent nod, keeping her eyes downcast. A moment later came the familiar scrape of metal on metal. The hair on the back of my neck stood up. *Why is he closing the door?* I raised my eyes only to see my host adjusting his silk trousers at the crotch. *Oh, jeez.*

"Some music?" David asked from the massive desk as a melody came to life from speakers around the room. "Let's relax a little bit until the others arrive. Do you like classical?"

Strange. The thought bubble rose above me like a balloon before I pushed it away. "Sure," I said, flipping my wrist to bring my watch into view. "I guess everyone is running a little late then?"

"Well, you know." David's perfect teeth shone against tan skin as he tucked an errant curl behind his ear. "It's Panama."

I nodded, eyes focused on my Blackberry, checking to see if Ana Maria had called. "So, I've learned." *It's so unlike her to be this late.*

"We'll just wait for them then." David came to sit beside me, his leg almost touching mine. My back straightened at the near contact as a flash of warmth ran down my spine. *What is he doing?*

"Oh, I thought you were sitting here." I patted the carved arm of the *Game of Thrones* spectacle to my right. "Let me move over."

"No, no, no," David reached out a manicured hand to pat my knee. "It's fine. Stay, stay. While we're waiting, we'll get to know one another."

I fought the urge to squirm as alarm bells began to sound in my head. My chest tightened. Forcing my spine even straighter, I cleared my throat. "Uh, David…"

"Are you married?" David interrupted as he took my hand to examine the stainless steel on my ring finger. "This is such a beautiful ring."

"Yes." I lowered my eyes to the ring I had personally designed. "I am and to a great guy. Just recently, in fact."

"Really?" David lifted an eyebrow as he turned my palm over to trace the Band-Aid at its center. "And what happened here?"

I jerked my hand back, color rising to my face. "Nothing," I stammered. "An accident."

David leaned back and let the plushness of the cushions envelope him. His hand came to caress the bottom of my skull. "And do you have any *ninos*?"

"No kids!" I rang out as I leaned forward. "And please don't get the wrong idea, David. I have no interest in you other than as a colleague."

David leaned forward to where I sat, his silk shirt gapped open, affording a front row view of his chest down to his navel. A few tufts of gray hair on otherwise smooth skin weaved their way around a long gold chain bearing an image of the Virgin Mary.

"Oh, that's too bad." As David's fingertips grazed the top of my left ear, the alarm bells in my muscles began to scream. Slamming my water glass to the table, I brushed his hand away. "Hey!" I turned toward him, panic rising in my chest. "What do you think you're doing?"

"I just want to get to know you," David's voice purred, his eyes sweeping across the outline of my breasts. "You're a beautiful woman. We need to have lunch sometime, just the two of us."

My voice raised an octave as my heart pounded out of my chest. "David." I turned to face him. "I told you. I'm a married woman. I'm happy to go to lunch, but only if the entire team goes along. We are doing business here, nothing more."

David leaned toward me so fast that his chest came to touch mine. I tumbled back on the couch in an effort to escape him, but he was faster and bigger than me, and in the blink of an eye, he had pushed himself on top of me.

"Stop it!" I pushed against him, though he outweighed me by at least 100 pounds. "What the hell do you think you're doing?"

"What I've wanted to do since the moment I saw you," his voice sneered as he yanked open my blouse and reached his fingers underneath my bra toward my nipple.

"David!" I shrieked. "Get the fuck off me!" I shoved hard against his frame, kneeing him in the groin. "Help!" I screamed as I scrambled off the couch to my knees. But as I struggled upwards toward the velvet curtains and the strains of Mozart, a heavy realization sank in. *Can anyone even hear me?*

David's hand caught my ankle, pulling me back down. "So, you're a fighter, are you?" The cackle that left his throat was pure evil. "I like that."

Just then, a knock came at the door. As if nothing out of the ordinary had happened, David lifted his head and shouted. "*Sí! Voy!*" Then, he forced his tongue into my mouth before releasing me. "Saved by the bell, I guess." He winked as he pushed himself up.

"Fuck you, you prick!" I wiped my lips with the back of my hand as I scrambled upwards toward the sofa, struggling to wriggle my bra back in place and tuck my blouse into my skirt. "Since when does no not mean no, you prick! I told you I'm married!" I wanted to explode at him, but I was afraid of who might be at the door.

"I'm married, too." He tossed the words over his shoulder as he strode for the door. "But what does that have to do with anything?" I heard the deadlock disengage a moment before he cracked the door. "*Sí?*"

The *empleada* stood there, two steaming cups atop a silver tray. David stepped back for her to pass.

I reached for my phone as I clamored to my feet, hoping I'd remedied my disheveled appearance. *I have to get out of here.*

David turned toward me, sensing my departure as a man's profile appeared in the doorway.

"Hey!" the man said, giving David's shoulder a punch. "What's up? Everyone's waiting for you in the conference room."

"Mario!" I shrieked, sprinting across the room toward the shorter, fatter version of my predator. "How are you?" My fingers reached out for the blue oxford at his elbow like a life preserver before I thrust my cheek at him.

"JuliAnne." Mario took a step backwards. "I didn't know you were here." He leaned in to give me a peck, narrowing blue eyes at his brother. "Good to see you. We were wondering where you were. Ana Maria arrived 20 minutes ago."

Color rose to my cheeks as I pushed past David to collect my things. "Really? I understood we were meeting in here. That's what David told me." It was an accusation, not a statement. My hands shook as I returned to the couch to toss my notebook and pen into my bag. "Let's go then." I took off down the hall, chest heaving, when I realized I had no idea where I was going. Turning back, I caught Mario arching an eyebrow at David.

"Mozart, huh?" he teased before punching David's shoulder with a wink and heading my way.

"Just give me five and I'll be there," David called after us.

Goosebumps crawled up my spine as my stomach heaved.

Five minutes later, Mario and I were settled in the conference room with the rest of the team and the meeting had started. Every time the door swung on its hinges, my breath caught in my throat.

As I sat there listening to the presentation, panic and surprise began to blossom into rage. *Did that even happen? It happened so fast! Mother fucker. I swear to God if that piece of shit comes in here, I'm going to go after him or come unglued. And probably both!*

But, time and time again, when the door swung wide, it was just the *empleada*, hands laden with more refreshments.

Needless to say, David never joined us.

My heart didn't stop racing until I got home that night.

David's calls to my cell phone would interrupt my evening hours for weeks to come.

"He's an ass, this guy," I replied when Joe queried why I kept avoiding my phone. "I've been crystal clear and yet he won't take a hint. It's not even worth discussing."

My husband raised his eyebrow. "It doesn't sound like you made it clear enough."

"Don't worry," I snapped. "I think I've got it handled." *But, do I?*

Guilt flooded my chest as I pushed the replay of the scene into the furthest corner of my mind. *Was there something I should have done differently?*

Never mind, Snickety waved a dismissive hand. *We have bigger fish to fry at the moment…much bigger fish.*

For whatever reason, I never told Joe the entire story because I was afraid…but of what?

What's the point? Snickety again. *You have enough issues without whining about this guy. The good news is nothing really happened.*

So, I held my tongue, my silence yet another betrayal.

CHAPTER 30:
The Doctor

"Wait here please." The nurse pushed back a retractable screen to reveal an exam room the size of a postage stamp.

"*Listo*," I replied, eyeing her lime green Crocs and the white triangular contraption that graced her head. The only nurse's hat I had ever seen like this one was one my mother wore in her graduation photo from nursing school. *And that was 1967.*

I scanned the tiny space in search of a place for my handbag, but found none. "*Y mi cartera?*" I held out the leather satchel. Panamanians believed that if you placed your bag on the floor, all the money would run out. I eschewed the silly notion but chose to keep my bag atop something since most floors in Panama left much to be desired in terms of cleanliness.

The orderly nodded toward a small hook on the side of a metal cabinet as she unwound a blood pressure cuff.

The clamp over my chest began its familiar squeezing as I sank into the chair. The fingers of my right hand clenched the front of my gown.

"*Tiene miedo?*" Her question sliced through me as she swabbed the inside of my elbow with a cotton ball. *Zing.*

My chin ducked ever so slightly. Her gloved hand patted the inside of my arm.

"*No te preocupes*," she said as the cold hypodermic entered my vein. "Don't worry."

The dark ruby of my blood spilled into one vial and then another. My face must have blanched as the nurse reached for a third. "*Tranquila*," she said. "It's the last."

A moment later, the *tick tick tick* of the wall clock above the narrow examination table was my only companion. My gaze followed the second hand as it swept around the dial. *Inhale,* I counted, forcing air into my chest. *Exhale. Inhale. Exhale.* The heart palpitations had started a month before. The first time they had struck, I'd been holding a staff meeting when a sharp pain pierced so deep behind my breastbone, I'd had to double over in my chair.

"Are you all right?" Ana Maria had bent her dark head toward mine.

"Water," I gasped as my heart began to race. "Just get me some water."

After two consecutive weeks of sleepless nights worrying that I was headed for a heart attack, Joe had insisted I see a specialist.

"Just to be sure," he said, rubbing my back one night when I lay covered in sweat, my breath coming in short pants. "I'm sure it's stress, but you need to be certain."

Footsteps squeaked to a stop outside my cubicle, heralding the physician's arrival. Polished black shoes came into view a few feet away before an invisible hand pulled back the folding door to reveal a smiling face.

"Hello," the man said in my direction, consulting the top of the clipboard. "Miss…JuliAnne." He extended his hand. "I'm Doctor Gonzalez."

"*Mucho gusto.*" Sweat slung upwards as I reached toward him. "*Disculpe.*" My face colored as I withdrew to wipe my palm on my gown. The doctor smiled when I re-extended the second time.

"*Español* or English?" he asked, wheeling a small stool from beneath the exam table, placing it in front of me.

"English is better," I said. "*Por favor.*"

"All right then." His eyes returned to his clipboard. "Mm-hmm." He nodded, flipping to a second page. "The test results from last week show that you are healthy, but your heart is under strain." His eyes squinted at me. "Are you experiencing a high level of stress?"

I nodded. *You could call it that.* As Curt's huffing and puffing appeared in my mind's eye, I winced.

The doctor's eyes scanned the length and width of my body.

"What we're doing today is an echocardiogram to confirm last week's test results were accurate, and that there's no damage of any kind to your heart." His gaze lingered a moment at the opening where my breasts hung braless before returning to my face. "Any questions?"

My face burned. "I don't think so."

"Ever had one of these before?" He tapped a machine behind him, from which snaked a bevy of dials and wires. I shook my head.

"All right then," he said, rising to his feet. "Get on up here and give me your best *Sports Illustrated* swimsuit edition pose." He let out a loud guffaw as his hand patted the exam table.

My smile froze as my mind began to race. *Where is the nurse?*

"Oh, I'm just kidding." The doctor's tone turned jovial when he saw my face as he pulled out a step stool. "But it's not every day I get to treat a pretty girl, you know. I have to make the most of it."

"Uh." I teetered on the stool, my fist still clenched at the front of my gown as I climbed up, attempting to maintain some level of decency. "Okay."

"Sí," he continued. "Most of my patients are a bunch of old guys," he winked, plugging the stethoscope into his ears. "So, your visit is a real treat."

Sirens began to blare in my head. I glanced toward the retractable door. *Should I ask about the nurse?* My head was spinning with all that had happened a few days prior to this routine exam that was once again, like with David, turning out to be another offense.

The doctor came to stand in front of me, stethoscope in hand. As the cold diaphragm found the center of my shoulder blades on my back, I bristled. A moment later, his fingers moved around to my front and tugged the gap of my gown open without a word to reveal my breastbone.

"Mm hmm," he said, pulling back to jot down a note on the clipboard. "You have a little bit of an arrhythmia." Turning back to me, the smile left his face. "Now what can we do to lower your anxiety level?"

As he began to attach a number of electrodes in and around my breasts, a cold sweat broke out on the back of my neck. *Perhaps men like you could stop harassing me for starters.* I narrowed my eyes, struggling to keep my face neutral. *I can't get a break anywhere I go in this country. None of you seem to have any fucking manners!*

The doctor kept on smiling. "All right. Lie back, face me, and recline on this arm," he touched the inside of my left arm, "and we'll get started."

Inhale. Exhale. I lowered to the table, turning to face him as blood continued to pound in my ears.

"And, here we go." He settled back to the stool before punching a square red button. The machine began to whir. "Do your best to relax."

As if on cue, the retractable door whipped open and the profile of a nurse's cap appeared. I exhaled as my body started to shiver. *Thank God.*

"That's right," the doctor said, glancing over his shoulder as the nurse came to take the clipboard from his hand. "Just keep taking deep breaths and relaxing."

As the nurse's face came into view, my lower lip began to quiver. *Thank you.*

"She's a little nervous, this one," the doctor said in Spanish. He smiled, patting my thigh. "*Tranquila.* It's okay."

But it was he who didn't understand. It wasn't my heart condition that had caused me to crumble; it was this guardian angel in white who now stood sentry at my feet who had saved me from once again collapsing under the scrutiny of men who saw me only for my gender. In that moment, I had realized anew how vulnerable I was, every which way I turned.

CHAPTER 31:
The Diagnosis

"JuliAnne!"

I looked up to see a woman on tiptoe wave above the crowd before a blonde bun began making its way toward me. It dodged one way and then the other to navigate around a crowd of men in black and navy suits. As she came bursting through, her diamond bracelet caught a man's cuff link, causing coffee to slosh out of the man's cup.

Oh, no. Horror flitted across my face, my hand coming to my mouth as the dignitary jumped back to avoid the imminent splash on his expensive tie. Then, *Thank God,* the saucer in his hand caught the spill.

The man lifted a bushy eyebrow as the woman continued toward me, oblivious.

"Patti," I said, taking her by the elbow and dragging her aside. "You almost caused the ambassador to spill coffee on his shirt."

"Did I?" She glanced back toward the short, bearded man who was still staring in our direction. "Oh, bugger!" She waved long nails at him. "Pardon me, Mr. Ambassador!" A nervous hand came up to smooth the back of her hair, a strand of which had come free.

I gave a slight smile as the ambassador lifted his chin to acknowledge the apology before I turned back to Patti. "Everything alright?"

"Yes," Patti stammered. "I mean, no! The chief correspondent for the Canal was supposed to speak in our next panel, and we've just received word he's not coming!"

"Oh, good Lord." I wrinkled my nose. Panamanian dignitaries were famous for showing up late, if they came at all. It made these global conferences much more challenging for local event planners, especially when the audience was composed of international attendees who expected everything to start on time. I scanned the sea of dark suits and the waves of slicked back hair. "Is there anyone else here that can stand in for him?"

I could feel the burn of Patti's gaze before I caught her eye and the blatant meaning in them.

"We were hoping you could," she said.

"Me?" I began to shake my head. "But, Patti, I don't think that's appropriate. I don't even know what the next panel's about; I wasn't even planning to stay."

Patti scanned to the second page of the program on my clipboard. "The panel is entitled 'How Sustainable Development is impacting Panama.'" She paused, biting her lip.

Well, shit. My mind began scrolling through any and all key messages about the project that would be relevant. *I know more than most people about that topic.*

"But." I lifted my palm in protest. "I'm really not prepared…"

"Stop it!" Patti pleaded. "I've seen you speak about Panorama at least a million times in the past two years. You'll be great!" She put a hand on my suit sleeve. "Plus, it's just a panel…"

I sighed as I stared at the pretty face inches from my own.

"Please," she begged. "You of all people know how it would look if I have an empty chair up there. Please JuliAnne, you need to help me out here." Her face registered sincere intent.

God damn it. "All right," I replied as anxiety washed over me. The reality was that a number of executives representing large British companies had flown in from the United Kingdom for this conference. Any exposure for us would be good exposure. "What time do you need me up there?"

Patti consulted her clipboard. "One o'clock, though we're currently running 35 minutes late." She twisted her diamond-encrusted watch around to look at its face. "It's 12:45 now so if you can come to the stage around 1:25, that'd be great."

Nodding, I flinched as the sensation of warm liquid filled my crotch. *Shit.*

"Okay, Patti. I'll do it. Now, if you'll pardon me," I said, as I headed off for the nearest ladies' room.

Inside the safety of the marble-tiled stall, I dropped my handbag, yanked off my suit jacket, and threw it atop the bag on the floor before tussling with the belt and zipper of my cream-colored pants. As the back of my legs hit porcelain, crimson flowed into the commode. *Jesus*, the worry line between my eyes twitched. *Where is all this blood coming from?* I reached in my bag for a tampon.

My period had far exceeded its normal course of five days; today was day 16. When I'd awakened this morning to a pool of blood around my hips, anxiety had clenched my head like a vice. My first inclination had been to stay home and call the doctor, but today was the British Chamber's annual event. With the ambassador's recent request that I join the Chamber board, I pleaded with my body to hang in for a few more hours. It clearly was not listening.

"It won't be long," I whispered as I reached for the string between my legs, "and then we'll stop by the gynecologist's office for that appointment I booked on the way here, I promise."

Everything in place, I flushed the toilet three times to get the bowl clean again.

Watching the blood disappear, Snickety took on a tone I was unaccustomed to hearing. *You're not taking care of yourself, little girl. You can't play Wonder Woman all the time. Pay attention to you, and forget all those assholes. Your body is screaming for help.*

Her words were kind, even compassionate. The softness in her voice surprised me; this inner critic who had always been my nemesis. Caring for myself was not something I was doing with regularity—whatever that meant. I kept taking them on the nose day in and day out from my male counterparts, only to go home and replay their harsh judgments against myself well into the night. I was anything but loving toward the part of me that felt entirely stripped of who I thought I was or toward my body, which was clearly suffering.

I rejoined a colleague at our trade show booth a few minutes later.

"Everything alright?" Madelaine asked, looking up from her cell. "You look a little pale, JuliAnne."

I looked away as I lied through my teeth, "I'm fine, thanks." Color flooded my cheeks, giving me away. "Just a little case of female stuff going on. Thanks for the referral to your physician this morning. I'm planning to go see him this afternoon."

A little case of the female stuff! Snickety screeched as her all-too-brief interlude was replaced with the critical voice I knew. *Can we get real for a moment? You've used five tampons today and it's only just past noon!*

"Ugh." My colleague rolled her eyes. "I hate it when that happens.

Do you need anything?" Her tone of total understanding brought me back from being berated by my own inner voice for being so stupid as to think that all this bleeding was simply going to go away. But, once again, I defaulted to the face I always put forward: capable, unruffled JuliAnne.

"I'm good," I said. "I'm going to get some tea before I have to speak. Want some?"

"No, thanks." Her brown head bowed again to the tiny screen.

Crossing the cream carpet, I walked to the food station and requested a cup of hot water from the attendant adorned in black and white. While he poured, I perused the plethora of tea packets. *Only in England,* I smiled. *Or in this case, when the English come to town.*

"*Gracias.*" I accepted the white cup and saucer from the waiter with a wan smile. A low dull ache had begun in my low abdomen. *That doesn't feel like cramps.* My shoulders shuddered for a moment as a chill wrapped around me. *That's weird.* Leaving the saucer on a table, I cradled the cup between my hands and checked my watch, once again trying to push through all the bodily protests that were mounting.

Ten minutes to kill before I need to put on some lipstick and get ready for the show. I pulled open an immense carved door to stand at the back of the ballroom to listen. A man with a clipped foreign accent was making his closing remarks from behind a glass-encased podium to 150 people or so in the audience.

As I brought the cup to my lips, the napkin I'd wrapped around it fluttered to my feet. As I bent over to retrieve it, a wave of dizziness hit me like a ton of bricks threatening to take me down. My hand went out to the wall as the room began to spin.

No. I clamped my eyelids shut. *Please. Hold on. Just a little more time. Please!!*

When my eyelashes fluttered open, my vision had returned. *All right,* I rose to my feet. *You're fine.* But, to my dismay, I was wrong.

My body had other ideas. As I came erect, another flush of warmth flooded down my thighs. I turned toward the door, grateful that the carpet absorbed the staccato of my heels as I ran for the ladies' room again.

Ten minutes later, I sat, head in hands, awash in sweat in the same stall. The last of my tampons was inside me, and I was out of back-up pads. My lace panties were lined with several layers of folded toilet paper to stem the tide of blood that was insistent.

This was not the best day to wear light-colored pants, Snickety sniffed.

"Please, please, please," I whispered. "Just give me another 45 minutes and I'll be out of here, I promise." I turned my wrist over to look at my watch. *Eight minutes until I need to be up on stage.* I wiped my brow with more toilet paper before I redressed.

A moment later, as I stood at the sink looking into the mirror at my ashen features, another wave of dizziness hit me.

Pull it together, said Snickety. *You can't collapse now. What will people think?*

"You can do this," I said to the blanched face in the mirror, pulling my compact from my handbag. "You can do this. I know you can." I powdered my face before reaching for my lipstick. "Hang with me, JuliAnne. Forty-five more minutes that's all. Power through. You can do this."

Then, taking a deep breath, I took one last look in the mirror and headed for the door.

~

Ding. What floor am I on? I stared up at the panel and saw the light illuminate floor three, an arrow pointing down.

My hand clung to the side rail of the cargo elevator like a claw. At the end of the short session that had stretched into an eternity, the ballroom had emptied and I had waited impatiently in front of three elevators. Though there were never less than 20 people on any elevator in this country, everyone had grown tired of waiting for the fancy one to return.

Now, I counted the seconds as 20 pairs of high heels and wing tips tiptoed around atop a good amount of dust on the cargo elevator floor. *Hurry, please, hurry.*

When it was my turn to extricate myself from the sea of sweating bodies heading to the parking lot, I summoned all my strength to make it the few steps across the expansive lobby to a bank of glass doors facing the valet stand. One doorman opened the door as I stumbled through; another opened the passenger door of my Audi.

"Hi, Miss JuliAnne." Tomas' voice was cheerful as I sank into the car.

"Tomas," I breathed, reaching for a napkin from the glove box. "We're going to Santa Rosa Hospital. I called my doctor and moved my appointment up. They're waiting on me."

Tomas' eyes widened to the size of platters as he maneuvered the car from beneath the hotel's portico onto the street. "Is everything all right, Miss JuliAnne?"

"Not really." I leaned back against the headrest, forehead glistening with sweat.

I felt the sedan lurch as Tomas accelerated to pass three cars in front of him.

"It's fine, Tomas," I said. "*Tranquilo.* It's not an emergency."

"No?" Tomas gave me a sideways glance. "You not look so good, Miss JuliAnne."

"I know, Tomas." I kept my eyes closed as waves of heat washed over me. "That's why I'm going."

"Okay," said Tomas as he eased his foot off the gas. "One moment."

"And Tomas," I said, "when we get there, I need you to park and walk with me upstairs."

There was a long pause. I had never asked Tomas for accompaniment unless I had things to carry. "Okay, Miss JuliAnne."

The car began to accelerate again.

~

"Señor Joe," the receptionist announced before pointing toward a door on her left.

Joe handed his copy of *Time* to Tomas and scrambled to his feet. When he approached, a buzzer sounded and the door clicked open. Joe rushed through.

A nurse in green scrubs greeted him. "*Venga,*" she said, turning on her heels. Joe followed her down a well-lit hallway to the last doorway. "*Aqui esta su esposa,*" the nurse said, pushing open the door.

Joe approached the examination table where I lay, wrapped in linens, a bandage on my left arm.

"Hey, how you doing?" he asked.

Still emerging from a sea of induced haze, I attempted a wan smile. "Hi."

Joe smoothed the wet hair at my temples. "How are you?"

"Hanging in there." My voice was faint, far from the high-powered executive.

"*Lista?*" A kind, oval face appeared on my other side.

"*Sí?*" I asked as the woman pulled me upright to sit. I searched her face for a moment, then she motioned for me to climb down from the exam table where the doctor had performed the surgery.

The room began to spin. I clutched her arm as pain shot up my groin to my stomach. "*Espera, por favor.*"

"Wait," Joe exclaimed, putting up a hand at the nurse. "Why does the doctor want to move you already? What is he doing?" The surgery had only ended 10 minutes earlier. Joe looked bewildered.

I blinked before looking toward the nurse, my brain computing in slow gear. *Of course, he doesn't speak Spanish.* I could hear the words in my head before they came out of my mouth. "*A donde vamos?* Where are you taking me?"

"*Alli.*" Her chin pointed toward the adjacent room. "I just want to take you to where you undressed earlier," she said.

Nothing was making sense. "Maybe they need this room or something."

A sudden storm crossed Joe's face. "Jesus Christ," he blurted. "Can't they give you a few minutes? This is supposed to be the premier hospital in the country! You just had surgery, for God's sake. Where's the doctor?"

In slow motion, my eyes went from side to side, but the doctor was nowhere to be found.

"*Vamos,*" said the nurse, nudging my elbow.

"All right then, let's go," I said, wincing as I eased one leg down and then the other.

The aide helped me take several steps to get out the door and around the corner when pain rippled through my groin, causing me to double over. A stream of dark blood ran down my leg, pooling onto the floor.

"Ow," I said, looking at the nurse before reaching toward my groin as I realized I didn't have any underwear or protection on underneath my gown. "*Señora?*"

"Let's get you to the bed," she said, but my feet dragged as if they were made of clay, refusing to move any faster.

Plodding through the second doorway, I began to sway. "Joe?" I cried as my knees buckled and I fell against the aide.

Joe pushed the nurse out of the way to catch me as I fell.

"Ow!" More blood poured from within me, splashing across the white tile. "Mother fucker."

The nurse appeared nonplussed and continued with her agenda of getting me dressed. Joe would have none of it.

"Come on," Joe grunted as he heaved me up to the exam table. "Work with me, Murphy."

"I'm trying." I gritted my teeth, doubling over. "But I can't do much. It's too high for me."

The aide stood to the side, frozen as Joe's massive size blocked her from intervening.

Once I was secure on the table, I leaned back, covered in sweat with blood trickling down my legs.

"*Señora?*" Joe shouted, glaring at the nurse, pointing to the mess on the floor. "Where is the goddamn doctor?"

She didn't speak Spanish but she seemed to get it. "*Momentito!*" She ducked out of the room.

Joe turned to me, clasping my head in his hands as lines of sweat beaded on my brow. "Hang in there. You're okay. We'll get you home soon now." Suddenly I thought back to how we were when Lily had arrived in Panama, totally riveted on getting her out of an abusive holding tank. We did what it took to free her and take her home for some real care, and in my heart, I knew that once again, Joe was saving one of his girls. But I was useless in my state to help him.

Suddenly, the doctor broke into the room. "Hello, hello, how are we doing?" He shook Joe's hand like it was any other day, before crossing toward me. "Uh oh," he said, glancing down at the bloody footprints his wingtips had tracked across the floor. He pulled up a nearby stool. "Let's take a look here," he said with a smile as if a lot of blood on the floor was the norm.

Glancing at my husband, my brow crinkled as the doctor carefully placed my feet in the stirrups. Even in my post-op hazy state, I felt exposed with the door wide open, and the aide and Joe standing behind him, staring at the mess that had been made. The doctor acted as if this kind of audience was nothing out of the ordinary.

I waved my hand at Joe to close the door.

The doctor lowered his head between my legs, this time with a small light to inspect what may have gone wrong. I winced as he poked and prodded, thankful that the anesthesia was still having some effect.

Joe moved around the table to stand next to my head.

"All normal," the doc said, coming up and removing white gloves spackled with red. "Do you feel well enough to get dressed?"

My head began to swim at the question. "Joe can help me, so, yes. Yes, I want to go home, I mean I can go. The blood is not a new problem, is it?"

The doctor shook his head as if all I had was a toothache. I looked toward my husband, who now had anxiety written all over his face.

Blood and your husband are not a good mix, Snickety said, nodding toward the floor. *Remember he discovered his own mother in a similar state of shock before she had her hysterectomy?*

"I'll see you up front in my office when you're ready," the doctor said as he backed out the door, barking something in Spanish down the hall.

The nurse appeared a moment later with my bag of clothes in one hand and a mop and bucket in the other. I flashed on the show *Outlander* where the main character had been a nurse in the war under barbaric circumstances.

My situation here, in the best hospital in Panama, was a pretty close runner up.

Joe took the bag without a word and waited for her to depart before he closed the door. We struggled against my inertia to get me back in my clothes. I pulled my blouse tight around me, compulsively making sure every button was in place.

A few minutes later, an orderly arrived with a wheelchair. As we exited the lobby, Tomas jumped to his feet. "Hello, Miss JuliAnne," he said in a soft voice.

"Hi Tomas." My voice was faint. I was too tired to meet his eyes.

Tomas shot a glance at Joe, who avoided addressing him at all. Tomas took my handbag that sat limp in my lap. "I carry this for you, Miss JuliAnne."

Isn't it a little uncomfortable for your driver to know you had female surgery? Snickety peered from behind a newspaper. *Of course, you know the gossip mill in this country. I'm sure everyone at the office will know within the hour.* She clucked her tongue. *That is, if they don't already.*

Joe and Tomas opened the double doors to the exit, as the orderly maneuvered the wheelchair down the hall.

At the elevator, Tomas waved him away and took over. "I'll do it," he told the man in Spanish. "And when I'm done, I'll put it in the lobby."

The orderly blinked before he nodded. "*Esta bien.*" Tomas took charge,

As the elevator doors closed, the three of us began our descent to the parking garage and eventually, home. Once they buckled me in the backseat and propped me up with pillows brought from home, Joe got in the front seat next to Tomas. My husband reached behind, searching for my clammy hand. But, before his fingertips touched mine, I was fast asleep.

CHAPTER 32:
The Nightmare

A bloodcurdling scream exploded from my lips.

"Help me." My arms flailed, desperate to latch onto something... anything solid.

But the sound never came. Liquid poured into my mouth, forcing my shrieks backwards. As the force of the pressure plunged down my throat, I choked, my tongue thrusting upwards and outwards.

Water. Is this what it feels like to drown?

A wave of adrenaline hit my bloodstream. *Paddle! Paddle!* came the frantic command from brain to limbs. *Swim, do something!*

I pushed upwards with all my might, attempting to reach the water's surface. But my movements were met with firm pressure. Sizable hands held me down—across my legs, across my torso, at the base of my neck.

I kicked, thrashing to be free, but my opponent's counter movements were bigger, stronger, and quite obviously male.

"She won't get away with it this time." The swirl of the water caused the voice to be chopped into sound waves.

My hands clawed upwards at the faded outline of four faces swimming above me.

"Help!" I screamed again. This time my words broke the surface far above in the form of tiny bubbles.

My chest began to cave as air squeezed from my lungs. My entire body bucked, frantic to break free from my captor, from this Leviathan of Job.

Above, the surface of the water remained still. In fact, the four men didn't seem to notice my plight; they went right on talking amongst themselves, laughing, as if I wasn't there.

Stars swam before my eyes as my vision faded, the life draining from my body. I gave one last struggle as I lost consciousness.

Blackness descended.

"Noooo!" As the scream ripped through the air, I bolted straight up in bed. Still caught in my dream, my fists shot out to pummel the man who kept me submerged. My nails raked down the sides of my neck to shred any remnants of his hold.

But my efforts came up empty. The ropes were gone. The faceless form had dissolved into the night. I scraped my fingertips along the surface of the bed, only to find the softness of the mattress. As I clasped my hand to my chest, I found it was slick with sweat.

I'm not drowning. I closed my eyes, blood pounding in my ears. Clenching my jaw, I pressed my palm into the damp skin at the center of my chest and waited.

My lungs filled with air. *I'm okay.*

Blinking in the darkness, I tried to get my bearings.

But it was so real.

My fingers crawled up to my face, brushing across my eyes, feeling the outline of my nose, the shape of my lips, the dampness of my tears. Relief flooded into my body, as consciousness returned. *Was it just a dream?*

A soft snore rose from Joe's sleeping form. I squinted to make out the shadow of Lily's bed on the floor.

I drew the cotton sheets into bunches between my fingers, willing their 600 thread count softness to protect me. My breathing began to slow.

I am here. Safe. In my home. In my bed.

There's nothing to be afraid of, sweetheart. At the sound of my mother's voice, I burst into tears. Clasping my mouth with my palm, I stumbled out of bed, feeling for my robe on the dresser beside me. The eerie glow of the LED nightlight in the hall directed me.

Stifling my sobs, I pushed through the swinging door to the kitchen. I turned toward the oven, squinting to read the green LED digits.

I had left my glasses next to the bed so I got up close, leaning over the stove to where the numbers seemed to mock me. *Right on time, four eyes.*

It was 3:30 a.m.

The next sob burst out as it surfaced, streaming tears down my neck, soaking my upper chest. I glanced back to make sure the galley door had swung closed behind me. *At least I won't wake him.*

Padding across the wide expanse of the marble floors to the island, I climbed onto the closest of eight barstools, laying my feverish head on the surface of the granite. Stretching my fingers out across the stone, I let its coolness permeate my palms. *Help me.*

The ticking of the wall clock was my only companion. After several minutes, my body stilled and my breathing returned to normal, but I was too tired to get up. Twisting sideways, I stared through floor-to-ceiling windows at the outline of the sleeping city. *Panama nights. The prettiest this city will ever be.*

Only a handful of windows in the buildings closest to ours stood illuminated at this hour. Unfortunately, my midnight rousing had become enough of a habit over the prior months that I could recognize which ones belonged to the laundry facilities and which ones were the maid's rooms.

My eyes sought out the shoreline behind the building next to us. Tiny dots of light flickered along the waterfront, ships waiting in line to traverse the Canal. My ears strained to catch the smash of the waves on the giant rocks at the ocean's edge. *Must be high tide.* Further up the coast, six lanes of coastal highway stretched into the distance, abandoned save a handful of cars zooming in the direction of the airport.

I squinted to bring the skyscrapers beyond the highway into view. Their ghostly outline never failed to impress. *Gotham*, I thought. It was my affectionate name for the dozens of towers that remained dark for the most part, even in the early evening hours. *Money laundering?* I often wondered. *Or just because no one's home?*

Home. A pang of nostalgia caused me to wince. The word rose like a beacon in the fog as images of our former life in the Mile High City began to cycle through.

What month is it? The gears of my recollection whirred. I lost track with the endless days of tropical sunshine and heat. *Right. April. The tail end of winter and almost spring.*

I closed my eyes, picturing neat lines of yellow crocus peeking through melting snow in Cheeseman Park. Joe and I wrapped in windbreakers and scarves walking hand in hand as Lily whipped around us, a Greyhound close at her heels. *The Cherry Creek Dog Park.* The crack of a baseball bat as we jumped to our feet with the crowd around us, beers and hot dogs in hand, at the opening day for baseball at Coors Field.

I sighed, pulling the thin cotton of my robe closer, feeling the chill.

If we were there, I'd be pulling the down comforter up to my chin before snuggling closer to Joe. My eyes closed again, remembering, as waves of comfort washed over me.

But when I shifted in my seat, my skin stuck to the bar stool reminding me of where I actually was. *You're in the tropics; there's no comfort here.* In fact, I had never felt more uncomfortable in my entire life, and it had little to do with the heat.

I turned back toward the buildings. *Will I ever be comfortable enough to call this place home?*

More tears splashed down my cheeks.

You're the one who brought us here, you know. Snickety wagged her finger at my face as I rubbed my temples. *And, it's because of* you *that all of them are here too.* She pointed her chin toward the bedroom where three furry bodies surrounded Joe. *You think they're having fun?*

I placed my forehead back on the granite as guilt pooled in my belly.

It was me who sold Joe on this country. I was the one who convinced him. I gritted my teeth as I recalled my own words as I'd stood there in our kitchen in Denver. *"This is where I want to be."*

Heaviness closed in on my neck again, as if my captor was back. And, though I knew he wasn't real, I squirmed, shrugging my shoulders and rolling my neck from side to side.

It's these feelings that hold you hostage. This time it was the gentle voice of my therapist. *No one can make you feel anything you don't want to.*

I'm afraid. Fear wound itself in and around the guilt. *That I might do exactly what I've wanted to do since the day we arrived in Panama: run screaming back to the airport.*

My favorite fantasy no longer consisted of beach scenes, massage tables, and mango margaritas.

Unfortunately, going home is no longer a viable choice. My hand came up to massage the tension from my jaw.

Joe and I had discussed it again the night before, our voices raised in battle. He threw all he had at me on how I had handled this move; I screamed at him for drinking and running away from reality.

"You can't just give up!" Joe spat, throwing a spatula into the sink with such force it ricocheted out and bounced to the floor.

"I'm not giving up! It's been 18 months!" I threw my hands skyward.

"But, Murph," he said, "you're a high-level executive now. Anything less than two years on your resume looks like you gave up."

"I just don't know if I can make it," I cried. "This is so much harder than I ever dreamed it would be."

"I know, I know," Joe said, coming over to envelope me in a hug. "But you're stronger than this. You have to pull through."

The aftermath left us both emotional and exhausted, which we were feeling together, all too often.

The ticking of the clock brought me back to the stillness of the kitchen.

A sob rose in my chest as I turned my gaze back to the window, to the darkness outside.

I got everything I asked for, but I never knew it would mean all this.

My face sank back to my hands as my shoulders began to shake again.

As grueling as it was, getting lost in the grief was the only place where things still made sense. Each day, I felt like I was unraveling and morphing into someone I did not want to be.

CHAPTER 33:
The Breakdown

The room began to whirl as I stood, packed between row after row of drenched bodies in formal wear at a Chamber of Commerce event a few days later. Shapes of the figures around me began to fade as if the lights had been dimmed, and stars appeared before my eyes.

What the fuck?

I inhaled, sucking stale air from the large events hall into my lungs, forcing it down my throat. The sound of my breath roared like a jet engine in my eardrums.

Breathe, JuliAnne, breathe.

Sweat beaded on the back of my neck as I cast my eyes to either side. Other members of Panama's business elite squeezed in around me, packed in like canned sardines. *I can barely move.*

A man in a three-piece suit droned on behind a wooden podium 30 feet in front of me.

My throat began to constrict, tension clawing at my chest. I tried to loosen a collar that didn't exist.

I can't breathe.

My vision seemed to freeze, the world around me moving in slow motion. The man's voice started to echo, sounding a million miles away. I blinked. Once. Twice. A third time.

I can't do this here. Not now.

The people around me turned cartoonish, swimming before my eyes.

No, I cried. *Not here, please.*

I struggled to focus on something—anything—to give anchor to the pressure on my temples. But all I could see was the outline of the navy blue suit on the stage. The suffocating crush of people around me felt like it was pressing inward.

Can someone enforce the fucking fire code in this country, just once? Snickety's silk-covered elbow shoved its way into the murkiness of my consciousness.

The floodwaters receded at the sound of her voice. I reached for her. "Snickety!" The croak left my throat before I could stop it.

"*Que cosa?*" A *whoosh* of hot air swirled above my head as the face of my companion turned in my direction. "What's that?" Skin the color of amber flashed a mere three inches from my forehead.

Focus, dear, whispered Snickety.

My neck stiffened as I nodded. This time it was Joe's deep baritone. *Get it together, Murph. You can do this. You're stronger than this.*

I waved my fingers in the direction of the leather bag at my feet. "Can you reach my water?"

My *compadre's* shoulders disappeared for a moment in the sea of humanity before re-emerging a second later, a bobber on the surface of a lake. "*Aqui esta,*" she said. Warm droplets of condensation dripped down to my feet as she handed me the bottle.

"*Gracias.*" I tilted the plastic skyward, my voice still enshrouded in sound waves.

"*Damas y caballeros,*" boomed the loudspeakers. Chairs screeched as the crowd scrambled to its feet in unison, bringing me along with it. My knees buckled as I came vertical, before my palm made contact with the cool metal of the chair in front of me. The water bottle jumped from my hand, splashing lukewarm water onto the tile. The women to my left shifted high heeled sandals in protest, long lashes casting an unspoken rebuke my direction.

"*Gracias por acompañarnos en este dia muy importante y la bienvenida a nuestros nuevos compañeros aqui en la Camara de Comercio,*" the words ricocheted as the sound system screeched.

"Today, we're starting this month's gathering with the recognition of our new member companies. Company representatives, could you please make your way to the stage?"

Icy hot began to course through my veins. *That's me. I have to get up there.* But my brain wasn't firing on all cylinders, particularly the ones that worked my limbs.

Get going, JuliAnne. Snickety's voice rang in and out like a foghorn above the swarming sea of humanity. *Others from the company are here, watching. You can't let them see you like this.*

I took a tentative step toward the center aisle, one foot in front of the other, a tedious march of gripping elbows and shoulders to navigate the attendees in my way. One by one, blank faces turned toward me before stepping back. By the time I reached the aisle, sweat was pouring down the middle of my scapula.

I paused, swaying at the end, my hand on the shoulder of some man I'd never met. "Señora?" he asked, lifting a bushy eyebrow a millisecond before another hand propelled me forward from behind.

"Going my way?" The familiar voice yielded reddish-blond locks framing a smiling face.

"Kent," I managed, my fingers clutched the inside of his proffered elbow like a lifeboat. *Thank God.*

People shuffled from one side of the crowded passageway to the other as Kent pushed us through. A moment later, we were ascending three steps to the riser. Kent released my arm only after placing me in the front row behind the speaker.

I blinked in the glare of the spotlights. Hundreds of people stood just beyond the white light, their shadows pressing toward us, vultures ready for the kill.

Keep your chin up, kid. You made it. Snickety smacked her gum, surveying the crowd. *Now, smile.*

I nodded, stretching the sides of my lips toward either cheek. *A few more moments, and you'll have done what you needed to. Then, we can get the hell outta here.*

A quiver ran across my lower lip. I forced my tongue across it, spreading my mouth wider. *Just two minutes more.* I latched onto the words like a mantra, my eyes searching out the path of least resistance toward the exit.

Two minutes more.

Just…two…minutes.

~

When I wiggled the door handle of the Audi, Tomas shot upward from where he'd been dozing in the bucket seat. "*Sí, Senora!*" he shouted, his hand grappling for the unlock button.

The white-shirted guard from the event pulled the passenger door open and I crumbled in without a word.

Tomas' eyes widened into saucers. "Miss JuliAnne? Are you all right?"

"Just get me home, Tomas," I whispered, turning my face away from him.

A pause. Then, "Yes, sir." One hundred eighty horses roared to life and gravel spun as Tomas hit the gas.

Twenty minutes later, I roused when Tomas tooted the horn at the wrought iron gates to our building. The night guard's head popped up from behind plate glass before he waved us through. I fumbled to bring my seat upright.

"What time tomorrow, Miss JuliAnne?" Tomas' voice was close to a whisper as he backed the car into our space.

"I...I...I don't know." My hand shook as I reached for the door handle.

"Do you need my help?" Tomas reached toward me where I sat swaying in my seat. I ducked my head before I shook it. *He doesn't need to see me like this.*

"I'm fine, Tomas." I ruffled fingers through my hair, extending my palm in his direction. "*Buenos noches.*"

"Okay," he said, handing me the keys. "*Buenos noches.*"

I clicked my way across the smooth concrete floor toward the stairwell. When I turned the corner, I caught Tomas' large form out of the corner of my eye. He was still standing there, eyes following my every move.

~

"Well, hello."

When I stumbled through the front door, Joe looked up from his copy of the *Miami Herald*. Then, a double take. "What the hell happened?"

"Fell asleep on the way home," I mumbled, navigating around Lily's prances to the kitchen table to set down my things.

"Murph, are you all right?" I never ignored my dog.

"No," I said, sinking into the nearest dining room chair and laying my cheek on the table. "I don't think so."

Joe jumped up, crossing the tile in an instant. He knelt beside me, placing a hand on the back of my neck. "JuliAnne," he said in a voice thick with worry. "What happened?"

I didn't answer.

"Murph." Joe sank into the chair next to mine. "When are you going to tell these guys to fuck off? You can't go on like this. It's killing you."

"It's not that," I said. "I can't breathe," I stammered, patting the area below my breastbone. "It happened again."

"Oh, honey." Joe's voice deepened. "It's stress. That's what the doctor said. Did you take your meds today?" His hand smoothed my hair. "Did you eat at the event?"

I nodded, then shook my head. "I didn't stay long enough for the food."

"Let's get you out of these clothes, and I'll make you some tomato soup with grilled cheese," Joe said as the warmth of Lily's tongue invaded my ear. "Oh, yes, your mom needs lots of love tonight. Come on," he said, standing up and patting my back again. "You'll feel better when you've showered and got something in your belly."

A moment later, pots clanged as Joe pulled the skillet from the cupboard along with a bottle of Patron.

If only food could fix this. I heaved myself up, feeling the weight of a thousand suns around my shoulders, and staggered toward the bedroom.

~

I stood like a sphinx in the hot shower for 20 minutes before collapsing into a naked puddle, shampoo pooling at my feet. Water cascaded from the showerhead up and over the back of my neck as I huddled in the corner, staring. When Joe discovered me in the fetal position a few minutes later, his rough hand shook my arm. The faraway voice that had been calling my name in my dream zoomed up to the forefront of my hearing.

"JuliAnne." My head turned in slow motion to see eyes staring down at mine, pupils the size of platters. "JuliAnne!"

When I opened my mouth, the spray from the shower coursed into it, jumbling my words. "It's all his fault," I mumbled, jutting my chin toward a tiny ant on the opposite wall. But the syllables that tumbled out didn't make any sense.

Joe reached behind me, twisting the faucet off. "Come on," he commanded in a tone he reserved for subcontractors, extending his hand down toward me.

"Nnn me shardon key." My hands were wound tight around my knees, my eyes trained on a visible hole in the corner of the tile.

"JuliAnne, get *up!*" Even in my daze, I recognized the stench of fear. A triumphant smile spread across my face.

"*No puede ser.*" My head shook from side to side, my eyes still trained on my tiny ant companion. "*No puede ser.*"

"All right then, have it your way," Joe muttered, throwing a plush towel around my shoulders. A moment later, his big hands invaded my arm sockets.

"No," I cried, swaying as he pulled me vertical, my knees buckling.

"Hold on," he said, wrapping my elbow around his neck as his arm encircled my waist. "I've got you. Step with me." But my feet refused to move. His opposite hand swept behind my kneecaps a moment before I collapsed. "Jesus, Murph, you're all skin and bone," he said as he deposited me on the bed and pulled a pillow beneath my neck.

His eyes came back into view. "Murph." His fingers brushed across my forehead. "You're scaring me. I need you to give me a sign that you're okay."

"I'm trying," I tried to say, but the low guttural sounds released were those of a wild animal. Sobs began to wrack my body. I curled up into the fetal position again.

Joe covered my body with his, cradling me. "Shit, baby." Hot tears dripped onto my neck as he clutched. "What am I supposed to do?" He was shaking.

A kaleidoscope of colors and shadowy objects began to collide across my vision, as a cacophony of voices cascaded like poison rain in my head.

You bit off more than you could chew, didn't you?

It's just like they said it would be. You knew you could never make it.

If they could see you now, what would they say?

Jeers rose above me, surrounding me, though the faces were blurred. I cowered, my hands coming up to cover my ears.

They're going to find out you're a fraud.

You're not so special now, are you, Miss Prissy Pants!

You're gonna end up on the street! another hissed. *Then, no one's gonna want you.*

Then the voice of my Sunday School teacher. *You're going straight to hell.*

Hands shook me. I opened my eyes to see Joe's moving lips, though I couldn't hear his voice.

You're going to end up broke and penniless on the street.

In the distance, a woman's voice began to scream above the din of the accusations. My ears dialed in, focusing beyond the constant buzz of white noise I'd picked up in the shower to her cries. The reverberations of her pain shook the room as her body came into view below me.

I'm on the ceiling.

A dark-haired man was holding her, patting her, rocking her. I watched as he covered her with a blanket and ran into the other room to pick up the phone. *Poor thing. He's calling for help.*

My eyes came back to the woman. For a moment, the tremors that shook her body rippled through my own. The wetness of her tears soaked my cheeks.

"No, no, no!" she screamed.

My hands went out to clutch the corners of the concrete.

And it was then, and only then, that I realized the reality. When I opened my eyes, the only thing I could see was a cloud of white. *What the...* I scratched the air in front of my eyes. The white form moved. *A pillow.*

"Nooooo." This time, her agony tore through my lungs.

And then it hit me, as I came up for air. *The woman on the bed is me.*

"Noooooo." Those sounds were coming from *my* throat.

My hand shot out to where Joe had sat a moment earlier. But, the bed was empty.

"Noooo," my voice faded.

A nasty voice. *There's no one here to save you.*

And then, like a curtain, darkness fell and the blackness of my mind enveloped me.

PART THREE

CHAPTER 34:
The Question

"Are you comfortable with that, JuliAnne?"

I had been observing my own index finger circle the rim of my thumbnail when the unfamiliar voice interrupted. Over and over and over again. *When did I start doing that?*

"Murph?" Joe's hand came into view, nudging mine.

A long moment ensued before my brain waves alerted me that I needed to respond. The echo of my voice reverberated in my ears when I answered. "Yes?"

"Now that I've heard from both of you, I'd like to have some time to speak with you, one-on-one." The man's dark hair was slicked back, his face partially obscured by stylish glasses.

Why is it so hard to judge a Latino's age? I thought. *Could he be younger than me?*

"Of course," I stammered, reaching for the small pillow under my arm and stuffing it behind me on the black vinyl couch. *Where am I?*

Joe gave my hand another pat before rising. "I'll be outside," he said.

My habit of forcing a smile failed me; I nodded. The soft whoosh of air heralded his departure. I turned back toward where the psychiatrist sat, twisting his pen in his fingers.

"Well then, let's get started." He tapped the pen on a yellow steno on his lap. "First, I need to ask you: Have you had any inclination of hurting yourself?"

I shook my head. "No."

The doctor made a note on his pad. "Any desire to cause harm to others?"

A gurgle rippled up from within me, out of nowhere. My hand came to my throat, a reflex. But the sound that came sounded more like a cackle than a laugh. "Yes."

The doctor peered at me before scrawling something else on the notepad. "Want to tell me more about that?" His finger came up to push up his glasses.

Leering faces began to flash before my eyes. Juan Carlos. Curt. David. The cardiologist.

"You'd feel that way too if you had to deal with the assholes I've had to." I snapped erect in my chair, eyes flashing. I looked around, surveying the small room as if searching for a safety net.

The doctor waited, watching me. "And?"

"I'm not sure, *doctor*." I paused for a moment, glancing at the certificates lining the wall on my right, searching for his name. "Doctor *Jiménez*." Propelled by the sudden force of anger in my belly, I leaned toward him, lifting a finger to point at him. "But first, there's something we need to get clear."

"All right," he said, meeting my gaze. "Go ahead."

"How do I know that what I say in here—to you—is truly confidential?" The words blurted from me, almost an accusation. "And don't bullshit me please. I know there's no HIPAA in Panama."

The doctor cleared his throat, straightening in his chair. "Correct, there is no HIPAA protection here." He motioned to a clipboard I had filled out earlier on the desk beside him. "You reviewed these forms before signing them, I assume?"

"Those forms don't mean shit," I spat. "You can write down whatever you want and within 24 hours, half of Panama could know everything I've said to you. As you well know, doctor, nobody in this fucking country can keep their mouth shut." I leaned back. "As an example, everyone in my fucking office knew my salary within a month of me starting work here."

"I see." The doctor grimaced. "Confidentiality is a big problem in Panama; that's true."

"*Entonces*?" I threw my palms face up, wide toward either side of the small room. "How do I know I can trust *you*?"

The doctor left the notebook on his lap as he removed his glasses and began to wipe them with a small rag he took from the pocket of his jacket. "You don't. But in order for you to feel comfortable with us proceeding," he swept a hand toward me, the proverbial olive branch, "you need to make a decision to trust that I will do what I say I will do."

"Uh huh." My eyes threw daggers his way. "And what recourse do I have if you don't keep your word?"

"There's the usual avenues for complaints." Doctor Jiménez held my gaze. "Medical board and all of that." He twirled his fingers in the air. "But the only basis for real trust is what we agree to. Either you have an agreement," he shrugged, "or you don't." He placed his glasses back on his face. "What does your intuition tell you, JuliAnne? Trust is simply a choice. And that choice is always yours."

As his words sank into the muddle of my brain, tears began to pool behind my eyes. I shook my head, the bravado siphoned away like water going down a drain. I reached for a tissue from the box on the table beside me, clutching it as tears began to slip down my cheeks.

"But how do I know for *sure*?" My hand shook as it came to my face to cover the beginning of a sob. "I'm not even sure I trust myself anymore."

"You can't know for sure." The doctor paused, taking on a gentler tone. "That's not reality. The reality is that you don't know. I can tell you whatever I want to but the reality is that anything is possible. But ultimately, the choice to trust is yours. And there is always inherent risk in choice."

A few moments passed before I lifted my eyes to his again. The understanding I saw there went straight to my heart; a heart that was tired from always holding up a shield. A heart that was worn out from dodging arrows. A heart that had been exhausted. My chest caved in as I doubled over, putting my face into my hands. I began to gasp for air.

"You're fine, JuliAnne. It's just anxiety." Dr. Jiménez's voice was quiet. "Open your mouth and take some deep breaths."

A minute or two later, I stopped heaving and opened my eyes. The wingtips of Dr. Jiménez's perfectly polished shoes were barely visible across from me, and the only sound was the ticking of a clock. My hand went out to yank tissue from the box on my right, though not a single tear had fallen down my cheek. "I'm sorry," I murmured.

"It's all right." His voice was quiet. Then, "Take your time." Dr. Jiménez sat as he had before, pen in hand. He gave a slight nod.

"All right," I said in a resigned voice. "Thank you." I grimaced as I inhaled, forcing air into the vice that had taken the place of my chest. Then, I reached for another tissue out of habit. "I guess we should get started."

~

"What do you mean?" I furrowed my brow as the strawberry ice cream in the plastic cup in front of me melted. This setting was hardly the scene I'd envisioned for a kick-off meeting with my new professional coach, the graying man in a three piece suit sitting opposite me. I'd been intrigued with his style from the moment I met him with his unusual name and his swagger; he had something—*something*—I was missing. And something I desperately wanted to replace the emptiness I felt all the time. So, I'd bit the bullet and hired him.

But now, like everything else in my Panamanian life, we were off to a disappointing start: Falc (which was short for his nickname, Falcon) had suggested we meet for our kick-off session at Panama's equivalent of Baskin Robbins.

"Consider the question." Falc's white teeth shone against a dark tan. His accent was confusing; I had guessed the United Kingdom, though he hailed from South Africa. "Who are you?"

I took a bite, squinting as the cold raced up my jaw into my skull. *Ice cream headache.* My tongue swirled around the middle of my gums to still the pain.

"Well." I dabbed a napkin to my lips. "I'm a lot of things. First of all, I'm an executive. At the same time, I'm a communications professional." I raised my index finger. "I've won my share of awards along the way for my work." My tone was matter-of-fact.

A polite mask fell over Falc's refined features.

I stopped. "What?"

"Hang on." Falc took a bite of the pralines and cream he'd been served at the counter by a lady in a paper hat a few minutes before. "Mmmm," he said. "This is so good."

All right. Snickety tapped the edge of her long white cigarette holder. Whistling *Tweety Bird, Tweety Bird*, her gloved hand circled next to her head before she cut an accusing eye at my coach. *And you're paying this guy how much money?*

I waited, surveying the silver coin ring on Falc's pinky, the thin chain around his neck, the Adam's apple bobbing behind his silk tie as he swallowed.

"The point is," Falc continued, "your answers would be fine if I'd asked you what roles you play. In fact, each of us play multiple roles in our lives." He chased a tiny pink spoon after the dregs of his ice cream.

"But that's not what I asked. What I am asking is who you are, when all the things you do melt away, like this ice cream is doing right now. What's left underneath," he took a final bite before tapping the edge of the miniature bowl with his spoon, "is what I'm interested in." He raised eyes the color of aquamarine to meet mine. They reminded me of a wolf the way he stared straight through me. His voice was calm. "So, I'm going to ask you again."

Suddenly, I was transported 26 years back in time to sixth grade. I was sitting four rows back from the chalkboard and Mrs. Smith had just called on me, but I didn't know the answer. A chill ran up my spine as I broke out in a light sweat.

Falc's eyes bore into mine. "Who are you, JuliAnne Murphy?"

My mouth opened. *Answer! Answer!* I could hear the chants of my fellow students. Then, Snickety shrieked, *You're no longer teacher's pet!*

But my tongue stumbled. No words came out. "I…," I started. Then, again. "I…" Then I stopped. *Who am I?*

My eyes dropped to stare at the empty cup as my heart sank like a stone. I could see it falling, falling, falling down to the floor of the sea into complete darkness, a place no one had ever gone before. In a moment, it was gone. For the first time in almost 40 years, my brain and my quick wit failed me. I had no inkling of what I was supposed to say.

"You're not alone." A kind smile spread across Falc's crag-like features. "Ninety-five percent of my clients can't answer that question any better than you have at their first appointment."

I sat, speechless.

"This is part of your homework." His eyes twinkled. "To contemplate this." He folded his napkin. "But be prepared that the answers may not be immediately forthcoming."

"You know, Falc, I usually figure things out faster than most people do." I cleared my throat. "I imagine I'll have something for you by our next session."

Falc lowered his eyes for a moment, attempting to hide a smile. "I have no doubt you will give this process your all, JuliAnne. But any kind of meaningful work we choose to do together in the future will be underlaid by the person you choose to be on the planet. Who you are *being* is much important than what you do and whatever roles you play."

My face contorted as Snickety started making noise again. His words were Greek to me. In elementary school, I had loathed word problems and puzzles; in high school, geometry had put me to sleep. *Who cares about all those angles and hypotheses? Just give me the bottom line.*

Falc shook his head. *Is he reading my mind?* "When did you decide to go into marketing?"

The pages in my mind's daily calendar whirred backwards until I saw myself in a silver Subaru wagon with my father. We were parked in the middle of an empty lot outside the mall in Northwest Arkansas, having taken a drive to catch up on one of my rare visits home from university. My future was the topic at hand.

"What's driving this change, JuliAnne?" My father glanced at me as the car had rolled to a stop. "I thought engineering was what you wanted to do."

I chewed my lip before answering. "Well, I don't really care for engineering," I said, keeping my gaze trained straight ahead. "And if I'm going to change, this is the time to do it. If I keep going in engineering, I'll lose credits down the line if I change."

"I see." My father went quiet. My breath caught in my throat before I plunged forward. "I was thinking maybe I'll look into medicine. You know, become a doctor, like you."

"Well," my father began to tick off on his fingers, "by the time you get through school, residency, and internship, the U.S. marketplace will be turning toward a socialized system. Doctors won't make any money." His head began to shake. "So, unless you're really passionate about it and don't care about the money, medicine doesn't make any sense for you."

"Oh," I said, uncertainty weaving its way across my young face. My father knew me well; I had an eye for the latest trends and the hippest fashions. Those things came at a cost.

Snickety started ripping a hole in my already holey jeans. *Well, if not engineering or medicine, then what? What are you going to do? What are you going to be when you grow up?*

"Any other ideas?" My father peered at me over his glasses.

"Well," I stuttered, clearing my throat. "I like to be around people." I attempted to bring a smile back to my face though I was beginning to feel as if an elephant with a purple tee-shirt reading *Future* had climbed atop my chest. "And I've heard marketing is fun, and that you can make lots of money. So maybe I'll go into that."

"When did you decide to go into marketing, JuliAnne?" Falc's British accent brought me back to the present, and the question of my future now, 20 years later. "How old were you?"

I blinked. "Nineteen."

Falc leaned toward me, bringing his eyes a few inches away from mine, too close for comfort. My pupils widened. "And, how much weight would you give career advice from a 19 year old at this point in your life?"

I burst into laughter, shaking my head. "Zero."

Falc sat back. "Exactly." He pointed at me. "And how much longer are you going to let your 19-year-old self determine the rest of your life?"

Zing. I gulped.

"Until you know who you really *are*." Falc pounded the center of his chest with his fist. "You'll never be able to figure out what kind of **work** you really want to do in the world."

"But I have no idea who I am," I whispered. "So, now what do I do?"

Falc handed me a napkin. "So, that's where we start."

Terror clenched my stomach. "And, by the end, will I have my answer?"

Falc's eyes were serious. "There are no guarantees, JuliAnne." He shook his head. "While I can guide you through the process, you're the only one who will be able to unearth whatever it is you're looking for." His eyes seemed to look into my soul. "The question is, are you willing to do the work?"

I stared back, the black chasm of my depths rising in me like the tide, waves of grief lapping underneath at my edges, the unanswered question of "Who are you?" threatening to break me wide open…again.

A long moment passed before I found my voice. "Do I have any other choice?"

Falc gave me a slight smile. "Usually by the time the Great Mother decides it's time." He held his hands out wide, referencing the years he had spent in study with the Navajo tribe. "You don't."

CHAPTER 35:
The Decision

I sat in near darkness in the bedroom facing the windows that stretched from floor to ceiling. The blackout curtains I'd had custom made to mask the noise from the street below hung to either side. As the sun set behind the mountain across the Canal, dusk fell. Because it was a weekday, the streets outside were absent of the party buses and the honking taxis. This was the hour I set aside to transition from the chaos of the office to coming home, a new habit I'd taken to as part of my coaching.

Nag Champa wafted from an incense burner next to me where I sat on the tile. The cats stretched out on either side, bellies rising and falling in the dim light. Lily kept watch on the three of us from her bed a few feet away.

Funny how this meditation thing seems to work for everyone but me. While my eyes remained closed, my mind was jetting from one thing to the next. Everything I had read said meditation was a balm for the soul, a step toward decreasing stress, the beginning of the path to peace. *God knows I deserve some peace.*

"Fuck," I said, bending from the waist to place my forehead on the tile. "But how long will it take to get there? All I want is to feel better." These days, post breakdown, it was all I could do to crawl out of bed and make it to the office by 8:30. Evenings weren't much different; when I came home, all I had the energy for was to meditate, eat, and crash. My need to focus on myself left Joe and I little time together, and the chasm between us was deepening.

There's a reason they call it the monkey mind. Snickety put a finger to her lips from where she sat half lotus in maroon yoga pants. *Relax.*

In spite of my fatigue, mischief spread across my face. *If people knew how much Snickety and I interacted, they'd lock me up for sure.*

Snickety shot me a look before she pushed her chin to her chest and folded her hands in prayer at heart center. *And may they never know. Now focus!*

"Oh, all right," I sighed, coming back upright.

If you can't concentrate with eyes closed, then find one thing in your present to appreciate. My eyes searched the horizon. *Something to appreciate.* Cars whipped by, radios blaring. The sizable park where Lily and I walked every morning rolled out below me like green felt on a pool table. Hundreds of trees bowed and curtsied in the breeze. Sunset cast shadows across the row of abandoned structures that had once served the U.S. Army. *Something to appreciate.* Farther out, my gaze caught the tail end of an immense blue tanker leaving the Canal. *Nordic,* the vessel boasted in letters that stood three stories tall. *They're a long way from home.*

Focus! screeched Snickety.

My heart opened as the canopy of a small forest came into view. I skimmed over it, then scanned back. *Wait.* And then my vision latched onto it like a guided missile finding its target: an enormous tree in the middle of the park.

I'd pointed her out to others who had visited us on vacation; that's how amazing this tree was. The name of the species escaped me, even now. *Who are you?* I asked. And then, as if she'd heard me, the name popped up. *Right! The Guayacan.*

The expanse of this tree's trunk could seat more than a dozen. Her branches stretched close to 100 feet wide.

Maybe 200, said Snickety, joining my admiration.

Okay, appreciation. I took a breath, addressing the tree. *Every time I walked under you, my body relaxed, and my heart opened. The smell of the earth underneath your bows rose to my nostrils, beckoning me to stay and take in the coolness of your shade.*

I squinted my eyes, inhaling. As the sun set, a host of blackbirds flitted and called from within her branches. Over the months, I had seen squirrels and iguanas screaming at each other as they raced up and down her trunk.

Funny, I thought, blinking my eyes to look at the tree again. *Each and every time I strolled beneath you, even near you, it felt like coming home. Like a refuge.* I regarded her now, from this different perspective several stories above. *I never considered you from this angle before.*

My hand opened atop my knee, palm lifted toward the sky. *How many times have Lily and I walked beneath you, a tennis ball in her mouth, her leash in my hand?*

In the months we'd been in this apartment, it was a rare occasion she and I strayed off the sidewalk into the grass. We'd visited this tree a handful of times. I was always running: to get to work, to get my mind off work, to escape, to decompress, to get ready to go out, always occupied, always jumping around, but never fully *there*.

The thought bubble rose in my consciousness. *Sounds like my entire life.*

Sadness surfaced. *This is not about you; appreciate her.* I gulped for air. "Thank you for the oxygen, even from this distance," I stammered. "Thank you for providing refuge for all those birds and animals, every single day. And, when I did take the time to come see you, thank you for providing those moments of safety and comfort." My eyes squeezed shut. "I guess I made the choice to overlook what you were offering me the rest of the time."

"You always have a choice, JuliAnne." It was Dr. Jiménez's voice. "What will you choose?"

It's all right, came the answer. *I'm still here. What's important is that you are seeing me now.*

Regret clenched my heart as I regarded her regal form. "I can't believe it's taken me all this time to *really* see you, to *really* appreciate who you are and what you offer. For God's sake, you're right here at my back door!"

Tranquila. The still small voice within me was hushed but firm. *And you? Isn't it time for you to take a look at who you really are, JuliAnne?*

I bowed my head, shame washing over me. *That's just it. I thought I knew who I was. But now, I realize, I don't. I have no idea.*

Then start with what you do know, came the answer. *Who are you not?*

I stilled as a light went on inside. *What?*

That's right, said the voice. *You don't have to figure it all out today, but for now, start with who you aren't.*

I shook my head. *I don't understand.*

Like what you will never be, the voice continued. *What you cannot stand. Say to yourself, 'I may not be this, but I am definitely not that.' Opposites are always a good place to start.* The clouds around my head began to dissipate. My memory latched onto the phrase like a life preserver.

"Opposites are a good place to start," I whispered, opening my eyes. "Opposites are a good place to start."

My eyes searched out where the tree stood, but darkness had fallen and she was no longer visible. But the truth of what I had heard locked in. "Opposites are a good place to start!" I scrambled to my feet, reaching for the bedside table, my fingers seizing pen and paper. I opened my notebook and flipped to a new page.

"Opposites are a good place to start." I enunciated the words as I wrote. Then on the line below: Who am I *not*? My pen underlined "not" three times.

Tossing pillows aside, I climbed onto the bed and began to write as the words began to pour from me like a fountain gushing forth from the side of a parched mountain.

~

Two hours later, I came up for air, my pen slowing to a stop. Like a slave under the watchful eye of his master, my hand hadn't stopped scrolling phrase after phrase in cursive onto the page.

But then, just like that, it was done. Everything in my head was there and there was nothing more.

But, where is the answer to the question? Snickety's finger was skimming line by line through my notebook. *Am I missing it?*

No, I said. *You're not. There is no answer, at least, not yet.*

Then I don't get it, she peered at me over the top of her cat eye glasses. *What's the point?*

I closed my eyes, a slight smile crossing my face. That had been my question too, earlier in the week, shot like an arrow toward Falc, who'd sat across from me in the restaurant at the Holiday Inn in Clayton.

"What's the point?"

Falc's wizened face spread into a smile. "I'm glad you asked." He nodded. "The point is to sit with the question and see what comes up."

"What do you mean, what comes up?" I sipped a cappuccino from the ceramic *taza* in front of me.

"What emotions or feelings come up in your body when you ask yourself the question at hand?" Falc asked, observing me as I shifted in my seat.

"I don't get it," I said, furrowing my eyes. "How are my emotions going to help me get any closer to where I want to be, if I don't have the answer?" The pencil in my hand began to tap against the coffee cup.

"Let's try it now," Falc suggested. "Why don't you close your eyes and turn your focus inward for a moment while I repeat the question."

I scanned the room, nervous that someone would recognize me and think I was crazy, closing my eyes in a business meeting. The restaurant was empty except for a woman cleaning a nearby table. I sighed as my eyelids came to a close. "All right."

"Take a deep breath," Falc instructed.

I complied, sucking air in through my nostrils.

"Now," Falc said. "I want you to tune into your body as I ask this." Silence hung in the air for a moment. "What if there is nowhere to get to?"

Nowhere to get to... A chill ran up my spine. *Nowhere to get to.* The cold clamp of fear clenched my heart. My eyes burst open. "Nowhere to get to?" I stammered.

Falc observed me, his eyes calm. "That's right," he said. "And I can tell from your response that you have some feelings coming up. What are they?"

I stared at him, pupils dilated, jaw open, breath coming fast. "Nowhere to get to?" I said again. "Holy shit."

"Take a breath, JuliAnne," he said. "This is exactly where we need to go. Tell me what you feel when I ask that question."

My teeth began to clatter together, though the room was far from cold. "I...I...I feel cold," I started. "And panicked." My hand came up to clutch my stomach. "And empty." My voice stuttered. "What do you mean by that question?"

Falc smiled. "What if there is no meaning?" he returned. "What if it's just a question, and nothing more?"

"But if there's nowhere to get to..." My heart was pounding like a drum in my ears now. I held my hands up. "...Then what is the point? Of all this? Of life?"

"Exactly." Falc leaned back in his chair. "What is the point?" His finger came up, a warning. "But don't look for that answer," he cautioned. "Let the question be with you, stay with you for a while." ·

I stared at him as my throat began to constrict. I waved a hand toward my neck. "I can't breathe."

"Ah," said Falc, reaching over to hand me the sweating glass of water in front of me. "Looks like we've hit on something we need to ponder for a while. Take a breath."

I sucked in the air, filling my lungs, keeping my eyes on him.

"Again," he instructed. "And take a drink."

I brought the glass to my lips and swallowed. My breath slowed before I raised shaky eyes to his.

"Good," he said. "This is going to be your homework for a while, so I want you to write this down." His eyes glanced at my notebook.

I drained the water from the glass before I reached for my pen.

"What is it like to simply live with the question?"

My hand shook as I scrawled the words onto the page.

"And any questions that come up, that is your homework. Simply to sit and observe what happens in your body when they do."

I gave a slow nod. "That's it? Simply sit and observe?"

"That's right," Falc nodded. "Nothing more." He repeated, "Simply sit and observe."

I reached toward the water pitcher to refill my glass again. "And when do I get the answers?"

"The answers may come when you've fully faced the darkness that arises from the questions," he replied, and then he shrugged. "But what if there are no answers? No right and no wrong?" His tanned face spread into a gentle smile as the color drained from my face. "A-ha! Another question. But for now, one step at a time."

CHAPTER 36:
The Escape

"I don't care what Juan Carlos said! I'm telling you what I want you to do!" Curt's voice reverberated through the earpiece. I held the handset a few inches from my ear to count.

One, two, three, four, five, six, seven.

The yelling began to subside. *Yep.* I brought the receiver back to my ear. "I understand your position, Curt," my voice was smooth as glass, "and, please know I'll make note of your requested change. However, this is something the three of us will need to discuss in our next marketing strategy meeting since this is different from what we last agreed." My heart rattled in my chest. "That said, I'll add it to our agenda. But for now, let me get back to work so I'll have something to show you guys tomorrow. Goodbye." With that, I replaced the receiver.

Snickety gave me a thumbs up. *Very bold.*

Slow down. I brought my hand to my breast bone. *You're fine.*

My therapist's voice joined in: *It's your choice, JuliAnne. No one is making you freak out. His outbursts aren't personal.*

Speaking of, Snickety waved a hand toward the small woven basket next to my keyboard, a new coping mechanism I'd implemented in my determined march back toward a healthier head space.

"Right!" I said aloud. "That episode calls for a slam dunk!" I turned toward three small shells lined up next to my desk phone. Scooping one up to examine it, I kicked my soles against the inside wall of my desk and pushed. My chair rocketed back, toward the wall.

"Which one do we have this time, JuliAnne?" My voice boomed like a broadcaster, the star of my own personal game. "Ah yes, the black and white one, a crowd favorite." The tiny mollusk was the perfect miniature of a species I'd never seen before coming to Panama. Miniscule spearheads covered the black exterior, making its capture by natural predators almost impossible.

And I have a few of them. I'd picked up shelling as a hobby when we've moved to Panama, but in recent months it had become my religion, a way to let the stress of the work week ebb from my mind like the outgoing tide.

Come on! yelled Snickety, bringing me back from the sidelines. *Sink it!*

I eyed the small opening in the top of the basket, bringing the shell above my head to take aim.

"Yes!" My fist clenched in victory as it sailed through the hole. "Take that, you asshole!" I rolled back to my desk with a smug smile. "And, thank you, doctor."

The game was one I'd devised with my therapist, another way to set bite-sized boundaries for myself at work. This one was specific to how much abuse I was willing to tolerate within one workday from Curt. The rules were this: every morning, I poured the shells from the basket, and started from square one. When His Assholiness chose to insert himself into my day with one of his screaming fits, I placed one in the basket. At any point during a 12-hour period, if all five found their way into the basket, I gave myself permission to gather my things and go home.

I glanced at the digital readout on my desk phone, considering the two shells sitting next to it. Two o'clock.

So far, so good. I sniffed. There were days I wished Curt would cross the line, so that I could make a mad dash for the door. The one time it had happened, I'd sent him a polite email feigning illness, turned off my phone, and spent the rest of the day in pajamas watching a movie. It had been kind of fun.

"Think of it like Curt providing you with a 'get out of jail free' card." Dr. Jimenez had smiled. "When you see it like that, it's like he's giving you a gift."

"I'll take that," I said. "Plus, this is something I'll actually *do*." I smiled.

The *mezcla* of the therapy, my work with Falc, and the meds were working; I was feeling stronger every day though nothing around me had changed. And, while my preparation for going to the office every morning still felt like girding myself for battle, little by little, I was attempting to give up my intense internal need for approval...from everyone.

Oh, good God. Snickety clucked her tongue from my shoulder. *Can't you just get it over it and move on?*

I broke into a cold sweat. *Maybe if you would leave the dark side and help me, I could do it a little faster, you bitch.* "God grant me the serenity...," I turned back to my computer, "...to accept the things I cannot change. Especially when it comes to other people, like these *idiotas* I work with and Snickety who just won't leave me alone."

~

My heels echoed across the courtyard as I crossed the near-empty restaurant to reach the group of women clustered around a circular table. "Sorry I'm late." I dropped my handbag in the empty chair before making my way around to kiss and hug my female counterparts.

"You are more than welcome." My friend Ida's English belied her Swedish roots. "We already started the introductions."

"Great! Carry on, carry on." I motioned to the *mesero* as I sank into a chair, "*Joven.*" When black shoes came to a stop next to my chair, I looked up from the menu. "*Como está, Jose?*" I smiled into the black eyes before my voice turned into a whisper. "*Todo bien?*"

The man returned my smile. "*Todo bien, gracias a Dios.*"

"*Ah, que bueno! Me allegro.*" My finger scanned the menu. "*Quisiera un mojito y un orden de el plato mixto, por favor, Jose.*"

The man scrawled something on his notepad and disappeared. I turned my attention back to the table to see that the woman to my right was speaking.

I'm next. My heart picked up the pace. *Stop it*, I breathed. *Be present.*

The woman gave her name, her title, her company, how she had found out about the group, and her thoughts on the evening's topic: her individual source of inspiration.

"I'm grateful to Jessica for inviting me," she concluded, glancing down the table on the other side of me. "There's nothing like this group elsewhere in Panama, and I'm excited to be here."

Her words brought a smile to my face. I nodded, touching my hand to her shoulder. "Welcome."

Ida nodded at me from across the circle. "JuliAnne?"

I shifted in my seat as 10 pairs of eyes turned my way. I cleared my throat. "Well, as most of you know, I'm JuliAnne Murphy and I'm from Denver, Colorado. I was fortunate enough to be introduced to Ida when we moved here in 2008." My eyes shone gratitude at the officiator opposite me. "She and I both had an interest in meeting other women like ourselves for fun, for support, for networking, and for friendship. But when we looked around the city, we realized that nothing like this existed. Or, at least not that we could find."

Several heads nodded. "So, we made the decision to meet, just the two of us, and to start inviting other sharp women…," I nodded toward two new faces I didn't recognize, "…like those you see around you and get together once a month."

Several faces broke into grins. "In the last year or so, we've been fortunate to grow to more than just two of us." My tone turned serious. "But what is really meaningful to me about these get-togethers is that we've created more than just a women's group. We've created a space where support and friendship are key." I scanned the gathering. "We don't judge here. We do our best not to gossip. And, we hold what is shared here with fierce confidentiality."

My eyes connected with each and every woman seated around the table. "That is of extreme importance to me, and I know it is to each of you, as well." I paused for a moment, the gravity of my words hanging in the air remembering the day I first met with the psychiatrist and heard myself say that my privacy was paramount.

"In terms of my profession, I serve as the director of marketing at Panorama, which is why I came to Panama. My husband and I relocated for my job, and that role keeps me pretty busy." My gaze connected with Ida and two other regulars within the circle, who nodded.

"As for what is inspiring me right now—" I ducked my chin as the chill of fear gripped my heart. I blinked, dropping my gaze to my lap. "I…I…have to be honest." My voice trembled. "I'm struggling." I took a slow inhale, counting to three.

"My life feels kind of like a tiny boat being tossed among some pretty harsh waves out there." Chuckles rippled through the group as some knowing glances were exchanged. "So, I guess that's it," I sighed. "As for inspiration: I need some. So, please, share some of yours. I'm all ears!"

Sharing my fears, my confusions, my life story with others had never been my strong suit, but now in utter vulnerability and in these months of barely hanging on, these moments of finding support outside my marriage was becoming lifeblood for me. Even so, connections with others in total honesty was a complete leap of faith.

Ida reached out to clasp my hand. "We're here for you." The lines around her crystal blue eyes creased.

Another hand came up to pat me on the arm. "We are," the woman whispered, as I turned toward my left. The green eyes staring back at me were filled with tears. Her hand gave me a squeeze. "Thank you for being so open," I looked from this one woman to Ida, "and for starting a group like this."

I took a gulp of oxygen as I nodded.

"Please. Go ahead and start." The dark head bobbed. "My name is Jessica." The Indian beauty shone dazzling white teeth across the room. "And, I too, could use some inspiration today."

~

"Joe?" My voice broke the silence.

It took a moment for my husband to tear his face away from his e-reader. "Hmm?"

"Thank you." I reached for his hand.

The tanned face broke into a gentle smile. He rubbed his big toe against my shoulder from where we reclined opposite each other in a rainbow-colored hammock.

"For what, sweet pea?"

"For everything." My eyes locked onto his before I broke away and took in a full sweep of the landscape. "For all of this." We lay at the center of a picture-perfect scene: alone, just the two of us on a boat dock, in the midst of an aquamarine sea. Local fishing boats droned on the horizon against the backdrop of a cloudless sky.

The worry lines on Joe's face relaxed. "You're welcome," he said. "How are you feeling?"

I gave a slight shrug. "Okay." The truth was my mind kept racing back to the morass of my office life, even amidst this paradise. It was an ongoing struggle to keep myself present.

"Good," he said with a wink, as he returned to his book. "Keep it up."

Our commitment to travel had been firm since the beginning. But now, since the "incident"—which was the word I'd taken to calling my breakdown—Joe and I had agreed that part of my recovery was having something to look forward to, at least every other month. For us, that was easy: more travel. Joe had agreed he could use the breaks too, as his consulting business was continuing to pick up speed…and stress.

In typical Murphy–O'Malley fashion, we'd amped up the frequency to Mach speed; now we left town every other weekend. In fact, we had been frequenting a tiny hotel on the Pacific coast beach of El Palmar so often that my husband had finally pitched the owners on giving us a better rate. And thus, we became regulars in *Habitación 15* at the BayView Resort.

On this particular three-day weekend, Joe had masterminded a puddle jump on Air Panama to an island in the middle of Panama's northwestern coast in Bocas del Toro. Our hosts had picked us up from a private dock on Isla Colon to skim across crystal blue waters in a flat-bottomed boat.

My eyes have seen the glory. The words from a hymn we'd sung in my childhood church had never made more sense as we navigated between emerald palms sprouting from white sand *islas* that protruded from an ocean the temperature of bath water.

This is truly paradise. I closed my eyes, letting the soft wind caress my face. Relief had washed over me when I'd perused our hosts' instructions as I packed. *Leave your cell phones behind; we don't have coverage.*

It was many a Monday I'd turn on my cell to find that Curt had left me a message or two over the weekend. *Sorry*, I'd text him once I turned my phone on and the ding came through. *We were out exploring the islands all weekend.*

"Boundaries," Falc encouraged me. "Once you have them, it's normal for those around you to test them." He nodded. "Especially when they're brand new. It's your job to create space for yourself to rest and rejuvenate so you can give it your all when you do return to work."

My face had blanched the first time he'd said it. *Shut off my phone? What if I miss a call? Won't that make me a bad employee?*

Falc read my mind. "Soon enough, you'll have trained those around you—including Curt—to give you the respect you deserve. But you must respect yourself first. Define your limits and guard them like a sentry. No one else, in this day and age, will do it for you."

I returned to the paperback in my right hand. Falc was right; it

was working. Step by step, day by day, Curt was backing off, at least...
on occasion.

Stop it, I chided myself. *Stop thinking about work; you're here in paradise, for God's sake.* Then, *Change your trajectory with gratitude.*

These days, I found I could appreciate just about anything. *Practice makes perfect.*

"Appreciate these guys, JuliAnne," Falc's voice resounded. "They may be assholes, but you never know, they might wind up to be your greatest teachers." He winked. "Remember the mantra: energy goes where attention flows."

My greatest teachers. As their faces stepped up into the spotlight of my vision like inmates in a lineup, anger gripped me. *The fuck these assholes will ever be my greatest teachers!* As zen as I was trying to become, this was not a concept I could embrace...ever.

Still, other lessons were piling up, day by day, like interest in a bank. I was learning to accept the realities of my life...sometimes. On some days, when I felt balanced, I maintained a good sense of humor and forgave those around me for being who they were, with granules of silent grace. On most days, I still wanted to box them around the ears for their stupidity.

Falc's voice chimed in like a grandfather clock. "It's your choice, JuliAnne. Which makes you feel better at the end of the day?"

Needless to say, just because I was recovering didn't mean every day was flowers and cake. In fact, in most cases, it was quite the opposite. Thus, I counted on these regular departures to maintain some level of sanity. One thing I could do—and tried to do, every single day—was to voice my gratitude, if only to myself. And so I did. Especially when my mind wandered back to stress monkey world.

Thank you, Falc, for introducing me to these truths. Thank you, Curt, for starting to back off, even a little. Thank you, Juan Carlos, for believing in me and giving me the original chance to come to Panama. Thank you, Joe, for getting me out of town so often. Thank you, God, for helping me recover and for helping me discover these moments of solace, even if they only flash in for a moment or two.

I closed my eyes and let the warmth of the beauty around me envelope me like a cocoon. *In this moment, I am grateful to be safe and sound, here with my husband, completely out of reach of anyone.*

Water lapped at the wood stanchions of the dock below us, suspending time in the warmth of the afternoon. And with it, we too succumbed to the heat and the quiet to fall asleep in the lap of Mother Nature.

CHAPTER 37:
The Descent

The sound of breaking glass ricocheted off the concrete walls, tearing me from slumber. I came upright, heart pounding as I reached for Joe. "What was that?"

But the bed was empty.

"Joe?" I called into the darkness. "Are you there?"

Lily came to a sit from her pillow on the floor.

My body relaxed a millimeter. *Surely if there were an intruder, she would have heard them.*

The fan on the AC unit above came to life, the gentle whirl pushing cool air down from the ceiling. *Wouldn't I have heard them?*

Our rented beach house sat at the end of the road in El Palmar. I'd discovered it on one of my first beach walks in the tiny Pacific side community and kept an eye on it for almost two years before it came on the market. Joe and I jumped at the chance to create a more permanent weekend retreat for ourselves, since we were already at the cozy Bay View Resort every other weekend. Though, our departure from the hotel felt akin to betrayal, since the local family who owned it had become friends. While the rustic "in the middle of nowhere" charm of our "away from it all" haven had appealed to us, it was not ideal for emergencies.

The muffled sound of moaning brought me to my feet. "Joe!" I yanked on my robe as I rushed toward the door.

But the hallway was empty.

Another moan.

"Honey! I'm coming!" Lily fell in close behind me as I ran toward the stairs.

And there my husband lay, in his underwear at the bottom of the stairwell, his frame splayed around a corner, head descending down the steps.

"Joe." I pounded down to reach him, taking in the catastrophe at a glance: foam splattered the walls, a plate smashed on the floor, the shards of a milk glass splintered into a million pieces. And blood. Lots and lots of blood.

The glass! Snickety screeched. *Your bare feet!*

My hands came out to catch me before I slammed against the wall. "Fuck!"

Joe gave another moan, arms clamoring skywards.

"Stay there." My voice shook as I reversed direction. "I'll be right back. There's glass all over the place."

Out of the corner of my eye, his blood-covered hand reached toward me. "Stay still," I screamed. "You'll cut yourself more!"

When I returned a moment later in my flip flops, Lily was standing over Joe's body like a sentry.

"Move, move, move." I waved my hand at her. "I don't need you to get glass in your pads, too!"

Pointy ears went docile as I moved beyond her. When I reached Joe's body, I stopped to survey the damage. His head was at a funny angle, an elbow stretched out below him. *Jesus Christ. Not again. Is his neck broken?*

I tiptoed around, crunching glass, trying to get a better look. A cold sweat broke out across my brow as I bent down and scenes from the last time, in our apartment, flashed through. *I still can't lift him by myself.*

For a moment, the only sound in my ears was the freight train of my breath before I sprang into action—grabbing a kitchen towel, stabilizing his neck, sweeping up the glass, and mopping up the liquid.

Joe began to move as he came to again, his eyelids fluttering. I scooted toward his face. "Joe, can you hear me?"

He gave another moan.

"You fell down the stairs." I searched the bloodshot eyes. "I'm cleaning up the glass so I can move you. Then, I'll take a look at your wounds and see if we need to get you to the hospital." *I don't know how but...*

"I'm fine," Joe slurred. He attempted to move again.

"Joe, wait." My voice was stern. "Let me get this cleaned up or you'll hurt yourself more."

The big body was still while I worked around him. Then, "Ready?"

He didn't move. "Joe?" I lightly slapped his cheek. "Wake up, God damn it, wake up!"

The closed eyes blinked open. "Huh?"

I patted his cheek again. "I need to move you, so I can see where you're hurt."

"I'm fine," the voice stuttered. "Just leave me alone."

"Nope." I poked him in the shoulder, this time hard. "Come on, damn it! Work with me."

The bloodshot eyes closed again.

I gave his shoulder a slight shake, my voice rising, "God, damn it, Joe. This is important!"

Joe's eyelids fluttered.

Adrenaline took over. "God, damn it," I yelled. "Wake up, Joe! You're hurt and I don't know how bad and *I need your help*!"

Joe's eyes shot open. "All right, all right," he stammered. "You don't have to be such a cunt!"

I fought the urge to punch him at the insult as fear turned to rage. "I'm the one trying to help you after you drink yourself silly and you call me that nasty word?" Instead I gritted my teeth. "All right then! We'll do it my way, whether you like it or not!" Using one hand, I lifted the tousled head to scale up and down the vertebrae of his neck with my fingers.

Everything feels normal. Pulling myself to stand above him, I turned his body toward me to probe down his back.

"Ow." Eyelids opened again.

"Does that hurt?" I retraced where I'd touched, pressing each vertebrae.

"I don't know." He pushed toward me. "Just let me get up." The stench of sour tequila and beer hit me full in the face, taking my breath away.

"Stop moving, damn it!" I crooked my elbow under his armpit. "Let's get you where I can see the rest of you." With some pulling and pushing and a few grunts, we heaved his body to a sitting position.

Two more swaths of blood pooled where he had been a moment before.

"Stay put," I said as I tracked my gaze up his leg to examine a small gash below his knee. I put a finger over the gash to find a piece of glass protruding. "Hang on," I said as I pulled the glass out. More blood followed.

"Ow," heaved Joe. "God, you're such a bitch!"

I ignored him, scanning the rest of his body. Another shard protruded from his forearm. I clenched my jaw before easing it out too. Another trickle of blood followed.

"Where you goin,' babe?" Joe's bleary eyes stared as I withdrew to put the glass in the trash.

"So now I'm your babe, when a moment ago you called me bitch and cunt?" I snapped, as my heart continued its staccato pace. "You're damn lucky I'm here at all!"

Stepping back around the corner, I found Joe pushing himself to his feet. "I'm fine. I just need to go to bed." He took a tentative step forward before one foot slid across the wet floor.

"Sit down, damn it!" My voice rose to a shriek. "If you hurt yourself more, I will never forgive you!"

He lowered to the bottom step, a frown on his face.

Bring it down a notch, JuliAnne. You can't argue with a drunk. "Joe, please," I pleaded. "Let me get this finished and we'll get you back to bed."

Joe took on the tone of a petulant child. "I'd like a sandwich."

I rotated Joe's arm to dab the antiseptic on the large gash. "I think you can wait until morning."

Joe snatched his arm away. "But I'm hungry now!" His bleary eyes shot arrows into mine.

Oh, children. Snickety rolled up her stethoscope and tucked it into her pocket. *In this case, I'd say placation is going to be much more effective than domination.*

"I am not finished examining you, damn it!" I snapped my fingers in front of his nose.

My husband stilled long enough for me to examine his knees. "All right," I said. "You're gonna feel banged up in the morning, but at least you didn't seem to break anything."

"I told you I was fine," Joe snapped. "Now can you just get me that sandwich?"

I came to my feet as blood rushed to my head. I bit my tongue before answering. "Why don't you get yourself back up the stairs? I can bring your sandwich to you in bed. Or wait a sec, and I'll help you."

"I'll go by myself," he grumbled.

Panic clutched me as I watched one foot and then the other take step after step until his feet disappeared.

I returned to the kitchen and began slapping peanut butter on bread from an open container.

Falc's voice rose in my consciousness. *Whose business is this, JuliAnne? Yours, his, or God's?*

"His," I snapped as I smacked the sandwich onto another plate and poured another glass of milk. "Or maybe a very unfair God's."

Then why not let him handle it—or the consequences thereof—himself? Haven't you given enough of yourself in managing the affairs of others who offer you little to nothing in return?

My hands stilled as I spied the remains of Joe's drunkenness in the trash can, the paper towels stained with beer and blood. Two soaked towels lay crumpled on the floor. I couldn't see the circles under my eyes but I knew they were there. *He's right. And the abuse...* Joe had developed a nasty habit of calling me horrible names when he was in this condition, but when I called him on it the next day, he feigned innocence. Or forgetfulness. I didn't know which.

"Oh, I did not!" he'd exclaim. "I'd never call you the c-word!"

My heart sank as I picked up the plate and the glass, heading for the stairs. To hear those words coming from the man I loved—and then to have him dispute it—that was the ultimate torture.

But when I reached the landing, I stopped. *So when am I going to change? When am I going to stop taking it?* I looked down at the sandwich and milk. *Because this is madness.* I shook my head, finding my voice. "And I can't do it anymore."

You always have a choice. What will you choose? Dr. Jiménez asked.

Reversing my steps, I walked to the front door and slid it open. Clattering down the outside steps, I crossed the lawn to where Joe's truck sat.

"This is my choice," I hissed as I pitched the plate forward and it sailed through the air toward the immaculate vehicle. The plastic ricocheted off the windshield after the sandwich sailed—the two pieces of bread separating midair—to land, peanut butter down, on the roof. "This madness stops right here, right now!" I slung the glass in an arc, spraying the hood with milk before dropping the cup into the grass.

And with that, I re-entered the house, climbed the stairs, stepped over Joe's still form at the top where he had passed out again, walked down the hall, and went back to bed.

~

Eleven hours later, I sat in the shade of the *bohio*, hugging my knees. My fingers clutched a coffee cup in my hand which had long grown cold. Streaks, where my tears had long since dried, stained my cheeks. I stared out at the waves crashing a few feet away.

All kinds of questions hung in the fogginess of my mind, but one kept resurrecting itself to taunt me. *So, now you're stopping the madness, but what does that mean?*

My gaze, which had been trained on nothing, was interrupted by the graceful arc of a sole pelican in flight. My mind whirred into gear, recalling what I'd read about the gawky sea birds. *Always in groups or alone, but never in pairs.*

The giant bird dipped into a dive, beelining straight for the water. A moment later, he emerged from the water without a fish, shaking his angular neck at the empty sky.

I know what that feels like. To come up empty handed, no matter how hard you try. I searched the horizon where murky skies blurred the line between earth and heavens.

Behind me, my ear picked up the whisper of the glass double doors sliding open, then closed.

Lily jolted awake where she'd been stretched out in the grass before jumping to her feet and breaking into a full run.

"Well, good morning." My back stiffened at the sound of the sugar sweet in my husband's tone.

His footsteps stopped to give the dog a pat. "How's my best girl today?"

I steeled my spine like a crash test dummy bracing for impact as he approached.

"Hey," he said as he passed, all semblance of joy leaving his voice.

"Morning." I watched him out of the corner of my eye, taking in the dark sunglasses, the issue of *Time* tucked under his arm with yesterday's edition of the *Miami Herald* in one hand; a dripping Corona in the other. My stomach clenched at the site of the beer. "It's a little early, don't you think?"

Let me guess. Snickety counted on her fingers as if to measure how far away the thunder would strike. *It's 5 o'clock somewhere.*

Joe ignored me. "Did someone piss in your mom's Cheerios this morning, Lily?" The dog had followed him, rubbing her forehead side to side between his legs after he sat, a request for attention. He brought a bruised hand up to pet her.

My mouth curled into a snarl before I could stop it. "I mean, don't you think you ought to lay off today, given what happened last night?"

Joe took a swig from the glass bottle. "So, I had a little accident." His shoulders shrugged. "Lighten up."

I swung my legs toward him as rage released into every pore of my body. "Lighten up?" I yelled. "Are you fucking kidding me?"

Joe waved a hand in my direction. "Not so loud, Murph. You'll wake the neighbors."

"The neighbors…," I shrieked, "…have been up for hours, unlike you. In case you haven't noticed, it's almost noon, my darling." I took a deep inhale. *Calm down, JuliAnne. Anger won't get you anywhere.* I pointed toward the bandage covering the gash where I had removed the glass in his forearm. "How do you feel today, anyway?"

He swung his neck from side to side. "I'm in one piece."

"You're in one piece!" My efforts to control my rage failed me as the panic and the uncertainty exploded inside me. The volume of my voice escalated. "But I didn't *know* that last night when your stumble up the stairs turned into a fall which shook the whole fucking house and woke me from a dead sleep, did I?"

My husband adopted the same blank stare Tomas did when he knew he was in trouble.

My finger shook as I pointed toward him. "And I didn't *know* that you were okay when I ran down the stairs to find you unconscious on those very stairs!" My voice crescendoed as my face twisted.

"And I didn't *know* that you were going to be fine when I came down to find glass and blood everywhere, which you were not even sober enough to clean up in your 'condition!' But I did." I waved my hands all around me, motioning toward my feet. "Everywhere, Joe! Not just a couple of pieces…all over the fucking floor! Milk splashed all over the walls! Your head twisted at a funny angle!" I stopped to take a breath, my eyes bulging, chest heaving.

Joe turned to look at me, taking another swig of beer.

"And we're God damn *lucky* I didn't have to get you to the hospital!" I continued to scream. "Because there's no *fucking* way I could have done it alone. I'm here—in the middle of fucking nowhere—and I have no one! No one to help me!" I lowered myself onto the couch, the force of my anger dissipating like a flashflood. "There's no fucking way I could have done it alone," I leaned back against a pillow, shaking my head. "Jesus, Joe." I looked at my husband. "You scared the living shit out of me."

A muscle rippled across Joe's jaw as he unfolded his newspaper. "I'm sorry I scared you." His tone was snide. "And I'm sorry I wasn't *there* for you." He snapped the newsprint in front of him. "But once in a while, you have to give me a break." He leaned forward, his eyes snipers.

"I've 'been there' for you for years now, JuliAnne. So what if I have a little fun once in a while? I have stress of my own these days, you know." He leaned back again, snapping the newspaper again. "It was an accident and I don't feel the need to apologize."

I leaned toward him, reaching a hand for his foot, which was now propped on the coffee table.

"It's not the accident I'm worried about," I said, knowing the words that had just left my mouth were a blatant lie. "It's you."

"I told you." Joe kept his eyes trained on the newspaper. "Focus on yourself. On your own recovery. Don't *worry* about me. I'm fine."

"You are definitely not fine when you can't even get up the stairs to get to bed," I snapped.

"And you are definitely not fine when you can't get up the stairs in the first place because of the deadly mix of sleep meds and tequila your body can barely handle. And nor are you fine when you almost set the house on fire like you did last weekend when you decided to barbecue at two in the morning and forgot to turn the fucking grill off!"

Joe snatched his foot away from my touch. "All right! Just fucking drop it."

"And nor are you fine when you call your wife—the woman you supposedly—" my hands came up to form quotations in the air—"'love with all your heart' nasty names when I try to help."

"Oh, I do not!" Joe's voice turned into a snarl.

"The hell you don't," I said, coming to my feet and gathering up my cup and water bottle. I shook the bottle at him in a huff as I rose. "The hell you fucking don't!"

I turned to stomp up the hill toward the house. I paused and realized I had said how angry and scared I was as Joe diminished any concerns, and that, in fact, I was not saying the one thing that had not been said all of this time. The one word that we had both never uttered.

I turned to face him as he buried himself in his magazine.

"Joe?" I waited for him to look up.

"What now, darling?" His tone was anything but endearing.

"I think it's time we face the facts. You have a drinking problem. And it's a big one. We can't pretend it doesn't exist anymore; at least I can't." There. I had finally said it out loud, the unforgivable truth, to myself and now to Joe.

"Holy Jesus, Murph, what the fuck?" He rolled his eyes before he laughed and went back to his reading.

I came closer and took his hand. "Joe, I'm not kidding. You need to see someone or your drinking will be the end of us."

Joe pulled his hand away and whispered from behind his magazine. "Anything you say, dear." I stood for a little longer, hoping to have opened the needed conversation but realizing that it was futile. I had learned a lot from Falc in recent months and one of the bottom lines was that denial is a ruthless shield against the truth. I could not force the issue on the man I loved when he was not at all interested.

Maybe I had said it because I needed to hear myself acknowledge how untenable my life with Joe had become. Maybe the decisions were not really in Joe's court but in my own. I needed something concrete to simply declare what I needed, wanted, and desired in my life, and allow Joe to make his own choices.

At that moment, I didn't really know what I wanted, but it was certain that what I did not want was for my marriage to Joe and the trainwreck of what our day-to-day life together had become to continue status quo.

This behavior—a vicious spiral into the abyss over which neither of us seemed to have any control—was on the verge of killing him, and it felt like it was killing me, too.

Head hung low, I turned and made my way up to the house.

CHAPTER 38:
The Prince

"Good morning, Miss JuliAnne." The Audi engine roared to life as I climbed into the front seat next to Tomas and threw my briefcase over my shoulder into the backseat the following week. That Monday, I had passed the two year-mark for my job in Panama. It felt like a major accomplishment, though there was zero fanfare.

"*Buenos dias, Tomas. Como está hoy?*"

Tomas ignored my question as he maneuvered the car down the narrow ramp. "Is this the big day, Miss JuliAnne?"

"This is it, Tomas." I flipped the visor down to apply my lipstick. "*El principe de Inglaterra, verdad?*"

"*Es correcto*," Tomas nodded. "Is this the most important visitor Panorama has, Miss JuliAnne?"

"Let's see, Tomas," I said, smoothing my bottom lip with my finger as my mind scrolled through the list of high rollers we'd entertained since the project had started. Our redevelopment methods had been the talk of the global marketplace before a shovel ever hit the dirt, mostly due to the project's behemoth size. At 3,500 acres, this would be the largest master-planned community in all of Latin America. I nodded. "I think so."

"And, Mr. Curt? Will he see the prince?"

"No." My eyes went skyward as I wiped a smear from my finger to a tissue. "*Gracias a Dios!*"

Tomas' laugh rumbled as he merged us with the ever-present traffic jam leading to the Bridge of the Americas. "*Y Mr. Ethan y Mr. Julio?*"

"No." I shook my head. "They didn't come."

"*De verdad?*" Tomas' green eyes widened as he shot me a glance. "They not come to Panama to see the prince?"

"*No, solo Juan Carlos y yo.*" I turned toward him. "Supposedly, this is the first visit ever by a member of the royal family to Panama!"

"Wah-oh." Tomas' eyes flashed. "A big day for Panama. A big day for Panorama." He nodded. "And a very big day for you, Miss JuliAnne."

I smiled at his pronunciation of "wow" as I dug into my handbag for my Blackberry. "Yes, Tomas, it's a big, big day for all of us." I cast my eyes heavenward to skies the color of milk. "I just hope it doesn't rain."

~

"Your Majesty." Steel blue eyes pierced mine as I dipped into a slight curtsy before the Duke of York.

Prince Andrew fought a smile as our hands shook. "Hello."

He's just like anyone else. Snickety did a quick appraisal of Fergie's former husband in his elegant striped suit. *Fit. Trim. Attractive. Mid 50s.*

I hadn't been sure what to expect. *He's aging well.* All the hassle in the weeks leading up to this moment seemed to fall away. The prince cut his eyes toward me as he stepped up to the large model of the project. "You're American then, not British?"

I kept my eyes on his, watching for the roving eye I'd become so accustomed to in this country. But the prince never let his gaze wander.

Upholding the Brits' reputation of keeping everything proper, said Snickety. *I like it.*

I nodded. "That's right. Denver, Colorado."

"Great skiing there," he said as he turned toward Juan Carlos, who was beginning a formal welcome.

Twelve minutes later, my finger tapped the silver timepiece at my wrist. Juan Carlos nodded and turned toward the Visitor Center's exit. A bevy of presidential security parted like the Red Sea as I motioned in the direction of the coaster outside. Though tours from around the world marched through our doors every month, the royal itinerary was one of the tightest we'd been asked to accommodate.

Tomas is right. This has to be our finest guest yet, I mused, as Her Majesty's ambassador to the Republic of Panama moved aside to allow me passage onto the bus. Like Tomas, I had been surprised that neither of our owners had made Prince Andrew's visit a priority; his official capacity as foreign investment officer on behalf of the United Kingdom made it even more important, in my humble opinion.

Curt, on the other hand, had not been surprised. "I need these edits made immediately," he'd roared that very morning when I'd reminded him the prince would be with us in less than an hour. "I don't give a shit who the guy is, unless he brings us sales!"

I had to admit that I, too, had my doubts initially when Juan Carlos had shared the email about the royal visit. *Is this what aging playboy princes do: tour the world under the guise of 'direct foreign investment?'* My patience for visitors ran thin by the end of every week when Curt or Juan Carlos pawned one group after another off on me after they deemed them "unimportant to immediate business."

Now, as my feet reached the top step in the bus, my heart jumped. The only seat left on the bus was opposite the prince. Before I sat, I raised a hand to do a quick count: Juan Carlos in the front, the ambassador behind, 16 members of security, and the chauffeur. I gave a thumbs up to the driver in the rearview mirror before sinking into the faded blue velour. The bus began to move.

"Quite an ordeal, isn't it?"

I turned toward the prince with a polite smile. "Sir?"

"You know." He waved his hand to mimic mine. "All this?"

"Well, it comes with the territory, sir." A real smile spread across my face. *He doesn't miss much.*

"Of course." He turned toward the lushness of the landscape outside. "So, how long will you stay?"

"Stay, sir?"

"In Panama." He cut his eyes back toward me. "A year? Two years?"

"Ah." I cast a glance toward Juan Carlos, who had turned his head back from the adjacent seat at the prince's question. *So nosy.* "I've already been here two years, sir."

"And when do you return?"

"I don't have an end date." I glanced at Juan Carlos, plastering the familiar smile across my lips. *Game face on.* "I suppose I'll be here as long as they'll have me."

It's never appropriate to tell a prince you're miserable. Snickety exhaled smoke from her perch on my shoulder. *Though he does look like he'd be fun to have a drink with.*

A moment later, we descended for a photo opp at a gentle rise in the tropical landscape. Radio Hill had been the transmission station for the former military base. Perched at the area's peak, the former airport tarmac stretched into the distance on one side, the sparkling blue of the Pacific Ocean on the other.

"Wow," said the prince, blinking in the sunshine. "This is something."

"Yes," I said, from a half-step behind him when I realized Juan Carlos was speaking to someone else. "It takes my breath away every time."

More members of the royal and presidential details spilled from a second bus which had just arrived behind us. People swarmed toward us like bees heading for the hive, eager to get close.

"So," the prince said, turning toward me, "walk me through what I'm seeing here."

"Certainly." I kept a close eye on Juan Carlos and the ambassador, who were engrossed in conversation. "Here on the far left, you'll see the beginning of the construction of the industrial area, which we call the Canal Point City Center." My finger outlined a large swath of red dirt to the left of the airstrip. "This is where most of the Special Economic Area activities will take place within the project."

"Third party logistics and so on?" the prince asked.

"Among other things," I nodded.

"And all this?" Prince Andrew pointed a manicured finger toward six blocks of aging white structures with red tile roofs. The monstrosity resembled an abandoned playground.

"The building closest to us is the second largest call center in the world for one of our Fortune 500 companies."

Prince Andrew crossed one arm across his chest, sinking his chin into his palm. The furrow between his eyes deepened. "How many people do they employ?"

"Close to 3,000, sir." I stretched out to indicate the land beyond. "And you can see the vestiges of the former administration buildings—quite obviously no longer in use. And, beyond that, in the middle, lay the old military parade grounds." Turning back, a smile crossed my face. "Kind of looks like a ghost town, doesn't it?"

"Indeed," said the prince.

"This is the site where we will construct the downtown area of Panorama with an outdoor shopping district, schools, and a new central park."

~

Seven minutes later, we were on the bus, roaring down the hill. In typical JuliAnne fashion, I'd maintained one eye on our surroundings at all times, and the other on the prince. Suddenly, out of nowhere, the driver slowed down to take a turn...a block earlier than the approved route.

Alarm bells began to sound in my head as the familiar anxiety poured into my stomach.

No, no, no! Snickety screamed, though the driver could not hear her. *What are you doing? We rehearsed this three times, you idiot!*

"Pardon me, Your Majesty." I cringed at the impertinence of interrupting a prince as I rose to my feet. *Desperate times call for desperate measures*, "but the driver just went off track. I'm sure it's fine, but I need to speak to him. Excuse me."

Surprise swept across his handsome features before he waved a hand forward. "Carry on."

But the aisle was 20 men deep between me and the driver. I tapped the shoulder in front of me, motioning toward the front. "*Dice el conductor que es necesario a hacer un turno en la proxima cuadra.*"

The guard stopped in midsentence, inclining his ear. With a nod, he tapped the guy next to him. The second man glanced back before reaching for the third. But number three was laughing with two other guys, and held up a hand.

The bus continued barreling down the block toward a barricade. *Fuck!* I waved a frantic hand toward another grim-faced guard facing my direction six men deep, when the prince's voice rang out from my left.

"Well, go on! Get up there, then!"

The ice in his tone caused me to freeze. I turned back toward the prince, who was waving a hand in my direction, and suddenly, there I was, transported back to grade school: a student being sent off to the principal.

"Go on," he roared. "It's obvious you're going to have to do it yourself!"

Setting my jaw, I dug my elbow into the side of the man in front of me before forcing my way forward, glimpsing a look of shock on Juan Carlos' face as I passed him.

Cheeks burning from the rebuke, my fingers came up to sweep my backside, checking for bite marks. *Jesus.* I remained by the driver's side to hide my embarrassment, even though the fuck-up hadn't been mine. *Fucking Panama,* I seethed. *So many people on the damn bus, you can't even move!*

When the bus pulled adjacent to a giant warehouse a few minutes later, I made my way back down the aisle. This time, it parted like the Red Sea.

"My apologies, Your Majesty," I said, forcing a smile. "This way, sir."

Avoiding my eyes, he gave a pert nod as he descended.

"Sir, we'd planned to take a photo of you atop this front end loader to commemorate your visit." I motioned like Vanna toward a new JCB machine parked in front of the warehouse. But seeing recognition of the approaching storm cross the prince's face, my voice trailed off. "That is, Sir…if you are so inclined."

His Majesty approached the equipment with suspicion, walking around it, inspecting it, and then shooting arrows at another machine like it further down the block. "I'm not doing a staged photo with this thing," he snapped. "It's obvious it hasn't even been used." He turned his heels and began walking in the opposite direction, away from me.

"Sir?" I double-timed it to catch up. "Well." I swallowed hard. *No need to lie.* "We had it delivered this morning, fresh and clean, just for you, that's true."

"Funny." The retort flew back over his shoulder. "But that other equipment there—the stuff that's been used," he thrust his chin toward the second machine, "has another company's logo."

I bit my tongue, cursing Juan Carlos, who had insisted on having a British branded machine delivered. "You don't think he'll notice that it's the only one on-site?" I'd insisted, but to no avail. Until this morning, the JCB brand of construction equipment had never crossed the project threshold; we were loyal to Caterpillar, who were building their Latin American headquarters on land that bordered ours.

It was my turn to shoot arrows in Juan Carlos' direction, who was once again lost in conversation with the ambassador. *Like I said, Juan Carlos, you can't fool a prince.*

Meanwhile, the prince had taken off, heading toward the far end of the warehouse structure, the roof of which had yet to be installed. The floor was scheduled to be poured that afternoon, weather permitting. In its place was the rich red of deep, damp clay.

"He doesn't have the right footwear to be touring the construction site," said Rodrigo, the British Ambassador's chief of staff who appeared out of nowhere.

"And, what am I supposed to do about *that*?" I hissed, watching as the prince brushed past yellow warning tape and headed inside the steel frame, alone.

"Get him back to the bus," my colleague hissed. "I don't have an extra pair of shoes, and we still have to go see the president!"

Gritting my teeth, I began to run. *God damn it! Since when did I end up being this man's handler?* By the time I cut across a wide expanse of dirt to reach the prince, sweat was pouring down the middle of my back. I slowed as I reached him, one hand coming up to smooth down my hair.

Prince Andrew stood peering into a thick canopy of trees.

"Sir," I said, stepping next to him. "I'm sorry to bother you, but we hadn't planned for you to enter this building in its current state. I'm aware you have other meetings this afternoon."

The prince didn't move. He stood there, hands behind his back, his head cocked, staring at a thicket of statuesque palms. It was obvious the prince was going to do what the prince was going to do.

What the heck is he looking at? I turned my gaze toward the same trees in search of movement. For a moment, the silence of the jungle enveloped us and the sounds of the delegation behind faded away. As I gazed into the forest, I felt myself relax. *Well, you can't force him. So, as the old adage goes, if you can't beat 'em, join 'em.* "It's a very unusual landscape for an industrial park, wouldn't you say?"

"It is," the prince nodded. "You know, it's the first time I've been to Panama." He glanced toward me and his eyes were serious. "It surprises you, doesn't it? It's much more than I thought it would be."

Surprise rippled through me as I held his gaze. The depth of his comment took me aback. Here I was worrying about shoes and schedules and this man—a member of the British royal family, no less—was present, fully enjoying the moment. I decided to join him. "Yes," I returned, a faint smile coming across my face. "Panama is indeed full of surprises."

A long pause ensued, both of us gazing into the treetops, saying nothing.

Finally, he turned. "Well," he said, offering me his arm. "Shall we?"

I blinked, propriety causing me to pause before a laugh broke free and I accepted the crook of his elbow. "Why not?" Because it wasn't every day that a girl from Arkansas could say she walked out of a tropical jungle on the arm of an English prince, who had insulted her mere minutes before and had left a string of tabloid hearts in his wake as a young man, when she had been just a teenager.

Needless to say, I had learned long ago that the adventure I had come in search of in Panama was far from a fairy tale. But in that moment, I decided to accept it for what it was, and not worry about what it wasn't. And with that, arm in arm, the prince and I headed back toward the bus.

But as we neared the entrance of the warehouse, the almost-like-a-princess moment ended abruptly when the prince shook himself free of my hand, dusted off the arm of his jacket and charged a few steps ahead of me as the delegation came back into view.

~

"Now, I have a story to tell about this young lady." Rodrigo, the Britsh ambassador's chief of staff cut his eyes at me and chuckled as he pulled out a chair to be seated.

A year had passed since the prince's visit and I had joined Rodrigo and another new acquaintance for a formal luncheon at the swanky Club Union, which would serve as the official Bon Voyage for the outgoing British ambassador.

Crystal tinkled as our host requested us to take our seats, and the three of us settled around the end cap of an elegant table set for 18. In typical Club Union style, the luncheon setting and decor reminded me of clean laundry hanging from my mother's line in small town Arkansas: plenty of hot wind blowing amidst rows of white upon white.

Heavy hitters from Panama's who's who occupied the 17 seats other than my own, including Juan Carlos, though he was seated further down the table toward the ambassador. Those fortunate enough to receive the etched invitation on Embassy stationery always made the effort to attend; to do otherwise was considered bad form, especially when the occasion called for the pomp and circumstance of the standing ambassador's imminent departure.

"*Gracias, joven,*" I said as white gloves carrying a sterling silver pitcher appeared beside me. A quick nod and water flowed into my goblet. Opposite, another pair of gloved hands fluffed a starched napkin before draping it across my lap.

Rodrigo's eyes sparkled. His appetite for a good story was almost as big as it was for a good joke. "Well." He leaned forward in his chair with a wink to my new acquaintance, a dark-haired Argentinian gentleman across from him. "Last year, you may remember that the Duke of York, Prince Andrew, came to Panama. "

"Oh." I cringed as a fierce blush climbed up my neck. "Surely you're not going to tell the one about how the prince treated me like Fergie on the bus." My colleagues at the office had had a good laugh the afternoon following the prince's visit. And to my dismay, news of that story had traveled beyond the project perimeter to many of my colleagues at the British Chamber.

Rodrigo wagged a finger. "Oh, no, no, no. This one is much better than that, *amiga*!"

Another waiter appeared with wine bottles in hand. "*Vino tinto o vino blanco, Senora*?" I pointed toward the white, never taking my eyes off the storyteller.

Rodrigo swirled his wine, clearing his throat. "Well, Panama was only one of a few stops on the prince's agenda last year." He took a gulp before tilting the goblet at me. "Though it was an important one, of course, because it was the first time British royalty had come to visit our premiere project in the country, Panorama."

Juan Carlos turned from the far end of the table to peer over his reading glasses toward us. Our eyes met for a moment before he leaned forward to grasp his wine glass, scanning the faces on either side of me as waiters around the room set chilled plates in front of each diner.

The man should have been a detective. This from the ever present Snickety.

"So, this lady," Rodrigo clasped a rough hand to my shoulder – a common gesture of friendship among Panamañians, "suffice it to say, the prince took a liking to her when he was on his tour." He guffawed, eyes roaming up and down my body. "But then, what's not to like?"

The Argentinian ducked his head.

"Oh, for God's sake, Rodrigo, stop it," I hissed, glancing back Juan Carlos' direction.

Rodrigo continued on, nonplussed. "Anyway," he speared a clump of arugula, "we had a very tight schedule that day." He twirled his fork in the air before bringing it to his mouth. "Including a visit with the president."

I narrowed my eyes at him as I brought my glass to my lips.

"And this lady...," Rodrigo smacked his lips, "...was in charge of the whole tour and did a bang-up job."

I colored again. "Thank you, my friend. But you know it wasn't just me. It was a team effort."

"Bullshit," said Rodrigo as the smile ran away from his face. "You did more than anyone else, and you were amazing."

I stopped chewing to cover my mouth with my hand. "Thank you."

"Anyway, there's more." Rodrigo clucked his tongue, shoveling more salad into his mouth. "The prince was so taken with this lady that he ruined a new pair of shoes just for her."

"What?" Now it was my turn to spew white wine. "You can't blame that on me! I didn't make him walk through the mud."

Our luncheon companion turned his head to me, observing our back and forth with a bemused smile on his face.

"A-ha!" Rodrigo snorted. "You didn't, but he did." He lifted his crystal goblet to guzzle more wine before motioning to the waiter behind him for more.

"Well," I shook my head, "you can't blame me for what he did. He's got a mind of his own, your prince!"

Rodrigo's laughter shook the table. "That he does. Indeed, he does. And while he chose to walk into the dirt with *you*," he crooked a finger in my direction, "he turned down a similar opportunity the very next day with Mr. Carlos Slim of Mexico."

The fork on its way to my mouth stopped. Carlos Slim was the wealthiest man in Latin America, one of the world's famed billionaires. "He did *what*?"

"Yep." A dab of salad dressing dribbled down Rodrigo's chin. "That's right."

The Argentinian piped up. "*En serio?*"

"Yes." Rodrigo's head continued its bobbing motion. "The next day after he was here, I flew with the prince to Mexico where he met Carlos Slim. Señor Slim has another huge project there—I believe it's bigger than our Pacific jewel here—and at the end of the meeting, he invited the prince to join him on a tour."

"And?" I inquired, my fork poised above my plate.

Rodrigo winked. "The prince refused."

"He refused?" My jaw dropped open. I scrolled back to my first day of work when I had met Carlos Slim when he'd flown in on his private jet.

The man had swept into the airport with his posse as if he'd owned the place. "*Mentira*, Rodrigo. You're making this up."

Rodrigo's eyes widened in protest as a beefy palm came up to cover his mouth. "No!" His head gave a violent shake. "I'm not!"

I stared at him.

"I promise you." His voice came from behind ample fingers. "He refused."

"The prince refused Carlos Slim?" I'd almost forgotten the Argentinian was still with us.

"Yep," Rodrigo nodded.

The prince chose to walk with me in the dirt and then refused a tour with Carlos Slim? Giggles started to spill out as Juan Carlos turned our way, his eyes full of questions. *Holy shit!*

Rodrigo turned to me with a look of triumph. "So, you *see*? And the shoes he wore that day on tour with you? The red clay stained them; they were ruined." He snapped his chin toward his chest. "So, Señora, I'd say you made *quite* an impression on our visiting prince. Quite an impression, indeed!"

I made an attempt to stifle my laughter. "Okay," I shrugged. "If what you say is true, I'll take that as a compliment."

Rodrigo lifted his glass in a toast with a wink. "As you very well *should*, my dear. As you very well should!"

"*Salud*," said our lunch companion, joining in on our tribute.

"*Salud*," I replied with a smile. *Wait 'til Joe hears this one!* My spirits lifted with our trio of wine glasses. But then I remembered the evening event marked on my agenda and anxiety snaked in to put a damper on things.

Snickety shriveled her nose. *Better wait, then. He'll be too far gone by the time you get home.*

She's right. My heart sank. I missed the days when going home to Joe hadn't been a crapshoot, when I was sure that my own Prince Charming would be in residence and not somewhere out to sea under the influence of a bottle.

The tinkling of a fork on crystal brought me back to the present as the ambassador stood up to make his speech.

CHAPTER 39:
The Talk

Thump thump, thump thump, thump thump.

A few weeks later, as Tomas maneuvered my car on the climb toward the crest atop the Bridge of the Americas, I balanced a mug of tea in one hand and scrolled through my Blackberrywith the other. The clock read 7:29 a.m.

"Let's see if Curt is on time this morning, Tomas." I squinted at the tiny screen, waiting.

Tomas had a way of parroting whatever I said when he wasn't listening. "Let's see."

When the minute number changed, my phone began to ring.

"A-ha!" I gave Tomas a sideways grin before I assumed my most professional tone. "Mister Curt, *buen dia*! How are *you* this morning?"

"It was great to see you guys at dinner last night," Curt's voice was smooth.

He must've gotten laid last night.

"We appreciated the invite." I bit my lip. *We both know the only reason we were included was to assist in recruiting our latest multi-national client. All gringo hands on deck.* Joe had succumbed to my plea to tag along when I'd reminded him we'd be right around the corner from his favorite cigar shop.

"Really?" Curt sounded surprised. "I thought those guys were pretty unexciting."

"Well." I exhaled, grateful he was in one of his reasonable moods. "To be honest, they were incredibly boring." That brought a chuckle. *Amazing how normal he can be when he wants to be, almost charming.* I waited, expectant. A long pause followed. *Already scrolling through his email?* A few taps in the background confirmed my suspicion.

"Anyway, what's up? I got your message a bit ago. You said it was important," Curt said.

"Yes." I swallowed hard. "Right. I did. Thanks for returning the call." My heart began to pound.

Showtime! said Snickety.

"I'd like to get your input about how the two of us could work together more efficiently, Curt," I said. "And I've put together some ideas. Are you available for lunch later this week so I could present them to you?"

"Can't you just come and show me in my office?" Curt's tone meant he was seeing signs of something he didn't like in his emails. "I've got a ton going on this week."

I deepened my tone like I'd practiced with Falc. "No, Curt, I can't." I cringed, waiting for an explosion, but there was none. I plunged forward. "This is really important to me and we get interrupted too much when we're in your office. I need your full attention."

Curt's sigh blew into my ear.

I counted to 10, wrinkling my nose, then holding my breath. Falc had predicted there might be a fight. "Show him what he gets out of it," he'd said. "Put yourself in his shoes, but stand your ground. He's used to your being a pushover; you are educating him about the new you and what you need in this relationship. It starts with not backing down."

"Tell you what." I broke the silence. "How about if we merge this stuff with our weekly meeting with the stipulation that we get off campus? That would free you up an hour on next Monday. Then you'll have an extra hour in your schedule you hadn't anticipated."

Curt's relief was palpable as he took the bait. "Great." The sound of his pen scribbling on his notepad meant he was convinced. "And, actually, I'm glad you brought this up. I do have some concerns about your department's performance lately that I've been wanting to talk to you about. And some ideas of my own."

My stomach did a flip flop or two. *Keep breathing.* "How about Thursday?"

I heard some tapping. "Thursday's good. Noon at El Formaggio?" Curt had a penchant for Italian food, plus the location across the Bridge would provide safe haven from other colleagues who never ventured that far.

"Perfect." My fist pumped. "Look forward to it. Have a good day." My finger pressed end before I rolled down the car window. "Yahoo!" I reached out to hand surf with the wind. The morning breeze rippled through my hair as the car began the ascent at the Panorama exit. "I did it! I did it! He said yes!"

Tomas' green eyes flashed, unaccustomed to this much exuberance from the *jefa*. "Good news, Miss JuliAnne?"

"Yes, Tomas." I let out an exhale. "Very good news. Señor Curt is in a decent mood today."

This announcement seemed to rouse my driver from his near slumber. "Yes? Waoooo! Congratulations."

I chuckled. "Yes, Tomas," I said. "In this case, it makes sense to congratulate me. Anytime Mister Curt is in a good mood, it is most definitely a day to celebrate!"

Peals of laughter shook the car as we joined the progression of vehicles toward the Panorama Business Park and my office.

~

When the Thursday lunch arrived, I got myself to our meeting place early to pick a table and get my game face on.

My internal circus had been going on all week; the exhilaration of scoring this meeting faded into the background as soon as I'd arrived at the office on Monday, and found Curt screaming about some exhibits he needed for a proposal. The rest of the week had become a tug-of-war between my flagging self-confidence and the newfound courage I was developing in my work with Falc.

"What's true for you about this meeting with Curt?" Falc's eyes had pierced me as he leaned forward in his chair to hear me above the din in the restaurant. I could see in moments like these why his Indian tribe had given him that nickname.

I took a deep breath. *Strength.* "I want him to stop treating me like shit."

"Right," Falc nodded. "And what does that look like?"

"I want him to stop yelling at me—at all of us—like we're children." I placed my coffee cup back in its saucer. *Why is my hand shaking?* "And to stop being unreasonable about deadlines. He's not the only guy I work for but he seems to forget that."

Falc regarded me. "Right. And what does Curt want, do you think, from this conversation?"

I frowned. "I don't know. Probably to bitch about something else he isn't getting fast enough and to tell me how to do my job."

"Right," Falc continued. "So, you'd told me what you don't want in this relationship. Now let me hear what you do desire within it." Falc was training me to use the word "desire" in lieu of "want." "By definition, 'want' means you are lacking," he'd said. "And, our goal in working together is that you attain what you desire. So, instead of *want*, please use the word 'desire.' It's a much stronger message to the universe. And, for practice's sake," he winked, "let's pretend I'm Curt, so you can get primed for the real conversation."

My stomach turned cartwheels as I scanned Falc's kind, wrinkled face. *Curt's countenance is anything but kind.* "All right." I sat up straight. "Curt, I appreciate your taking the time to meet with me today."

Falc narrowed his eyes in an effort to look gruff. "Sure. So, what's on your mind?"

A laugh began to form, but I forced it down. "I have some concerns about how the two of us have been interacting."

"Hang on," the gruff mask evaporated. "That's not what you've been telling me, JuliAnne. Do you really have concerns about how you have been acting with Curt or are you just being nice?"

I thought for a moment. "I guess I'm just being nice."

"Okay, you're done with being nice, remember? Being nice has gotten you run over, felt up, tossed around like a noodle, and made you feel like shit!" Falc leaned halfway across the table. "And you've told me you are done being treated like shit. Is that correct?"

"Yes!" My nod was vigorous.

"So, no more Mr. Nice Guy." He thrust his hand in my face. "Are you at a place where you feel you deserve something different?"

"Yes!" I exclaimed.

"And do you feel desire for something different from this guy, or don't you?"

"I do!" My head continued to bob.

"Then, JuliAnne," Falc's eyes pierced me like arrows. "You need to go in like a lion, inform him of your new boundaries, and tell him what's going to happen when he crosses them!"

The force of his tone caused me to cower. Just a bit. *No wonder Falc is so successful. Now I see why he has such a prestigious reputation for being called in to negotiate tough multimillion-dollar deals.*

"So, strap on your big girl pants and get out there and lead the conversation!" Falc roared. "And let him see the you that's been standing in the background all these years—the one who knows what needs to happen, how it needs to happen, and doesn't take any shit. Show him why he needs to give you the respect you say you deserve." Falc leaned closer, his voice dropping to just above a growl. "Are you ready for that, JuliAnne?" His palm came up in front of my nose where he clenched it into a fist. "Because it's there for you. All you have to do is command it."

I began to pull myself erect again from where I'd begun to cower when Falc had raised his voice.

"That is exactly what I desire…" My voice came out a squeak before I shook my head and coughed. *No.* I raised my eyes to his, forcing the muscles in my belly to tighten. *Energy goes where attention flows. This is my choice.* This time, my voice was anything but a pushover. "That *is* what I desire," I said. "But how do I do that without coming across as a whiny bitch?"

Falc grinned. "Great job coming back to your power just now. Because this…," his index finger pointed at me, "this is a powerful woman!"

He picked up a spoon. "To answer your question, I have a trick I'd like to show you that will level the playing field with Curt from this point forward." He twirled the cutlery between his fingers. "So much so that he will never treat you in the same way again, at least as long as you hold your ground. Because with this trick and the part when you tell him what you require in how he treats you—he may even *forget* that you're a woman."

Coming back to the present moment, I smiled at the thought of what Curt's reaction might be when he saw this trick I had learned from Falc.

I sat at the four-top with my back against a wall, waiting. My heart rate had cooled but the trapeze act in my stomach continued.

"When you get anxious, bring your focus back to your breath," Falc had said. "Bring your energy down to your belly and feel your core connect to the very center of Mother Earth. Like that giant tree you told me about. You are immovable."

Out of the corner of my eye, I watched as a silver SUV whipped into the restaurant's entry, screeching to a stop. Curt catapulted from the driver's seat, grabbed his suit jacket, and tossed it with his keys to the valet. Covering the short distance to the hostess stand in a few strides, I could see him scan the room. *Here we go.* My throat tightened as I lifted my hand. *I am strong.*

Curt took the stairs two at a time to reach the landing where I sat. "Hey!" I stood to offer my cheek. "How's it going?"

Curt leaned in and I felt the air swish between our faces, though his skin never touched mine. *He never touches anyone,* the thought rose as we took our seats. *Except for the occasional high five or fist bump.*

Our waiter appeared to get Curt's drink order.

"So," Curt never wasted time, "what's all this mystery about wanting to get me away from the office?"

I smiled, Falc's voice resounding in my ears. *Don't be surprised when he tries to take control of the conversation.* "Let's get our order in first, shall we?" I picked up my menu. "So that we can beat the crowd a bit, before we get right to it."

"All right." Curt followed suit. He flipped a page in the three-ring binder that resembled a book.

"*Estamos listos a ordenar*?" The lapel of the waiter's white shirt was worn; a stain the color of molasses marked his pants at the knee.

I raised my eyes and smiled. "*Sí, por fa.*"

"*Señora.*" His pen scribbled as I ordered. "*Y el Señor.*"

When Curt finished placing his order, I smiled. "Your Spanish has come a long way in two years."

Something between guilt and embarrassment crossed his brow. "Yeah," he grinned, "it has." He dropped his napkin into his lap. "Yours is pretty good, too."

"It's my private lessons," I said. "About four hours a week."

"Hmm." Curt set down his glass, motioning toward my notebook. "You ready?"

"I am." I flipped open the spiral to a paperclip and placed it behind the vase that sat between our placemats. Inhaling with intention, I turned to look him full in the face.

"But first, Curt, before I get to sharing, I'd like to say how much I appreciate you making this time for us to talk. The way in which we work together is super important to the company, as much as it is to me. You are unstoppable in making sure this company is selling at its maximum and that the team is producing as much as it can. Your North American drive to success is something I admire in addition to your efficiency. So, I appreciate you. And I want to tell you that first."

Curt's eyes widened as if he were in the spotlight before he averted his gaze. "Um, sure. But, that's what we're here for, isn't it?"

I clenched my stomach muscles. "It is, which leads me into what I want to share with you first." I picked up the pen lying next to my notebook to keep my hands occupied. "As I mentioned on the phone, I'm interested in working with you in a way that supports the goals you have for the part of the business you manage and what we're building overall, and also gives me the support I need in marketing and communications to achieve the things the board has asked me to do. But I need to know, first, are you interested in working together more efficiently as a team?"

Curt's eyes glanced off mine before he looked again toward my notebook. "Of course."

I placed my pen atop the notebook.

"Great," I said. "But I think it's important first that I own up to a couple of interactions we've had recently that don't work for me. Because I have a feeling, they don't work for you either but neither of us have had the nerve to bring it up."

Curt lifted an eyebrow.

"Give an example," Falc had coached. "But only one. Be specific and own up to your part, whatever that is."

I gulped. *Go for the gold, JuliAnne. Be kind but speak your truth.* "Remember when you had that corporate presentation on Tuesday and you called me from the Visitor Center five minutes before you started to ask why the laser pointer was not in the conference room?"

The duck in Curt's head was slight. His eyes narrowed. "Yes."

"My experience was that you spent four minutes yelling about why the pointer wasn't there." I looked straight into Curt's eyes. "The thing is, Curt, when you yell at me, I can't hear anything you're trying to communicate. All I hear is yelling."

Color rushed to Curt's face.

I pressed on. "Yelling does not work for me. What I need in order to perform is to be treated with dignity and respect. And that does not include yelling."

A bead of sweat broke out on Curt's brow.

"What I'd like to tell you is that I screwed up in not coming to you sooner with this issue." The pen danced amidst my fingers. "I'd like to apologize for that because it wasn't very respectful of me or of you. I was afraid that you would demean me for coming to you about how I felt, or that you would think it was stupid or that you would yell more." My voice was coming fast.

Slow down.

I inhaled, counting to five. "The bottom line is that, in not speaking up about what I needed, I disrespected me," I paused, "which made me feel resentful. Plus, I didn't give you the opportunity to do anything different. I apologize for not valuing our relationship enough to come to you immediately."

The cloud of suspicion on Curt's face began to lift.

I plowed forward. "So, in the future, I'm going to make a commitment to you, Curt. As soon as I realize I have a problem related to any interaction we have, I am going to come to you. I am going to tell you where I'm at, hear where you are at, and then we can talk about it. Because I believe that's one way we can work better together—much better—for the good of the company."

Curt shifted in his seat, blinking.

Ask the question, Snickety danced.

Clinch the deal! Falc thundered. *You need his agreement!*

"Would it be valuable to you to know that you have someone else in the office who's committed to making things work as smoothly as possible between our two departments?"

Curt gave a vigorous nod. "Yes. Though I've always felt that way about you. And, I don't think you did anything wrong."

Surprise flushed my cheeks. "Thank you," I said. "But I made some assumptions. In the future, I won't make that mistake again. I'll simply come to you so we can talk. I know if there's anything you're interested in, Curt, it's efficiency. *This*...," I tapped the table, "...will make us more efficient. Sound like a deal?" I extended my hand.

He lifted his hand to shake mine. "Deal."

"Great!" In his eyes, I saw something new. *Admiration?*

Snickety drew a large check next to the first item on my mental chalkboard.

"All right," I said, turning to the next page. "In that spirit, there's something else."

Curt sat up straighter. "All right."

I picked up the spoon from the silverware in front of me. "I'm going to use this to show you."

Curt's brow crinkled.

I held the spoon up, so that its profile curved between us. "Now, as you can see, this spoon has two sides." My finger traced the backside. "Let's consider that each side is one perspective. Now, depending on where each of them are sitting, two people looking at this spoon from different angles will probably describe what they are seeing in very different language."

Curt's face twisted into a frown.

I continued, "But in reality, those two people are talking about the exact same structure. It's just that the manner in which they are languaging is probably foreign to the other person…"

He's getting impatient, Snickety screeched. *Speed up.*

I reached out to place a hand on Curt's shirtsleeve. "I know this may seem silly, but this analogy will help me prove my point, Curt. So, hang with me." I thrust the spoon at him. "And take this."

Curt's reluctant hand received the spoon. He turned it sideways to inspect it.

"Notice," I continued, "that when you hold the spoon, you hold it in a different way than I did."

Curt nodded, eyes trained on the spoon.

"Imagine how different the use and perspectives would be if either of us was from a different country or a different culture!"

"Bring the analogy home to how it relates to the two of you by asking a question about a shared experience," Falc had said.

I brought my eyes back to Curt's face. "And, you, Curt—you and I— we experience these cultural differences every day in our office, do we not?"

Curt's eyes rolled skyward as he nodded.

"So, the point is, that the spoon is like our shared goals and vision of creating success and abundance in our work at Panorama." My finger pointed toward the Canal where the crown jewel of Panama's reclaimed lands lay. "The spoon is the thing you and I share—we both want the same thing and we're on the same team—but sometimes because our training, our expertise, and our backgrounds are different, or because I juggle direction from you and from Juan Carlos, our perspectives look more different than they actually are."

Curt's chest began to cave in at the mention of Juan Carlos' name.

"But, you and I, Curt," the use of his name caused my boss' neck to snap back up, "you and I have a *shared* vision." I let those words sink in as Curt stared at me. "It's just that sometimes we have different paths of getting there." I held my palm out, fingers beckoning.

Curt returned the silverware to me.

"Now," my heart picked up the pace, "all that said, I have to be honest."

Bad news! Snickety hid her face in her arms. *Batten down the hatches!*

My voice dropped to just above a whisper. "I only recently got this concept and realized—again—that I had made the mistake of judging you because I thought you were just being unreasonable with me about things. I thought that when you pushed and pushed and pushed that you were just being a dick."

Curt's eyes widened, though he didn't move a muscle.

I didn't drop my gaze. "But then I realized with this analogy," I glanced again at the spoon in my hand, "that perhaps part of the problem was my perspective."

Though not all of it, Falc had said. *Speak your truth.*

My throat went dry as a flash of anger washed over me and I stared into the eyes of my transgressor. I put a finger up as I reached for my water, draining the glass.

You are strong, whispered a voice. *You've got the floor. Take your time.*

"But, I am also realistic that I need to speak up when I need something." I wiped my lips with my napkin. "So, this is me speaking up."

Curt's eyes followed my every move, his face frozen.

"In some of our past interactions, the ways I allowed you to treat me do not ring true with how I allow myself to be treated." I felt the blood rush pound in my veins. "One of the values I hold most dear is that I treat people with respect." I ticked my fingers in the air like I was checking off a list. "For example, I return phone calls. I reply to emails within a few hours, or at the most within a day. I listen. I allow others to have their say. I don't yell and I generally consider that every person has their own burden to bear, and I am gentle with them."

Curt still had not moved a muscle.

I leaned back. "I have a personal belief that people deserve my respect, that every person is *worthy* of respect. And I feel that I deserve theirs." I paused. "In our case, Curt, there are many things about you that I respect. I do feel that I treat you with respect in our interactions. Would you agree that's the case?"

Curt looked like a deer caught in the headlights. "I think so."

"Great," I leaned toward him. "And you like it when people treat you with respect, don't you?"

"Yes." A muscle next to his eyebrow twitched.

"Great," I said. "So, what I am asking is that you treat me the way you like to be treated—with respect."

Curt erupted, "But no one treats me with respect in our office, especially not Juan Carlos!"

My breath caught in my throat, though I held my ground.

The wisdom from Falc might as well have come from Yoda. *Face your fear. What's the worst thing that could happen?*

"But I do." I stressed the word *I*. "And we're not talking about anyone else other than the two of us here." I tapped the table with my finger. "We're talking about you and me. So, I'm going to ask you," I leaned forward, eyes boring into his, "is there any reason why you won't treat me with the same respect you would like for yourself from this point forward?"

The steam in Curt's face evaporated and for a moment, the person I glimpsed in his eyes looked more like a scared little boy than a senior level executive. He cleared his throat. "No reason," he said. "You absolutely have my respect."

"Great." Triumph flooded my chest. "That means the world to me. Thank you."

Just then, the waiter appeared at my elbow, tray in hand. "*Su comida, Señores.*"

"*Muchas gracias.*" I leaned back for the steaming plate to be placed before me. I reached for my lemonade as the man rearranged some things to make room for Curt's meal.

"Well," Curt picked up his fork as the waiter took his leave, "shall we eat?" He glanced at me, a shy smile spreading across his normally stern features. "But maybe this time, we could use forks?"

Relief washed over me. "Yes!" I scrambled for my fork, bringing it up to clink with his. "*Salud!*"

I gave an inward smile as I lifted the first bite to my mouth.

Falc's voice came again in the background. *Well done,* he nodded. *Well done.*

On my way back to the office in the safety of the car, my throat tightened and I struggled to breathe.

"Everything all right, Miss JuliAnne?" Tomas had somehow noticed I wasn't tapping away on my handheld like usual.

"Sí, Tomas," I managed as my fingers came up to clutch the middle of my chest. The anxiety I'd had before the meeting had now settled into familiar waves of *What the heck did I just do?* after the fact. I popped a Xanax and swallowed it down. All these new techniques I was putting into place were hardly a guarantee of instant peace and calm, at least not for me, not yet.

"The steps you are taking," Falc had said, "do lead to your taking the reins of your life back. The body is often the last to catch up, the last to understand that there's no more need for the fight or flight response. So, just keep breathing when you feel the anxiety come. It too will pass."

So that's what I did, day after day, time and time again, when I took a new baby step toward my sanity and my freedom. *Breath in, breath out, breath in, breath out.* And I tried…I really tried…not to worry about the future.

CHAPTER 40:
The Change of Tides

As we reached the peak of the hill, daylight crested, splaying yellow and orange rays of sunlight across the façade of the city's 100-plus skyscrapers.

"Wow," I breathed. "We're so lucky to get to see this, aren't we, baby girl?"

Lily looked up from the end of her leash, panting.

A flash of color dipped and glided above our heads. I caught the crescent shape of a yellow and black beak out of the corner of my eye. "That's three toucans today, baby girl!"

Lily stamped her feet and gave a slight pull.

"All right, all right, just a second." I bent down to tie my shoelaces when a familiar voice cut through the tranquility.

"Hey! JuliAnne!"

My stomach did a flip-flop. I sprang to my feet, squinting. *Please, no.*

There's an alternate route, Snickety squealed, pointing toward the street we had just passed. But the square-shouldered figure had advanced in the dim light. *If I take off now, it'll be too obvious.*

"Hey!" Curt cupped his hands to form a microphone as he emerged from the canopy of the street below.

Fuck. I lifted my hand as the hair on the back of my neck bristled. "Oh, hey." My hand smoothed over the top of my headband. At 5:30 in the morning, I never looked in the mirror before Lily pulled me out the door. It was rare, if ever, that I ran into anyone at this hour, especially since we had moved into our new condo at Panorama. We had been the second family to move into the first residential building. It was just a few of us amidst a multitude of abandoned buildings. Curt and his girlfriend moved in the week after we did.

"Are you coming this way?" I yelled, hoping we'd leave it at hello and continue on our separate paths.

"What?" Curt huffed, pulling out his earphones. "Hang on! I'll be there in one second."

Lily emitted a low growl as Curt's companion, a small dog, came into view.

"It's okay, girl." I pulled the leash in tight next to my hip. "We've met Ringo before." In our previous meetings, the black and tan miniature pinscher had shown more affection for Lily than she had for him.

As Curt approached, Lily gnashed her teeth at the petite dog. Curt came to an abrupt halt, eyeing her. "Will she...?"

"Just keep walking toward us on the right," I said, turning in the opposite direction. "It's a dog pack thing. You have to take the lead and let 'em know who's boss. They'll get used to each other again in a second." I took a few steps. "Come on."

"Okay." Curt kept an eye on Lily and pulled Ringo in close before falling into stride beside me. "How's it going?"

How can he be cheerful at this time of the morning? I ignored the question. "I didn't know you got out this early."

"We don't usually, but I'm trying to get back in shape." Curt patted his belly. "So I'm changing things up a little bit with my workout routine."

The last thing I want to discuss with my former arch enemy is his desire to get skinny for his new Panamanian girlfriend. Curt and his first wife had split the year prior; she had returned to the U.S. with their kids.

Though you have to admit, his moods seem much more stable these days.

I changed the subject. "Did you see the toucans as you came out of Calle Quetzal? There were two hopping around in there when we went through." The tree boughs above this particular street hung heavy with overhead vines, providing a perfect hiding place for the famous Fruit Loop bird.

"You know everyone keeps telling me about all the toucans in this country, but I've never seen one."

My jaw dropped. "You've lived in Panama for three years and you've never seen a toucan?"

Curt shook his head. "Not in the wild."

"Wow. They're all over the place, Curt. How is that possible?" Then I spied the white cord around his neck. "Ah, wait. Do you always have those in?"

Of course, he does, Snickety sniffed. *This is the guy that wore earphones the entirety of his first two years in the office.*

"I do. I download a lot of the news podcasts and listen to them," Curt said, relaxing his hold on Ringo, who began to wander my direction.

Lily lunged toward him, snapping and snarling. Curt came to an abrupt halt.

I wound my leash back to the hilt and reached fingers toward Curt. "Hand me Ringo's leash."

"But won't she…?" The trepidation in Curt's eyes caught me by surprise.

"Just give him to me," I commanded, "and follow my lead."

Of course, his wussy dog has a wussy leash. My palm closed around the hard plastic handle of the retractable. I picked up the pace, both dogs in tow. "Come on!" I tossed over my shoulder. "We have to walk fast, so they stay focused on keeping up. It diverts their attention."

Curt ran the few steps to catch up.

"So, anyway, about the toucans," I continued. "You usually hear them before you see them, so it might be a good idea to do some walking without your earphones."

"How often do you see them?" Curt began to gasp, his breath coming faster.

"Every day," I replied, keeping my attention on maintaining space between our mutts. "Sometimes twice."

"Really?" He crooked his head toward me. "Every single day?"

"Of course," I nodded. "They're all over."

"Have you seen more than one at a time?"

"Sure," I nodded, fighting to keep the incredulous look off my face. *Where has this guy been?*

"Usually where there's one, there's a second. The max I've seen in one day out here is 12. Over time you'll get familiar with their call, which is usually how you'll catch them. I hear them first before I see them."

"Can you show me sometime?"

My breath caught in my throat before I sent him a sideways glance. It hardly seemed plausible that I had once considered the figure next to me, covered in sweat with hair sticking up in all directions, my nemesis. And now he was asking me to show him the toucans?

"Really?" I said, before I could stop myself. "You want me to show you how to find the toucans?"

Color rose to Curt's cheeks. "I mean, only if it's not too much trouble."

His discomfort caused me to smile. "All right," I replied. "But it has to be early, like this, or we'll miss them."

"Great," Curt said as we reached the door of our building. "Let's do it."

I handed him his dog's leash and motioned the two of them inside. "You first."

Lily's nails clicked as we climbed up the tile steps after them.

"Thanks for the education," he called as Lily and I peeled off on the second floor. "And, have a good day!"

"You too," I said. "Good to see you." And for the first time in three years, that phrase didn't feel fake.

Snickety was staring at me, mouth agape, shaking her head from side to side. *Holy shit!*

"No kidding." I looked at Lily, who took a sit as I turned the key in the lock at our apartment door. A laugh began to rumble from deep within my belly. "This is one of my greatest teachers, huh? And now he wants me to show him how to find a toucan? Holy shit, indeed."

I closed the door softly before hanging the leash on a hook behind the door and walked to the kitchen. My iPhone signaled that I had a text. It was from Juan Carlos.

"I need to see you first thing. Let me know what time you'll be in, please," the text read.

All remnants of humor evaporated like the Ghost of Christmas Past as I ran for the shower.

~

My pulse thumped when I heard the signature steps echo down the hallway toward my office.

"*Que paso?*" the familiar voice inquired with the tenor of a schoolboy.

But my stomach affirmed the fact that this was no fresh faced juvenile as it wrenched in my gut. Danger, it squeezed. Danger, danger, danger.

The steps grew closer. A smattering of female voices transformed from giggles into polite containment. "*Hola, Señor Juan Carlos,*" they rang in unison.

I could see his eyes narrow as they swept the room, as his feet advanced my direction, ascertaining in the blink of an eye if something was amiss, off. The man rarely missed a beat. When I closed my eyes, the image of a hound dog came to mind, long snout to the ground, ears flared, eager to seek out whatever was coming… *Whether or not anything is really there*, my mind accused.

The vision of the dog evaporated as my heartbeat began to pound. My hand went out for the glass of water beside my keyboard as the auto-reflex to cough forced the wind from my larynx. *Oh, for fuck's sake, perfect timing.*

"Everything okay?"

Water spewed from my mouth, streaming from between my fingers as my head went into the auto-pleaser nodding sequence. My other hand grasped the Kleenex to my lips with record speed as my voice forced its way through the liquid. "Yes, yes, everything's great." *Crap. That sounded weak. Try again.*

"Come in, come in." I waved the Kleenex at him, motioning toward the chair facing me. Air continued to fight for passage with the tickle in my throat. *Holy crap! What is my problem? Why do I fall back on this pattern of bracing myself for the worst, instead of waiting to see what he wants?* I reached for a pen and paper as I tried to pull strength into my core.

Juan Carlos arched an eyebrow as he came in and closed the door, along with the compulsory, "Are you getting sick?" The room in the air seemed to thicken as he settled himself into the chair across from mine, shuffling a stack of papers from the crook of his arm to the seat of the other chair.

"Just inhaled the wrong way, nothing more." The even tenor of my voice surprised me.

"Hum," came his signature reply. I watched his eyes scan the small room: my tidy stacks of paper atop the shelves, a small fountain supplying a steady stream of white noise on the file cabinet, the characteristically messy surface of my desk wiped clean except for a single cream-color manila file by itself in the corner. I half expected to see his glance return in suspicion to the file folder, like a cat ready to pounce, and his chin to extend in its direction, *Do you have something for me there?*

But today, it appeared my inner sense was off. There was no second glance, no question. "How was your trip?"

My body relaxed, if only slightly. *Of course, the niceties first.* "Right," I said. "Really good, thanks." My brain calculated the days. It had been almost three weeks since I'd seen him between Hanukkah and our trip back to Denver for Christmas. "Though it seems like a year ago already. Yours?"

"We spent some time in Chile, then we were here."

I nodded, attempting to mask the tension wrapping around my midsection with a polite smile.

"Nice. Are the kids still on vacation?"

"Yes, until the ninth."

Why the hell is he making small talk? "That's nice." I nodded again before holding my tongue. One thing I'd learned in the past years of working with this man was to wait him out versus attempting to ask him anything; one of the direct benefits of the expensive coaching I'd invested in.

He licked his lips, running a hand through his thick dark hair before reaching toward the hidden stack. A moment later, he brought a single white envelope to the surface of the desk.

My gaze flickered to it. Number nine. Standard size. It bore my name in carefully typed letters. My interest piqued though my face revealed nothing.

"Right before the end of the year," Juan Carlos began, "the board elected to distribute annual bonuses."

My head snapped up. Now, he had my full attention. Bonuses had never been paid prior to March 31, not for the executive team.

"I came around, but you were out, so I held on to this until you got back."

My eyes narrowed as I steeled myself for the fight that was sure to come. Juan Carlos had a habit of pointing out that something important always happened when I was on vacation. After the first two years, I'd ignored the innuendo and I would do the same today. *I deserve every fricking minute I take outside this fucking office.* I bit my tongue, waiting for him to continue. *Come on, let's get it over with.* A moment ticked by, then two. But to my surprise, when I lifted my eyes back to his, I saw a smile there.

My guard came down, just a little.

"Congratulations." He extended the envelope toward me.

My hand went out to meet his, receiving it. "Thank you," I replied, though I didn't have a clue what I was thanking him for.

"The board decided to award you your full bonus this year."

My pupils widened as I turned the envelope over and removed the check. *Full bonus.* I dropped my eyes to the numerical figure typed into the little box on the right side and my jaw dropped. *Holy shit.*

"The board is happy with your performance." Juan Carlos watched me, taking in the shock washing over my features.

I looked at him again. *Full bonus.* Then I looked at the check. *Well, knock me over with a feather.* "Thank you!" I stammered before shutting my mouth. "Wow. I don't know what to say… Thank you." Tears pooled as the full force of this thing hit me and I remembered what my old boss in Denver had once told me. *When you get to this level, the only way you'll know they're really happy is when you get paid your bonus.*

I let the appreciation sink into my skull, relishing in the unfamiliar feeling before reality sank in. As it did, my head began to pound again. *Uh oh.* My eyes darted sideways to the single file on my desk. *Shit.* The file held a resignation letter that I had drafted earlier in the week with Joe; I had finally had my fill of Curt. While things had improved, they were still far from perfect. It was time to move on.

Snickety nudged me. *Go ahead. No better time to get out than when you're on top!*

I hesitated. *Maybe I'll wait 'til the check is cashed.*

Juan Carlos was smiling, oblivious to my internal dialogue. "Oh, and there's one more thing."

I dragged my eyes up from the check in my hand, where I couldn't stop staring at that number. It was bigger than what I'd hoped for, much less the biggest bonus I'd ever had in my *life.* All the carefully-arranged composure I normally employed had gone right out the window.

"We're making some structural changes to the org chart."

Still immersed in the check and what it would mean for my impending resignation, I shook my head, trying to refocus on Juan Carlos. "Okay." There had been some talk about an org charge shuffle in a recent director's meeting, though it had nothing to do with me.

"We've decided it makes more sense for marketing to be a corporate function, versus answering to sales."

The fog in my brain evaporated. The man now had my complete attention. "I'm sorry…what?"

Juan Carlos pulled his reading glasses down from the top of his furrowed brow to peer at another piece of paper he'd freed from his hidden stack. I recognized the tidy little boxes stacked atop one another as an org chart. He laid the paper on the desk in front of me.

"That's right. Effective immediately, you'll be answering to me."

The pen in my hand clattered to the floor.

~

As soon as Juan Carlos departed, I shredded my resignation letter and tucked its remains into my handbag lest anyone discover it by accident. Then, I called Joe on his office phone.

"Hey." I could tell from his voice that he was knee deep in construction drawings.

"Are you in the middle of something?" The urgency in my tone seemed to wake him up.

"Yes, but I'll always make time for you."

"I'll be right down." I slammed down the receiver and ran out the door, down the hall, clattering down the front steps and around the corner to the building's basement level which had been only partially built into the ground. Swiping my badge, I waited for the latch to click before I heaved the heavy door open and galloped down the hallway toward a tiny office at the very end. Joe's consulting with Panorama had led to a free office space for him and an employee, which meant that, on most days, my husband could be found bent over plans a few feet below me. I was the one who had brought us here, but the ultimate irony was that this project had us both intertwined.

I burst through the closed door like a time bomb.

Joe looked up and gave me one of those smiles I'd fallen in love with so many moons ago before the reality of our demons had complicated everything. "What's up?"

I sank into the chair opposite him and stared open mouthed at him.

The black leather chair creaked under Joe's weight as he leaned back. "Well? Don't keep me waiting, Murph."

I put up my hands to silence him. "For once," I panted. "No, scratch that. For the *first* time since I've worked on this project, Joe O'Malley, I have some very good news. No! Not good news! Some great fucking news!"

CHAPTER 41:
The Practice

Curt answered. "Hey." His voice was the softer version of the one that had attacked me earlier in the day, which meant his meeting with the client that afternoon had gone well. The man was still adjusting to our new roles, which made him my equal instead of me being his subordinate.

I, on the other hand, had taken no time to recalibrate. "Got a minute?" My tone was matter of fact.

"Sure." Papers rustled. "What's up?"

"Remember when I told you at lunch that I would talk to you if I had a concern?"

The rustling stopped. "Yeah."

"Well, I have one today about when you called me a few hours ago."

It sounded like Curt was holding his breath. He said nothing.

"My concern is two things, Curt. First, as you know, the company is paying me a shit load of money to do my job. That phone call took several minutes out of our busy schedules today—yours *and* mine—and it didn't accomplish anything. Second, as I told you last week, I will no longer respond when you call me and yell. You did it today and I did not feel respected. So, in the future, I want you to know that if it happens again, I am simply going to hang up and talk to you when you calm down and I can actually hear what you are saying."

"Well." Curt cleared his throat. "I'm sorry. I shouldn't have yelled at you like that, but I was stressed."

"And you don't think it's stressful when I pick up the phone to have you—a fellow director—yelling at me?" The tenor of my voice began to rise, belying my anger. "Anyway, thank you. I accept your apology."

"The presentation went great," Curt said, his voice brightening.

"I'm glad," I replied. "But I still need to understand something, Curt. Why is it that you continue to call me—to cost the company time and money for the two of us to talk about something as simple as pointers—when you can call the receptionist, your secretary, anyone else in the company, and they can help you? Why do you continue to call me about every little thing?"

There was a pause before he replied. When he did, his voice was so faint, I had a tough time hearing him. "What was that?"

He gave a fake cough. "I said the reason I keep calling you is you're the only one who picks up."

My heart sank like a rock and for a moment, I didn't know whether to laugh or cry. *Of course, no one else picks up. Why would they when they know you're only going to yell?* I shook my head, picturing how frustrated he must feel as he tried number after number after number to no avail. *No wonder he's a screaming mess by the time he gets to me.*

The steady green light on my console reminded me he was still on the line.

"Okay." I said. "Got it. So, I guess I'll take that as a compliment."

Curt's voice was serious. "You should," he said. "You're the only one I can depend on in this company. Everyone else seems to avoid me. With the exception of, maybe, Jackson."

Jackson was the only other gringo in our office.

"Well," I said. "Thank you for your trust. But in the future, if you need help with a pointer, I need you to save the company some money and call the receptionist or somebody else."

"All right," Curt said. "That's fair."

Remember, Falc's voice intoned. *These guys may end up being your best teachers.*

"Great," I said. "Talk to you later." The handset came to rest in its cradle.

~

The Visitor Center was crammed to the gills with staff members. All attention was focused on Curt, who stood without a microphone at the front of the room.

I stood in the back, behind everyone, so I could give Curt some cues he'd requested.

Two more bodies crammed in beside me. *Latecomers,* I thought.

Not your business, I heard Falc say.

Right, I smiled.

The room was silent, except for the two bodies next to me. In my periphery, I identified our sales manager and another guy, shoulder to shoulder.

Their whispers led to chuckles, the volume of which kept increasing. My ears perked up, trying to catch their words, and I fought the urge to take my eyes off Curt, who was butchering the Spanish language from the front of the room. *Action speaks louder than words*, my mother had said. *Lead by example.*

The whispering continued.

These guys aren't getting the hint. Snickety put a finger to her lips. *How rude!*

Finally, the temptation was too great; I glanced toward the men with a frown. *Get a hint!* Then, did a double take when I saw the second man was Juan Carlos.

Oh, Lord. He gave a polite nod when he noticed my stare. As if on cue, he nudged his fellow offender and the two turned their gaze forward.

Way to set a good example. Scorn dripped off Snickety's every word.

A moment later, quiet laughter erupted, causing several heads to turn back to where Juan Carlos stood. I glanced back to see that he and our sales manager were holding their Blackberries at arm's length. The phones appeared to be protruding from their hips.

Juan Carlos caught me spying. His cheeks flushed before he mumbled something in Spanish. "*Vista...ital.*"

His counterpart's shoulders began to shake.

I acknowledged the words with a lift of my chin before turning my gaze back to the front. *School boys and their innuendos.*

Two minutes later, applause broke out, signaling Curt was finished.

Juan Carlos stepped toward me. "Did you understand me? What I said in Spanish?"

"Sí," I replied. "*Vista digital,* right?"

"No." A smirk crossed his face. "*Vista genital.*"

"Oh." My face turned red. "Okay."

"You'd better be careful." He wagged a finger. "When you act like you understand things when you don't, it can get you in trouble."

My eyes flashed as I turned to leave. *And it's appropriate for you to* chide me *when you were interrupting a staff meeting with a foul joke?* Snickety waved a middle finger salute over my shoulder as I walked away.

"Don't take it personally," I could hear Falc say. *"Ask yourself in every situation when you feel yourself react in anger or irritation toward someone: Whose business is this? Mine? Theirs? Or God's?"*

"His," I muttered as I burst through the double glass doors into the sunlight.

"If it's not yours, then don't give it another thought. It's not personal. It has to do with them. Think of it as practice."

"Practice." My palm clenched into a fist as I stamped out onto the sidewalk. "I'm getting pretty fucking good at this thing called practice."

"Remember," Falc's voice continued. *"Your greatest teachers…"*

"Oh, shut up!" I hissed as I walked across the parking lot. "Just shut the fuck up."

CHAPTER 42:
The Request

"Hey!" The voice behind me sounded like it was from a long way away. "Wait up!"

I turned to see Curt and Ringo beelining down the hill toward us. *Is he running?*

"Whew!" Curt's face was flushed the color of beets. "I've been trying to catch up with you since you made the turn back there."

"Sorry," I said, pulling the single ear bud from my right ear. "I had Katy Perry cranked pretty loud."

Snickety covered her mouth with her hand. *Do you think he heard you singing?*

"I thought maybe we could catch up," Curt panted. "But I didn't realize how fast you guys were going."

"My post-work blowing off steam pace, I guess." My heart pounded out a steady beat. "Do you care to join us around the back side? We're going the long way tonight."

"Sure." He and Ringo fell into stride with Lily and me.

Lily crossed in front of us to noodle Ringo in the rear end. The smaller dog whirled around to snap at her. "Come on, guys," I said, pulling at Lily. "No time for romance."

"It is amazing how much they like each other." The look on Curt's face could only be described as bemusement. "It really didn't take that long either, once Lily figured Ringo out."

My face broke into a smile. *Kind of like us.* "You could say that. Lily has the tendency to rule the roost," I nodded. "Did I tell you she was the test dog for my entire doggy day care in Denver?"

"Yep," Curt replied. "The one they put in with all the newbies, right?

To see if the pack would accept 'em."

Since we'd become neighbors, Curt and I crossed paths inadvertently to walk together about twice a week.

Proximity makes for strange bedfellows, Snickety reminded me every chance she got.

"So, I wanted to share something with you before you hear it elsewhere," Curt started. His smiling face melted into a somber expression I did not think I had seen before.

"Yeah?" I looked sideways at him. "About business?"

"Of course." Curt's wavy hair obscured his face as he ducked his chin. I'd had to twist his arm the week before to get him to admit he'd finally asked his Panamanian beauty to marry him. They'd been dating for quite some time.

"I mean, come on, Curt," I'd teased. "It's been more than two years. She's Latina. Of course, she expects you to marry her!"

Now, I mimicked Curt's famous question. "So, what's up?" Then, I bit my tongue. His answer did not come immediately so my jovial mood took a back seat to mounting concern.

Last one to speak holds all the power. Falc had never spoken a truer word. I'd seen it play out again and again and again at the office.

Mostly because you've gotten pretty darn good at holding your tongue, Snickety gave me a wink.

"Well." Curt cleared his throat. "The thing is, I'm leaving the company."

I snapped my head to look at him. "What? When?"

"I don't have an end date." Curt's cheeks flushed crimson for the second time. "Juan Carlos and I are still working out the details."

Lily pulled on her leash before I realized my feet had come to a stop.

"Well, what does that mean?" I demanded, searching his face. "And, where the hell are you going? I mean, are you happy about this? Or is this just about your contract coming to an end or…?"

Curt's shoulders bowed a bit though he kept his face straight ahead. *Is he ashamed?* "Well, it's a lot of things… It's no secret that Juan Carlos and I have never been best friends."

I bit my tongue. *That's the understatement of the year.* "Right, I know."

"And, being family, he's decided he wants to continue on with the company. His decision doesn't really leave me a lot of growth opportunities as were originally discussed for my position."

Snickety inclined her ear. *What's that? The company golden boy didn't get what he was promised either?*

I kept quiet.

Curt glanced my way. "Did you know that I was supposed to be named managing director within six months of my start date?"

I swallowed hard as my stomach did a flip flop. *That certainly would have changed things.*

I shook my head. "I had no idea."

Curt's voice wavered. "Then Juan Carlos decided he wanted to stay…" he shrugged. "It's been a fight ever since."

Do you see? Falc's voice piped up. *Do you see how difficult ego makes things?*

"Wow," I stuttered, my mind still whirring from the news. "So, are you leaving on good terms?"

"I think so," Curt nodded, though he wouldn't meet my eyes. "We've still got some contract stuff to work out, but ultimately, no one can argue with the results I've produced here."

I chewed the inside of my lip, watching his body language out of the corner of my eye. *I'll be damned. Has he been asked to leave?*

The man has never looked so, Snickety paused, searching for the word, *humble?*

"At any rate, I wanted to share this with you for two reasons."

Curt dragged his gaze up to meet mine for a millisecond before he turned his gaze toward the dogs. "First," he cleared his throat, "you've been a good friend to me in the past months." A cough. "As a thank you, I wanted you to hear it directly from me."

A wave of a nameless emotion washed over me. *Tenderness? Regret?* "Thank you." I regarded him with solemn eyes. "I appreciate that."

"I've already had some questions about it." A muscle in Curt's jaw tightened. "Which means Juan Carlos has told some people before we've settled everything." He shook his head.

"Oh, no, never." I cut my eyes toward him. "I don't believe it! Someone revealing something they're not supposed to… in the country of secrets?"

Curt's face broke out into a grin. "Right," he paused, steeling himself. "And second," he glanced toward me, eyes hopeful, "because I may need your help."

Whhaaaattt? Snickety's voice screeched like a needle reaching the end of the soundtrack. She put a hand up. *Stop the music.*

Tears sprung to my eyes as Falc's deep voice resounded. *When you stand up for yourself and you stick to your boundaries, it changes everything.* For the second time within the conversation, words failed me.

Curt began to stammer at the silence that hung in the air. "I mean, I'd appreciate your help. But, only if you have time. I mean, I just wanted to run some things past you and get your ideas." His final words tumbled out, in a rush. "You don't have to."

I put a finger up in his direction to buy myself some time. "Wow, Curt," I choked. "I don't know what to say." My hand came up to wipe away a single tear that had trailed down my cheek.

Curt's shoulders began to collapse inward, like I'd seen him do a thousand times in the board room. The man had never been at ease with emotion: his or anyone else's.

"Hang on." My tears continued to slip out unbidden, one after the other. "You don't need to say anything. Just give me a second."

We walked along in silence for a minute.

"I won't apologize," I started, catching my breath.

"No, no." Curt waved a hand. "No need."

"It's just…," I paused to inhale. "You just caught me by surprise," I said. "I mean, we've been through so much together, you and I."

Curt glanced at me before looking away, confusion crisscrossing his face.

"This is big," I shrugged. "I mean, your departure impacts me too, you know? With Jackson leaving soon and now you are going, I guess I'm gonna be the last gringo standing." I smiled.

Curt ducked his chin again before he smiled. "You're right," he said. "I hadn't thought about that. I'll bet you never thought this would be the case, huh?"

A chuckle broke free from me, gurgling unbridled in my throat, as the four of us came over the last hill to see the sun drop down behind the Panorama Mountains.

"No." I shook my head. "Believe you me, Curt, I *never* imagined any of this." I paused, seeing that Curt was more vulnerable than he had ever been, and I was certain this entire change, on top of asking for my help, was not easy for him. I took a deep breath and turned to face him.

"I know that change can be hard. I've faced some tough personal decisions myself that challenged every fiber of me. I would never have thought that I'd still be here in this country, as a matter of fact, but here I am. I'm sure you are surprised to be where you are now, but Curt, I do believe that change…especially unexpected change brings…opportunity." I paused, stealing a glance at him before finishing. "So, all that said, I am happy to help you in any way I can."

Curt stared. He had no words but simply gave a halfway grimace, and we continued to walk.

As we rounded the last curve toward home, our shadows stretched out before us on the pavement, a most unlikely motley crue: big dog, little dog, and two former arch enemies who had somehow muddled their way onto the pathway to peace and mutual respect. All I could see in my mind's eye in that reflection was a broad smile on Falc's face.

Curt and Ringo peeled off for one more loop as Lily and I took the final half-mile. Our pace slowed when our building came into view, not from fatigue but the feeling of mild desperation I couldn't keep from blooming in my mind.

While Curt's news had caught me completely off guard, and brought up some emotion I had not anticipated, I was now faced with going home and not knowing which of my husbands I would find: Dr. Jekyl or Mr. Hyde. While the frequency of Joe's drunken bouts had increased, it was a crapshoot. I was never sure how the evening would turn. I entered our home as if I were walking on eggshells. Anxiety clawed at the edge of my temples every night as I turned the key.

My home life was fast becoming an endless merry-go-round of angry interchanges and disappointments interspersed with flashes of time where my husband would resume his role as my Prince Charming. *I wonder what tonight will bring?*

The last rays of sunshine splayed from behind Panorama's western mountains.

Everything is changing so fast, I mused as the kaleidoscope of colors merged from yellow to orange to red to purple. *I hacked and scratched my way to the top of the heap at work, finally answering to the boss I was supposed to.* I shook my head at how my reassignment to Curt had been at the crux of my entire experience entering this country, and had damn near cost me my sanity. *And, now, my nemesis is leaving…and he's asked for my help.* I swallowed the knot in my throat. *What he doesn't know is that I won't be far behind.*

Juan Carlos and I had begun our own negotiations for when I too would depart the company. *So, Curt doesn't know it, but I'll only be the last gringo standing for less than a year.*

And you don't owe him any updates on that! Snickety sniffed. *The man never did you any favors, even if he is playing nice at the end.*

Endings. I smiled through my tears as I reached for the door handle. *Panama, Curt…what else?*

Snickety raised an eyebrow. *What else?*

Everything has its price. I wiped the tears from my cheeks as I unhinged Lily's leash from her collar and stepped over the threshold into our apartment. "Hello?"

~

The years—close to six of them—that passed played out in a manner different than I ever could have imagined. I renewed my contract—twice—before my eventual departure from Panorama after having received international recognition for my final marketing campaigns.

A couple of weeks before I wrapped up, I made one last presentation to the board.

"And, that, gentlemen, wraps up quarter one and quarter two's successes." I turned back toward a room full of the usual characters: Ethan in his signature Ralph Lauren; Julio, relaxed in his high-backed chair, a finger under his nose; Franklin, the CEO for the Middle Eastern interest who were latecomers to the investment team; and Juan Carlos, shuffling through his never-ending mess of paper.

I moved to my chair next to Franklin as I scanned the room for anything brewing beneath the surface. "Any questions?"

"I have one." Franklin rolled his chair up to let me pass. "Well, two, actually."

"Sure thing." I settled into my seat, the adrenaline high washing over me in waves. *Amazing how my presentation style changed once I got my mojo back.*

Snickety waved a black and white flag from my shoulder. *This was your last presentation here ever!*

I bit back the grin that had begun to spread across my face.

Franklin turned toward me.

"First off, I'd like to say to thank you," he said. My eyes held his. "We at Zufar Development have been very impressed with what's happening here, on the marketing side. In fact, we're restructuring our internal communications functionality within the main arm of our development company and with your permission," here, he gestured toward Ethan and Julio across the table, "I'd like to send my top guy down to spend some time with JuliAnne in the next few weeks to get her input on some ideas."

My eyes followed Franklin's across the table. *Have they not told him I'm leaving in two weeks?*

A black leather chair squeaked as Julio shifted his weight from one side to the other. He turned without a word toward Ethan.

Snickety raised an eyebrow at me. *I'll take that as a no.*

No one moved a muscle until Ethan spoke. "Of course, of course. Whatever you need."

Julio chimed in. "All we'd ask is that you coordinate with Juan Carlos on the details."

Juan Carlos shot up in his chair at the mention of his name. "Sure, sure," he clamored, lifting his eyes from his iPhone.

"Thanks for the compliment, Franklin. I'm more than happy to help out as long as we can coordinate dates," I turned back to him, keeping an eye on the three other men, who sat frozen in their chairs, still as sphinx.

Franklin nodded. "Great. We'll look forward to it, JuliAnne. Our guy will benefit greatly from your knowledge and expertise." He stood to his feet to shake my hand.

"Thank you," I replied.

Julio interrupted. "We need to move on. We'll be served lunch during the financial presentation."

Franklin turned back to his seat as I gathered my things.

Juan Carlos rose to walk out at the same time I did. When we reached the hall—both headed for the bathroom—he cleared his throat. "Ahem."

I turned back at the sound, accustomed to this being my boss' way of trying to get my attention. "Hey there."

"Uh, JuliAnne," he hurried the few steps to come alongside me, "I've been thinking…"

I stopped moving in order to hear him out.

"Well." He looked at me over his reading glasses. "I think for your going away, I'd like to do something between you, me, and the directors... maybe a dinner or something."

A soft smile spread across my face. "Oh, well, that would be nice." Curt's going away had coincided with the company Christmas party, which had turned into quite the showdown.

Snickety crinkled her eyebrows together. *So, the man gets a better send-off than the lady? I'm not surprised.*

"You know," Juan Carlos continued. "Since you were one of the first people to come on board here, I figured something more intimate would be more special."

A soft warmth invaded my chest. "That sounds nice, Juan Carlos. Thank you."

"I'm out of town next week," Juan Carlos looked me straight in the eye. "So, I'll be in touch the following week and we can figure out a date."

The following week was to be my last week in the office. "It's a plan," I said, turning back toward the ladies when it was obvious we were through. "Thanks again, Juan Carlos. I'll look forward to it."

Juan Carlos nodded, ducking his head as he pushed his way into the men's room, and that was the last time I saw him.

While my marketing staff held a small party for me the next week, the call for the director's dinner never came.

And just like that, with no fanfare and no official send-off, my time as a high-roller executive in Panama's limelight came to an end when I walked out of that board room. I departed just as I had entered with only the things I carried on my back—a suit coat, a briefcase, and my purse. But this time, I bore the thing that no one could ever take away from me: the battle scars and stories from a lifetime of lessons in the field, learned the hard way in a period of less than six years.

CHAPTER 43:
The Confrontation

"Well, I don't see what that thing has to do with the other!" Gin sailed into the air as Joe waved his martini one way and then the other.

Embarrassment washed over me as our friends across the table leaned back to avoid the liquid splash in front of them. *Here we go again.* The year was 2015, and we had gathered to celebrate a friend's birthday and to commemorate the seventh anniversary of our coming to Panama. While a year and a half had passed since I had concluded my work with Panorama, Joe's consulting in the market continued to flourish, and so we'd stayed in country.

"Shit! Sorry!" my husband guffawed, motioning to the waiter. "Guess I'll need a refill!"

I rolled my eyes before turning to the waiter with an imperceptible nod. The man lifted his chin to signal he understood. *No more.*

The girlfriend next to me leaned in. "How're you doing?"

"Hanging in there," I replied with a tight smile. My closest friends knew I was hanging onto the thin thread that kept Joe and I still tied together, as he refused to make any changes in his drinking patterns. But for how long?

"You know, we're all pretty worried about him." She flitted her eyes toward Joe, who was waving his arms above his head toward the group at the other end of the table. My husband's decline was becoming more and more apparent to everyone, and was something I could no longer cover up with niceties and excuses. On most days, he wasn't even getting out of bed until 11 o'clock.

"Is there any way you could get him to a meeting or something?" As a recovering addict herself, I knew which meeting she was talking about.

I followed her gaze. "Thanks for your concern, Miriam. But if there's one thing I've learned about men, it's that they're not ready until they're ready." I turned back to look her square in the face. "Whether we're talking AA or anything else."

She nodded as she withdrew a cigarette from her purse. "Come with me?"

"Not this time." I glanced back at Joe. "I need to keep an eye on the peanut gallery over here."

"Who're you calling a peanut gallery?" Joe swung his face back, inches from mine.

I narrowed my eyes. "You," I hissed. "Because you're the one that's acting like a cartoon with all that gin in you!"

"I am *not*!" he snarled back, loud enough for our friends to turn toward us with knowing glances. Then, he lowered his voice. "And you don't have to be such a spoilsport every single time we go out and have some fun! You're turning into quite the bitch, you know." My face went slack, the wind of my emotions becoming gale force.

I lowered my voice to a vicious whisper as I came to my feet. "Maybe that's because my husband turns into such an asshole when he drinks!" Snatching the bag off the back of my chair, I stomped off toward the waiter's station to pay the check.

"I'm leaving in five minutes, so be ready or I'll be **happy** to leave you here!" I threw the comment over my shoulder in Joe's direction.

Joe turned a surly face back toward our friends. "Well, I guess the princess has had her fill of you people!" He pushed himself up to his feet, where he gave a mock salute. "Which means we'll be taking our leave."

Three minutes later, I returned to make the rounds of hugs and air kisses.

"Best get him to bed," one friend whispered in my ear.

"Good luck," said another.

"You can always come stay at our house," Miriam said with a smile as she kissed me on the cheek, "in case he gets too rowdy."

I nodded, all smiles, though I said nothing. *What is there to say when your husband is a mess and everybody knows it? Yes, it gets old, but I can't control him or his antics.* My tolerance for his shit had hit an all-time low.

Blue rings of smoke floated from the passenger window of the Audi as I approached. *At least he found his way to the right car.* I got in the backseat. "All right, Tomas. Let's go home."

"*Sí, Señora.*" The car pulled into the street.

What would life be like if you weren't managing the business of Joe drinking too much? My mind slipped this one in as I struggled to inhale one deep breath after the other in order to calm my racing heart. It was a thought I did not want to address but it was too late; my mind had run with it.

"Well, it would be refreshing," I muttered to myself, though I could not imagine a life without the tall, dark man in the front seat at this moment in time, no matter how bad our home life had become.

"*Señora?*" I didn't realize I had spoken out loud until Tomas looked at me in the rearview mirror.

"It's okay, Tomas." I waved a dismissive hand at him.

"What's that?" Joe turned bloodshot eyes over his shoulder. "You say something?"

"Never mind." I turned toward the outline of skyscrapers as the car screamed down the freeway. I didn't even have the energy to remind Tomas to slow down.

Snickety followed my gaze to the city skyline. *And what would you do if you left him? Stay here in Panama? Get an apartment by yourself here in Gotham?*

My stomach sank as uncertainty wrapped me in its tentacles. *Fuck. I don't know.* The only thing I did know was that the chasm inside kept getting bigger and deeper with every passing night while my husband drowned himself to deal with stressors and feelings that he kept locked away. I had given up long ago, trying to get inside my husband's head. Now, at the levels of drunkenness he was attaining five nights a week, the man I was living with here in Panama was miles from the one I had married. It had to change.

Nothing changes until something changes.

"I don't need you right now, Falc," I murmured. "I have to figure this one out on my own."

What else do you possibly have to think about? Snickety considered me. *At what point does your happiness come first? Otherwise, he's just taking you down with him.*

I winced as the truth hit home. *She's right. Staying on a vessel that one party has already abandoned...for well, more than two years now, I might as well jump ship, too. Either that, or we're both going under.* I hugged my knees into my chest in the darkness. *I don't want to leave...but am I willing to continue living like this?*

My handbag buzzed. The backseat was illuminated by the eerie green light of the incoming call as I unearthed my handheld. It was Miriam. "Did you guys already leave too? The party seemed like it was just getting going."

"It's not that," Miriam sobbed through the line. "We just got a call from the doctor. It's really bad news."

I bolted upright. "What happened?"

"It's not me," she sniffled. "It's Daniel. He's been diagnosed with cancer. He goes into the hospital for surgery tomorrow."

~

Four weeks later, Joe sat in a chair in Daniel and Miriam's dining room, a towel around his shoulders. I stood above him, armed with clippers.

"All right," I said, tears welling up as I took the first lock of his brown waves between my fingers. "Are you ready?"

"Ready as I'll ever be!" my husband bellowed before he wiped away a tear of his own.

"Victim number two." Daniel stood to one side, beer in hand. We'd shorn his hair a few minutes before to even out the patchwork that had emerged on his head, thanks to the chemotherapy.

Miriam came up to hug him from behind. "Who knew this is where we'd be today?"

"Who knew?" My heart thudded as the whine of shears meeting hair indicated that Joe would also soon be as bald as a baby eagle.

"But we're with you guys!" Joe sang in a sing-song voice. "And you know we love you!"

"We love you, too." Daniel regarded Joe with a newfound gentleness in his eyes. "Both of you."

I paused to take the tequila snifter from my husband's clutches and handed it to Miriam. "Let me take this before you cut one of us please."

"Oh, stop being such a kill joy!" Joe smacked me on the behind, hard.

"You stop it!" The bittersweet joy of Joe's gift to Daniel in shaving his own head and being with our friends during this tumultuous time had fast melted into full-blown fury as my husband had downed one drink after another at a faster pace than usual. *On a night like this? Have you no respect…for me? For them?*

Joe reached for my hand, a silent apology, but I yanked it away. "I'm busy here, sailor." It had been a fight to rouse him at 4 p.m. to get his ass up from the couch after another drunken night on the patio. Any patience I had for his hangovers had been siphoned away by grief and exhaustion.

And even still, Daniel could die. Every time I thought of our friend's diagnosis, it felt like I'd been hit in the gut with a fly ball. The reality of life and its fragility had come home to roost like a homing pigeon that had found the wrong house. It had pecked away at the cloudiness of my mind and my uncertainty with ruthless precision about what I was doing with my life, with my job, with my happiness, with my husband. There was simply nowhere left to hide.

The questions piled up. *What if tomorrow never came? What if it were me instead of Daniel? What if I only had three months to live? Or a year? Would I stay? Would I go? Is any of this worth it?*

Tears continued to fall as I buzzed one row after another from my husband's head, revealing the tender white skin of his skull.

Everyone thought that I was crying for the loss of his splendor; my husband's thick head of hair was indeed an anomaly at 55 years old.

But I wasn't. I was crying for me, for him, and for the impending loss of the world as we knew it.

~

The next morning, Joe stumbled into the living room, rubbing his eyes. The clock read 11 a.m.

I looked up from the dining room table. "Hey," I said. "There's coffee for you."

"Well," he rubbed his eyes. "If you made coffee for me, then you must want something." He shuffled to the counter to pour himself a cup before bending over to scratch Lily's ears.

"When you've had a few minutes to wake up, yes." My voice was quiet. "We do need to talk."

Joe held up a hand. *Too early, too much information.* I had figured as much, which is why I had already packed and put two suitcases in the car.

I was heading up to Miriam and Daniel's home in the mountains of El Valle to get some much-needed perspective and R and R.

Lily danced around Joe's legs as he made his way to the couch. "Come on, girl." I closed my laptop. "I'll take you out." The dog bolted toward me as I walked toward the front door.

A moment later, the two of us descended into the coolness of the parking garage. The guard lifted his chin at us before he buzzed the door open.

"This may be our last walk here for a while, Lily." I pulled my sunglasses down from my forehead to combat the midday glare. "If not, the last one ever…in this apartment….as we are today."

The dog turned her brown eyes toward me and gave out a long low whine, as if she understood.

"Let's just do our 15 minutes, and then I've got to go back up and talk to your dad."

As we made our usual midday circuit up and down the dead end street across from our building, I let the tears fall unbidden. *How many times have I run screaming to these streets in my angst? How many times did the jungled hillsides hold me, taking my burdens from me, so that I could make it through one more day? What surprises came from our time here in this place I built and in which I worked and I lived? The surprises, the betrayal, the relentless pace, the exhaustion, the exhilaration. The hidden moments of beauty, the unexpected friendships. The person I thought I'd always have—*Joe's face came into view—*that I'm leaving behind.*

The cream and yellow façade rose before me as we turned back; our building had been the first of its kind in Panorama when we'd moved in four years earlier. Now, with the wear and tear of the humidity and the rain, the paint was beginning to peel around the edges.

Just like Joe and me: frayed from lack of proper maintenance.

Snickety snapped her fingers. *But you tried, JuliAnne. You really did. The fault is not yours alone.*

My heart hung heavy as Lily and I marched back up the stairs toward the inevitable conversation. *But even my efforts—imperfect though they have been—weren't enough to save us.*

Joe and I sat across from one another on the couch. His eyes were cast downward, listening, as I read everything I wanted to say. I'd long found that writing down my thoughts about anything emotional was the best way to capture them in totality.

"And that, Joe, is why I am going up to the mountains for a few days to decide what is next for me." I folded the paper in half as I brought a shaking hand down to pat Lily, whose body was pressed next to my leg. "And I'll be taking Lily too."

The color drained out of Joe's face. He sat frozen for a moment.

I waited, unsure what to do next. The wall clock ticked in the silence.

Finally, my husband seemed to snap back to attention and as he did, rage unfurled across his features. "Fine!" he shouted. "As usual, it's all about you, JuliAnne. What *you* need! What *you* want! You never seem to care about what's best for *us*, or what I might need."

I crossed my arms across my chest. "Do you even know what you need? It seems to me you're so busy drinking that you don't even have time to think!"

"Oh, don't make this all about my drinking because it's *not!*" He heaved himself up and began pacing back and forth in front of me.

"As a matter of fact, if you would stay sober for more than half a day, I imagine we'd have a lot fewer problems!" I shot back. "Whether or not you like it, you *are* an alcoholic, Joe. It's impossible not to see that!"

"Fuck you!" he shouted, pointing a finger at me. "I am *not* an alcoholic! I'm Irish and I just enjoy my drink. Drinking relaxes me."

"Well, I can hardly call 'enjoying' what we do most nights these days," I seethed. "You turn into this other version of yourself when you drink as much as you do—you become this messy, mean, nasty guy—and no one—not even our friends, enjoys being around you! And, especially not me." Lily cowered at my feet. It was my turn to point around the room.

"And this—this life—where we sit around and I cry while you get trashed is no way to live anymore, Joe! Whatever happened to the fun we used to have? Whatever happened to the jovial guy I knew when we got married? Where did you go? What happened to us? Why did you abandon me, abandon us?"

Joe stopped pacing to stare at me. "He went away when we moved to Panama and he had to pick you up from the floor, time after time and time. Do you think that was any fun for me, to have to be the strong one day after day after day after day…for years…when you could barely get out of bed to even function?"

My heart thudded to the floor.

"Well, it wasn't," he snapped. "So, you can barely blame me for enjoying a few cocktails every now and then, because the truth is *you* abandoned *me* long ago. It was all I had to pass the time, while I waited for you."

"I'm sorry," I whispered, as tears flooded down my cheeks. "I know I've made a ton of mistakes and I've hurt you. But I can't go on…we can't go on…like this. I'm unhappy and it's obvious you are too. Otherwise, you wouldn't be…drinking this much, every day."

"How would you know how I feel?" Joe seemed to tower over me at that moment. "You never ask. All you do is try to get me to do this, or do that, or stop drinking. You've become a nag and a bitch. You're not the wife I married either, you know!"

My tears dried up as I swallowed hard. "That may be true," I managed, "but at the moment, the reality is—no matter who's right and who's wrong—this is just not working." I stood to my feet. "I love you, Joe. But for now, I simply need time to myself."

"Then go ahead and fucking do whatever it is you need to," he raised his fingers in fake quotations, "'once again' take care of yourself! It's the same old story, JuliAnne! All about you!" He stomped toward the bedroom, but before his welcomed retreat, he snatched a half bottle of Herradura off the table and headed down the hall. "Don't let the door hit you in the ass as you leave!"

The bedroom door slammed so hard it shook the building. Lily raised her head from where she'd hid underneath the coffee table.

"All right, girl." I blew my nose into a Kleenex. "That's our cue." I crossed to the dining room table, tucked my laptop into my briefcase, threw my handbag over my shoulder and hooked Lily to her leash. Lily looked up at me as my hands shook. She leaned over and licked my hand, which brought the reservoir of tears spilling over. In an instant, the door closed behind us, in a whisper.

CHAPTER 44:
The Wrap Up

Months passed. Curt and his wife had long since moved back to the U.S. My contract with Panorama had been over for almost two years. A number of our other expat friends had relocated to new jobs, leaving gaps in our hearts and our social calendars by their absence. My time on the isthmus was coming to a close. For Joe and me, it meant we were finally going our separate ways.

"Over here, Tomas." I pointed with my neck toward the pickup truck. "I need those two boxes over here. They go to storage."

"All right, Miss JuliAnne." I gave the hulking form sufficient room to exit the doorway, balancing one foot against the door jamb to keep the wind from slamming it shut.

"And this, Miss JuliAnne?" Tomas pursed his lips toward the inflatable ball rolling around in the breezeway.

"*Aye, sí.*" I craned my neck around the corner so the wind didn't blow the door shut and lock me out. "*Olvide eso. Sí, se puede pero lo haremos mas tarde*. That can go in last."

"*Listo.*" Then the elevator dinged and he was gone.

"*Oye, Omar*," I said, as a younger man bounded up the stairs. "*Necesito su ayuda con la pintura en el baño al final de la tarde.*"

"Okay, Señora Murphy." Omar's never-ending energy belied his youth, taking the two boxes I'd been juggling without missing a beat. "*Y donde está?*"

"*Creo que en el deposito.*" My oval-faced maid appeared behind me, sliding yet another plastic *caja* toward me across the tile floor. I turned toward her. "And what's this?"

"*Platos de la cocina, Señora.*" The box came to a stop a few inches behind me. Jovanna took a paper towel to my dripping brow as

I straightened upward.

"*Gracias,*" I said. "That's fine there."

"*Yo la llevo en un momento.*" Omar threw the shout over his shoulder. "Give me five."

~

"What do you *mean*, you're getting a divorce? *Que paso?*" Maria Carmen's fork flew across the table with her final syllables.

"*Oye, cuídate.*" My fingers caught the fork before it clattered to the floor. "I know it's a shock, but we've been having problems for a while. We separated for the first time last year but I didn't tell anyone because we got back together and tried to work it out."

"Oh, *amiga.*" Maria Carmen's face crumbled. Divorce in Panama was still considered a social failure of sorts. "*Estás bien? Necesitas algo?* Do you need anything?"

My hand searched for the crinkled Kleenex in my handbag. Seeing how much my friends cared for me always made me cry. I was existing in a perpetual state of sensitivity these days. I excused myself to make the familiar pit stop in the ladies' room only to stand in the stall and weep in silence, collecting myself, refreshing my makeup, and returning to the table. While I dug in my purse for a lipstick, I stared at tired eyes looking back at me in the mirror.

"What do you want from me?" Joe's face appeared in my mind's eye, across the kitchen counter from where I had stood at the sink.

I had tasted blood after biting my tongue to keep my emotions at bay. Joe, as always, was revving up his own anger as well as one more drink. I stared in disbelief as he railed one more time against my accusation that he was an alcoholic. "When are you going to grow some balls and ask me for a divorce?" His face was red, his nostrils flaring like a mustang.

My hand shook as I raised a glass of water to my lips and drained it. Then, I set it down on the counter and moved toward the stairs. The letter I had written him asking for that very thing was tucked in my purse, sealed in a plain, white envelope.

Are you sure, JuliAnne? My mind refused to accept the truth that the agony we'd been enduring for the past year was irreparable.

"God, damn it!" His cup slammed into the coffee table with a bang. The impact shook the floors beneath me.

My fingers fumbled with the zipper on my jacket. I forced myself to inhale, once, twice, three times. Then, I gathered my bag and removed the letter, turning it over in my hands before I began my descent back down the stairs.

My husband sat embroiled in his own private hell on the couch, hands wrapped around the thigh of his good knee, the knee he'd had surgery on two weeks before. The same knee he had re-injured that first fall down the stairs that he had said was "nothing at all."

"I'm going to my appointment," my voice was barely audible, even to me. I cleared my throat, as I stopped beside him.

Joe kept his eyes straight ahead, his nod imperceptible. I could feel the defeat in the shrug of his shoulders.

"I'm sorry, Joe." I had laid the envelope on the side table next to him. And then I turned, before I lost my nerve, and walked out the door.

"Oh, honey, I'm so sorry." With a British accent, the words somehow came out more chipper than expected as the three of us sat there at our girl's lunch, though I knew Suzy didn't mean them that way. I snapped back from my own thoughts.

I nodded as her hand reached out to mine to give me a squeeze.

"So, now what will you do?" The worry lines on her kind face always reminded me of my grandmother, which nearly set me off crying again. "Will you stay in Panama, or go back to the States?"

"I don't know yet." My shoulders reached toward my ears. "Short term, we've separated, and I'm heading to Costa Rica to consult on another development project. A few months there will give me some perspective and a needed break from all the gossip about our split. As you know, Panama is very small."

Suzy nodded. "Of course, the *bochinche*. You came to Panama together so, of course, it's all people know."

I drained the last bit of wine from my glass. "Even so, I am weary of telling the same story over and over again. And for some people, I don't want to explain."

"How long will you be in Costa Rica?" Suzy's eyes took in the furrows between my eyebrows, which had accumulated over the last few weeks fresh from our split. "You have so many friends here, you know. You'll be missed."

"Three months," I replied. "Madelaine and I should wrap this thing up by the end of August at the latest. It's on the coast, so that will be a nice change of scenery for me."

"Oh, good," my friend nodded. "Being in nature as much as possible is just what you need."

Yes, being in nature...

~

"Miss JuliAnne." Tomas' baseball cap loomed in my vision, jolting me to the present from my reverie. "*Estamos listos* with everything." He waved his large hand around the now empty apartment. "Are you going to ride with me in the big truck or with Omar?"

"*Voy en cinco minutos.*" I jumped down from where I had ended up perched on the kitchen counter.

Tomas disappeared out the front door, slamming it in its heavy frame behind him. The crash didn't even faze me.

Look how far I've come. I put my hands out to the still air as I walked from room to room, taking in the empty shelves of the life Joe and I had had together. *When I first got off the plane, that noise would have sent me out the roof! Now, I barely even notice.*

And, here we are. I crinkled my mouth up as I self-corrected. *Well, here I am anyway. Packing up. Moving on. But to where? To what? What do I want?* I was immediately back, sitting with Falc the first day we worked together, with him asking me who I was. Telling me to sit with the question and now I had the same need. I had to sit with the question "what do I want" and this time, I found it an exhilarating question to pose.

"Thank you." I spread my arms toward the bare walls. "Thank you for how you held us, how you protected us, the life we had here—the precious moments and the shit, too. Thank you for giving us safe haven, in the midst of everything." Once again, a voice emerged to tell me that I would someday thank the very people who had challenged me the most. Thanking them for making me who I was that day.

I just never thought that Joe would be one of those teachers. I paused for a moment as tears slid down my cheeks. "Thank you, Joe. Thank you, Joe, for loving me, for believing in me, for teaching me how to be strong, even in all your imperfection. I learned so much from you." I reached into my pocket for the ever-present Kleenex, bowing my head as I lifted it to my eyes.

I walked to the door and opened it for the last time.

"Thank you." This time it was a whisper. Then, I let the door go, knowing the breeze would take the latch to its final resting place, behind me.

But this time, instead of a mighty slam, there was only a quiet click.

As I walked toward the exit, a string of faces scrolled through my mind's eye. Joe, Juan Carlos, Curt, Ethan, Julio, and all the men who had been harsh mirrors to look in as I had to face my own demons in all the years in Panama.

I pushed the doors to our building open, and was again engulfed by a wall of Panama humidity. I wiped my eyes and erased all the faces off the screen of my mind. I looked up, and standing a foot away with a broad smile and an outreached hand was the loyal face of Tomas, who reached out and took my briefcase.

"Where to first, Miss JuliAnne?'

I could only smile.

CHAPTER 45:
Stand By Me

A yellow taxi pulled curbside in front of the airport terminal. My eyes took in the flash of skin colors merging in and out of the dirty doors, like salmon spawning at the confluence of two rivers.

An audible sigh escaped my lips as I turned to look at Tomas.

Green eyes caught mine for a moment, brimming with unspoken emotion. "Okay, Miss JuliAnne, whatever you need, just say me."

My vision blurred with tears. My hand shook as I reached inside my handbag for a tissue. "Well, Tomas. I guess this is it, isn't it? I don't need anything else right now. Thank you for…" I could no longer hold back the wall of emotion that had been building in me for weeks.

He shifted in his seat, nodding, eyes looking everywhere but at me. "Yes, sir, this is it."

I blew my nose before tucking the tissue in my pocket. Door hinges squeaked as we opened them in unison.

A moment later, a battered black *maleta* loomed over a smaller one on the curb. Tomas closed the trunk with a bang. "You, Miss JuliAnne, are a beautiful person to me. I am privileged to be here for you all these years. I thank you for all." He lowered his head.

"All I have done for you, Tomas? It is the other way around! What would I ever have done without…you?" My tears spilled over as I reached for him, not as his employer, but as his friend.

Tomas instead held out his palm for me to shake, as if we are meeting for the very first time. "Remember, Miss JuliAnne, whatever you need, *cualquier cosa en Panama.*" I reached past his outstretched hand and threw my arms around his thick neck, standing on tiptoes only to reach the middle of his broad chest. My tears cascaded down all over his starched shirt, which was already drenched in sweat from the heat of the coming day. "Thank you for everything, Tomas."

He lifted one arm and placed it around my shoulder, his discomfort palpable at this unusual show of affection. Hugs in Panama are reserved for family members and the closest of friends, considered more intimate than the air kiss.

"*Cualquier cosa*, Miss JuliAnne." His head bobbed up and down as we moved apart. "I am here for you." His immaculate size 14 Nikes stepped back toward the driver's side.

I wiped the tears from my cheek. "I know, Tomas. Thank you." My chin lifted skyward in that familiar Latin way I had learned—the way that said, "Got it," before I turned my body toward the gray concrete building. My hand hung in the air a moment later, in a final wave.

A moment later, the cab was gone and I was left with my years in Panama filling my mind with all the triumphs and failings that I faced, all the wins and losses. *If I'd had any idea what this dream job—this dream life—I had imagined, would cost, would I do it again?* I pondered for a split second, seeing how I was a stronger person, had accomplished more than I set out to achieve, and yet it had cost me the foundations of everything I had known myself to be before: my sanity, my health, and my marriage. *Was it worth it?* Only time would tell. I was awash in the conflict of gratitude mixed with deep, deep grief.

Falc's face came into view for a split second and without a word, his sly, confident smile held the answer to the question I continued to ask myself for months to come: Was it worth it?

~

Ding.

Juggling a Styrofoam cup of Kotowa Chai, I stuck my ticket between my teeth and pulled my iPhone from my bag.

Ding.

"All right, all right," I mouthed around the paper, squinting to see which icon was notifying me of new messages. One-handed, I swiped the screen to unlock the phone. I paused for a moment, feeling that it might be Joe and not wanting to encounter any new wrinkles. I just needed to disconnect, but I took a breath and clicked the icon.

In WhatsApp, Tomas' face beamed from the top of the screen. My face broke into a smile.

After the porter had dumped me at the front of the line at the ticket counter, I'd tapped in one last message.

Thank you again, Tomas, for everything.

My lips curved up.

Remember, you are very special for me! Then the emoticons: Thumbs up. Hands in prayer. Hands clapping.

I smiled, bringing the phone back to its resting place in my handbag.

Ding.

I brought the phone back up to my line of vision and was caught unaware of what the sentence would mean to me.

Stand by me.

Stand by me!

Stand by me!!

My throat tightened as another wave of emotion broke. I glanced around, heat flooding my chest for a moment. In a sea of passengers waiting to check in, would anyone even notice a middle-aged woman crying? It was unlike me to show emotion in public. The woman I had been in Panama had always been in control; at least, that was the version of me most people saw. This *was* the country where appearances were everything.

Yes, said Snickety, *but you're finally leaving!*

"Thank God." I set my cup down on the floor to type a reply.

"Gracias, Tomas. And you to me. I am grateful for you. God bless you," I typed.

I bent forward as silent tears of gratitude flowed freely. *What this man had come to mean to me, over the years.*

Around me, tourists giggled and grumbled and shuffled forward, the nationals' noses buried in all sizes and shapes of tiny screens, oblivious to anything around them.

I stood there, an island, surrounded by babies howling and people laughing, noses blowing and a number of loud cell phone conversations, just as it was when Joe and I first landed and felt like fish out of water. And, I realized, for the final time, here in Panama, how alone I had been in this country.

But this time, it didn't bother me. The strength I'd found in myself now buoyed me. I was heading toward a future that had yet to be written, a future I did not want to control or about which I had to know every single detail, a future where I hoped to be a better version of me...a better version of myself...grateful every day for the lessons I had learned, the hard way, in Panama.

White noise from the intercom crackled for a moment before a Latin voice smoothed across the airwaves: *"Damas y caballeros, ahora la puerta principal ha cerrado. Por favor apaguen todos sus aparatos electronicos para preparar nuestra salida."*

As I clicked through my phone into settings to switch it into airplane mode, the sense of déjà vu rose upward in my mind. *How many times have I done this, on my way in or out of this country?*

And, yet, this would be the last time.

A torrent of memories began to flow.

My feet exiting that very first plane on Thanksgiving Day 2007, Joe's towering frame following close behind. The wide, self-assured smiles on our faces, his confident stride, our exclamations as we walked up the jetway, the heat hitting us like a ton of bricks. North American optimism positively dripping off of us.

"Flight attendants, please take your seats."

Emerging two hours later from Customs into the sea of people clamoring outside, our eyes like platters, bodies covered in sweat, searching for the man we'd been told would be there with a sign. Tomas materializing in his white shirt and khaki pants with the sign that read, Joe O'Mealey. "Mr. O'Mealey? Nice to meet you." His ever-present smile. "Okay."

The wheels of the aircraft bumped across the runway.

I stood atop the crest of the hill overlooking Panorama with Juan Carlos, my hair ruffling in the heat of the midday breeze. Behind me, Joe gazed in the opposite direction toward the ocean. *I can do this,* I thought to myself, as my eyes scanned the outline of city skyscrapers in the distance that sharply contrasted the abandoned military buildings carved into the jungle.

The walls of the plane vibrate as the engine picks up speed.

"Okay, Tomas." The door to the Audi is pulled open by a gloved hand at the Club Union. "I think I'll be done around 10." He nodded as I gathered my evening bag and took the outstretched hand to exit.

"Mr. President." I shook hands with the white-haired man who was built like a bull. Bulbs flashed around us as we give each other a polite nod and tight-lipped smile.

"Señora." Our faces turned back to the cameras. As we pulled apart, he wagged a finger in my face. "Ah, yes, I remember…my friend from Arkansas."

The tremor of the tires shakes the seat beneath me as the plane gains speed across the tarmac.

"I don't care what Juan Carlos says." Curt's volume threatened to flatten me against the door of his office. "This is what I am telling you, so just *do* it!" His face contorted like a wild animal, close to frothing at the mouth.

The plane spun at the far end of the runway before turning toward its final path in the direction of the Canal for takeoff.

I see myself on my yoga mat atop the rooftop of our building in Amador, shaking with sobs. The sunrise broke across the horizon in a fantastic display of red and orange.

Bursts of color whipped past the window as the plane traveled down the runway past Albrook Mall outside my window.

Joe's hand squeezed mine as the photographer placed us with two other couples next to a man dressed as a member of the British National Guard. When we were finished, the men whistled as we women shimmied in our heels and long gowns to the dance floor.

Joe and me, stifling our laughter in the elevator after catching Tomas walking Lily in circles in the parking garage because it was raining outside.

The plane gains speed. I inhale, letting the air expand my lungs. *This is it.*

"When are you going to have the balls to ask me for a divorce?" Joe's eyes bore through me from the couch. My hand shook as I refilled my water glass.

As the jet plane takes off, my breath releases into a small sob.

I watch as the shadow of the plane crosses the blue cranes in Balboa Port, the muddy water of the Canal, the steel expanse of the Bridge of the Americas. Sunlight highlights the carpeted green that is Panorama, the new city I had built, the gym, our apartment building.

So, this is the end.

The plane climbs, the world below me getting smaller and smaller until finally I can no longer see it behind me.

My mouth forms the words, *Goodbye, Panama. Goodbye, Panorama.*

Goodbye Joe.

My heart expands wide as I realize anew all that this small country gave to me.

Correction: *What I had the courage to give to myself.* The journey. The struggles. The expansion. So much in my relation to men and now so much more in my relationship to my own self, my power.

Inhaling, I close my eyes, and bring my hands in prayer to my forehead.

Thank you for all those teachers that were brought into my life in this chapter. The lessons were different from what I thought they'd be. And the people that came and went, including Joe. Again, Falc's voice intoning, telling me that these amazing, difficult, lost men were the teachers I needed. How I had railed against the idea, over and over and over. *And now, I probably would not be making this move, had they not been my trial-by-fire.*

My eyes fill with tears as they flutter open.

Ding.

Wait a minute!! One more text came in. One more reminder from this gentle giant of a soul who stood in the shadows of my life, always there, always there. *Always!*

"Remember me, Miss JuliAnne. I am always here for you." The soft baritone of his voice rose in my ears. *I am here.*

My pupils widen, my mouth drops open as the realization breaks over me. *Oh, my God.*

I scramble for my phone, swiping to bring up the text before. And there, it blinks at me from the screen. *Stand by me!*

Steady and true. Simple. Always there. *Just like him.*

I bow my head toward the coastline which appears endless to the horizon, as my hands came up to my temples. *My God, I can't believe I didn't see it before. I never got it. I never saw that he was the one man who stood by me, no matter what.*

My hands clutched at the center of my heart as the tears fell again. *Tomas was the one man who was there for me* all along.

I bow my head towards my chest and whisper to myself, "I just now got it. Thank you, Tomas." And the tears flowed, unstoppable. "Thank you, thank you, thank you."

His answer rang out on my left as if he were there next to me, like he had been for all those years. "Yes, Miss JuliAnne. Yes, sir."

And then the plane turned and it was ocean as far as the eye could see.

EPILOGUE:
Three Years Later

The bell jangled, announcing my arrival as a burst of wind slammed the door into my backside and shoved me into the narrow entryway of My Brother's Bar in Denver, Colorado. Ten heads turned as a young man approached, wiping his hands on an apron. "One for lunch?"

"I'm meeting my…uh…" My voice caught as I scanned the faces behind the man. A tall figure beckoned in the dim light. "That's him!" I ducked my head as I pushed past the waiter.

Snickety's voice invaded the calm I'd just spent five minutes composing outside. *Did you just hesitate to call him your ex?*

It's nothing, I hissed. *Just a weird moment, that's all.*

I unwound my scarf as I dodged tables and chairs to get to where Joe stood. "Hi!" I beamed as he bent down to hug me. "Good to see you!"

"You too." My heart did a little flip flop when our eyes met, but the fairy tale spark we'd had for years was gone; all I saw there now was kindness. "You look good."

"Thanks." I shrugged off my coat and handed him my handbag before collapsing into the seat across from him. My eyes did a quick scan of his physique in that familiar way that only an ex-wife can. "You look good, too." The man that sat across from me was an earlier version of the Joe I had been married to. This one seemed to have reappeared from a long time ago—before the heavy drinking and the disappointments between us had piled up with the years.

Now, the wrinkles around his brown eyes creased when he smiled. The bags that had taken residence under them for years had disappeared, as had a good 30 pounds from his midsection. I raised an eyebrow at his belly. "You look *really* good, in fact."

Joe flashed me a row of pearly whites.

"Whoa!" I reared back, pointing toward his teeth. "What? Let me see 'em!"

Joe's face colored.

Is he embarrassed? I leaned in with the smile of a Chesire cat. "How do you like them?"

He shrugged. "They're fine."

"Fine, my ass!" I leaned forward. "Holy cow! They're gorgeous! You look amazing!" For years, Joe had hid behind a closed lip smile because he'd been embarrassed about the stains 30 years of smoking had left behind.

A waitress appeared at my elbow. "Something to drink?"

My eyes never left my ex-husband's face. "An Arnold Palmer for me, please."

"Same." Joe nodded. "Well…," he said, as he waved his hands around. "Here we are…the scene of the crime."

We burst into laughter as we both looked around. The low-hanging ceilings showed a space packed to the gills with the lunch crowd seated at modest tables around us. The rumble of midday conversation bounced off the walls, but was quickly absorbed by the dark wood of the antique bar behind us.

"Indeed," I returned. "It only seemed fitting. How long has it been, anyway…two…?"

Joe held up two fingers. "Two years," he said. "It was two years ago this month that we signed the final papers in the attorney's office."

"Incredible," I murmured, staring into the crystal blue eyes I had once known so well. They hadn't changed much—except now, two and a half years into sobriety, they simply looked clear, happy.

We both smiled before turning to the menu.

The waitress returned to take our order. I observed him—this former husband of mine—and marveled at how kind the aging process had been to him, given all that he had given her to reckon with. His dark salt and pepper hair remained thick, even though he'd celebrated 60 just a few months back. Lean muscles rippled down his arms, affirming his continued commitment to the gym.

When Joe noticed me watching him, he shot me a wink. *So much the same, and yet, so much has changed.*

I set my elbows on the table, chin coming to rest in my palm, a pose I'd struck with him a million times before. "So, tell me everything. What's new? With you? With Panama?"

Joe leaned in, mirroring my pose, and there we sat. I felt the hands of Father Time swing backward as I listened and watched and laughed with this man who still to the day held the record for sharing my bed.

"What's the latest on your book?" Joe posed the question in between bites of our longtime favorite: the famed jalapeño cream cheese burger. I grinned as I scrolled back our history in this place—we'd called it *our place*, back then—because it was at this very hole-in-the-wall—and probably at this very table—that it—*we*—had all started…16-plus years ago.

Back then, we'd been unlikely colleagues, brought together by the architectural monstrosity that sat across the highway, a stadium that kept changing names except for its tenant, the NFL team, the Denver Broncos. It was in the throes of the stadium construction project that we'd discovered each other and a playful friendship had formed, which had blossomed into a torrid love affair, a 14-year tumultuous relationship and marriage, and most recently, our divorce.

The memories came tumbling back—one after the other after the other—as I listened to him.

And maybe it was the recollection, or the ghosts of Joe and JuliAnne past in this locale, or maybe the color in his cheeks and the expression on his face, but whatever it was, I felt something swell in my chest…a wave of sadness…remorse?

Snickety, as usual, nailed it. *He looks like the man you fell in love with.*

My eyes scanned him again: the way that rogue curl wrapped around his left ear, his ever-present grin, the continual twinkle in his eyes. *Wow, she's right.*

Do you regret it? Her question hung in the air as all the oxygen seemed to disappear. *Would you go back if you could?*

With a measured inhale, I checked in with my heart. And the answer was swift, firm. *No,* I replied. *I don't.* The constriction in my chest evaporated as I watched the animation in Joe's face and he concluded his story. *He seems so…happy.*

As the last of the words tumbled from his mouth, I reached my hand around the mustard to touch his.

His eyes widened. He looked at me.

A tear slipped down my cheek before I could catch it. "You seem happy, Joe." I paused. "Are you?"

Joe brought his grizzled hand atop mine before handing me his napkin and giving me a somber nod. "I am," he said. "I really, really am." Then, he winked again, the Joe of 16 years prior returning. "But, then, I did recently rid my life of some serious drama!"

I wrenched my hand back. "Well, good," I retorted as I took the napkin and wiped my cheek. "I'm glad that worked out for you!" My voice quavered. "Never failing to interrupt a thoughtful moment with humor, of course. I guess some things never change."

Joe's face grew serious as he pulled some bills from his pocket. I reapplied gloss to my lips before beckoning toward him for my handbag. The bag found my hand before the request even left my lips. I smiled. *Some things never change…*

Our eyes reconnected as we rose, and he reached out a hand to help me with my coat. When he bent to hug me, I returned his hug with the fierceness of gratitude that now swept over me.

"I love you, Murphy," he said.

"Thanks." My eyes shone through the mist. "I love you, too, Joe, and I'm so glad you are…," I circled my glove in the air in front of him, swirling as if encapsulating the man I had known so many years before who seemed to have found himself again. "…back," I finished.

We walked to the door, together, and with one last brush of each other's cheek—the greeting we'd adopted from all those years in Panama—we went our separate ways.

As the winter wind blew me back to my rental car, the tears returned amidst the waves of memories that continued.

Snickety chimed in on my reverie. *If it weren't for you, Joe never would have started that business. And if it weren't for you, he wouldn't even be in Panama. And if it weren't for you…*

I know, I know, I said. *And, I'm happy for him. And I'm grateful he's happy. I'm grateful it was my job that led us to Panama, that led to him starting a business, that led to the life we had there, that led to my financial stability, that led to me becoming a writer, that led to the wherewithal I've had to be able to write about my roller coaster in Panama…*

Snickety's eyes widened for a moment. *But does that mean…?*

It does. I set my jaw, drowning her out. *It means I'm grateful for our divorce, too, which led to Joe getting sober and finding himself again… though yes, it meant that we would never be together again. I'm even grateful for those pricks at Panorama who found me and hired me because that's what got us to Panama in the first place.*

Snickety shook her head. *You're thankful for them? Even for those jerks who chewed you up and spat you out and showed you so little respect?*

Her words gave me pause. My hand hovered, poised to insert the key in an ignition that didn't exist. I searched my conscience…*Could I? Be grateful? For them?*

When my words pierced the quiet of the car's interior, their resonance rang true. I spoke aloud, "Yes. Even for them. Even for everything that happened in Panama. Because somehow we all made it through for the better, even though we got lost along the way. Somehow we made it through and we're better people because of it."

Snickety plucked a Kleenex from her pocket and handed it to me.

I took it and wiped the single tear that trailed down my cheek as I chuckled. "You're right though, Snickety…who would ever think I'd be grateful for all of that *locura*? It took a long, winding road to get here, but once again…wonders never cease."

I started the car with the push of a button and eased out of the parking space.

Snickety's final words rang in my ears as I joined the line of traffic heading for the freeway. "If all that's possible—" she paused for effect, shaking her head, her eyes wide with disbelief, "—then, what else is possible?"

"Right," I murmured. "*Así es*. What else *is* possible?"

And with that, I merged onto the access ramp and joined the hundreds, then thousands of commuters on the interstate heading south to God knows where…and whatever the next chapter would bring.

ABOUT THE AUTHOR

JuliAnne Murphy is a two-time bestselling author who has overcome unbelievable odds and found success in many aspects of her life. She has served as one of the only women in leadership on the building of the Denver Broncos NFL stadium, and acted as a lead communications strategist for a $1.7 billion transportation expansion project in Denver, Colorado. She also served as the Vice President of Marketing for the largest international airport redevelopment in the United States.

JuliAnne grew up in a small town in Arkansas and set her sights on breaking the glass ceiling for women. She attended the University of Arkansas, receiving her education in marketing and communications, and has twenty-two years of experience in real estate development, specifically launching start-up landmark properties. She redefined the role of a marketing and communications executive when she worked for an international developer in Central America. In this role, she managed the global launch of a massive redevelopment of a former U.S. Air Force base into a new city. She has since partnered with a real estate consulting firm in Latin America, working with major corporations on high-end and luxury properties.

JuliAnne and her husband Yor live *la vida loca* in tropical Costa Rica, where they started an innovative real estate sales and consulting office, South Pacific Costa Rica Real Estate. JuliAnne has founded an international Professional Women's Networking Group in three countries, the United States, Panama, and Costa Rica, and she is now hard at work on her sequel to *Dream Job*.